1994

No End to Her

No End to Her

Soap Opera and the
Female Subject

Martha Nochimson

UNIVERSITY OF CALIFORNIA PRESS

Berkeley / Los Angeles / Oxford

University of California Press
Berkeley and Los Angeles, California

University of California Press, Ltd.
Oxford, England

© 1992 by The Regents of the University of California

Library of Congress Cataloging-in-Publication Data

Nochimson, Martha.
    No end to her : soap opera and the female subject / Martha
Nochimson.
        p.   cm.
    Includes bibliographical references and index.
    ISBN 0-520-07763-6 (alk. paper). — ISBN 0-520-07771-7
(pbk. : alk. paper)
        1. Soap operas—United States—History and criticism.
    2. Women in television.   3. Sex role in television.   I. Title.
    PN1992.8.S4N63   1992
    791.45′6—dc20   92-26
                                                                   CIP

Printed in the United States of America

9 8 7 6 5 4 3 2 1

"*I'll be somebody's wife. I'll be faceless. Anonymous. I wanted to be the star. I wanted to have my own game show. I wanted to dance with the Rockettes. Once. I want to replace Sandra Day O'Connor on the Supreme Court. Because you know they'll never appoint two of us.*"

Julia Wainwright, to her Matron of Honor,
contemplating her imminent marriage to
Mason Capwell, *Santa Barbara*, June 2, 1989
(Patrick Mulcahey)

"*When is it going to be my turn? You keep wanting to be the star of my life story. Well, you can't be because I want to be the star. I was doing very well, you know, before I met you. I never was lonely and I never needed anything that I couldn't get for myself. Until you came along and started treating me like a conquered nation, and I let you, and maybe I want to let you again, but so what? I mean, what the hell good is life if you don't learn anything from it?*"

Julia Capwell, to Mason Capwell, evaluating
their marriage, *Santa Barbara*, April 5, 1990
(Patrick Mulcahey)

"*Be bold, be bold, be not too bold.*"

The writing on the wall for Britomart,
in Book III, *The Fairie Queene*,
Edmund Spenser

Contents

Illustrations

Acknowledgments

First, although I had my own industry experience to guide me in writing this book, I am deeply indebted to a large group of generous, creative people from the soap opera community for augmenting my own small perspective: Sheri Anderson, Richard Biggs, Lane Davies, Bridget and Jerry Dobson, Nancy Ford, Michael Gliona, Nancy Grahn, Leah Laiman, Terry Lester, Douglas Marland, Patrick Mulcahey, Stephen Nichols, Agnes Nixon, Barbara Perlman, Jill Farren Phelps, Al Rabin, Charlotte Savitz, Anne Schoettle, Charles Shaughnessy, Courtney Simon, Millee Taggert, and Steve Wyman. Here's to all of you, who seize the moment and make it glad you did, as you create, through daily magic, a dramatic experience unlike any other.

Next, to my academic colleagues I owe a great deal for their considerable help and encouragement. Thank you to Elaine Hoffman Baruch, Miriam Fuchs, and Patricia Ondek Laurence for reading my manuscript in its early stages. Thank you to President Jay Sexter, Provost Peter French (both of Mercy College), and to Henry and Phyllis Beinstein, Nancy A. Benson, Lynne and Joshua Berrett, Sydney Callahan, Fay T. Greenwald, Betty Krasne, Robin Landa, Charles Merzbacher, and Barbara Traister for advice and collegial support. Thank you to the Faculty Development Committee at Mercy College for generous financial support. Thank you to my students at Mercy—their bright eyes lit my way many a time—and to my students and colleagues at the Tisch School of the Arts at New York University, whose passion for that flickering screen kept my batteries charged.

At all times, I was grateful for access to the treasures of the libraries at Mercy College and New York University. *Soap Opera Digest* was kind enough to permit me use of its photoarchives. Thank you to the very gracious people—especially Charlotte Lowther—at Tree Music Publishing for granting me permission to quote from "Crazy." I was fortunate in being permitted to use the Irna Phillips Papers at the State Historical Society of Wisconsin.

At the University of California Press, I owe much to project editor Pamela MacFarland Holway, a careful *and* buoyant trail companion, and to copy editor Anne Geissman Canright. And to acquisitions editor Naomi Schneider for jumping in with so much enthusiasm midway through the project. Special thanks to my editor, Ernest Callenbach, for those long, literate, supportive letters, for lunch, and, above all, for believing in me.

Finally: thank you to Dale Ortmeyer, a very important friend and mentor. Thank you to my dearest children, David and Holly, who change me every day through the *amazing* difference of their texts from mine. Thank you to my permanent (steadfast, wise-and-gentle) gentleman caller, Richard Nochimson: "feather of lead, bright smoke, cold fire . . . waking sleep that is not what it is. . . . God help me, I'm in love" (*Santa Barbara*, June 2, 1989).

Prologue: An Invitation to Recovery

The combination of a dissertation-in-progress on my desk and a baby or two in every other room of a small apartment forced me to desperate measures. Housebound for the first time in my adult life, I turned on daytime television as an anodyne—with great reluctance, as I had always imagined soap opera in the demeaning terms in which it is conventionally discussed. Much to my surprise, though, I discovered that I liked the daytime serials. Once I became part of the daytime audience, it did not take me long to discover that my contempt for soap opera was an attitude I had adopted never having seen a soap opera, on the recommendation of social commentators who had also never really seen a soap opera. Among the many others (of all educational backgrounds) who have made the same discovery, some, like me, have come to the conclusion that the critics are in error, but more daytime viewers furtively watch soap operas hoping that no one will find out, convinced that their pleasure, which conflicts with the dicta of social authorities, is unworthy of validation.

In the modern world, where technology imposes authoritative discourse so efficiently on daily life, we find that many of the prismlike facets of private encounter avert their faces from the gaze of public Truth. Indeed, Hans-Georg Gadamer held that no one's life is reflected accurately by most of public discourse and has called the first task of philosophy the exploration of "how our natural view of the world—the experience of the world that we have as we simply live our lives—is related to the unassailable and anonymous authority that confronts us."[1]

Here, Gadamer suggests that resistance on behalf of the marginal is a major priority. Resistance is my task in this study.

What do I resist? In the tradition of previous psychological readings of screen fiction, particularly those of Tania Modleski and Mary Ann Doane,[2] I resist media marginalization of feminine discourse. However, my reading of soap opera represents a significant change from previous critical methods. Most feminist film criticism has unmasked the way the Hollywood movie assumes essential, biologically determined female and male gender and then encourages the female spectator to buy into the inevitable, "natural" domination of the female by the male. In other words, it exposes Hollywood's sly reinforcement, through narrative fantasies, of the masculine politics of both the industry and the society that produce cinema. Regarding soap opera, the task is different. I shall argue that soap opera *is* a kind of feminine discourse. As do the movies, soap opera assumes an essential femininity and masculinity, but there the similarity ends, for soap opera looks with a very critical eye at Hollywood's rigid interpretation of gender roles: women tucked securely under the influence of men. Hollywood fantasy is the fantasy of patriarchy. In soap opera, by contrast, another kind of yearning emerges, one rarely permitted expression in our culture. Soap opera includes a female subject.

The proposition that soap opera is a resistant feminine discourse will excite many people who have secretly harbored like-minded intuitions. However, it flies in the face of strongly defended assumptions, both conventional and radical. First, so many mainstream discourses have defined soap opera as the backward child of media that a thesis such as mine has the appearance of nominating the student ranked lowest in the standings as class valedictorian. This study will aim in part to demonstrate why consensus among a great many very knowledgeable people does not necessarily point the way to truth. Second, my claim may outrage those concerned with marginalized discourses and populations, who understandably criticize network broadcasting as one of the major producers of texts in which women, non-Christians, people of color, and gays and lesbians are presented as objects of the white, male, Christian subject. In part of what follows, I will discuss how contradictions within the patriarchal network system have ironically made soap opera, a feminine text, part of that system's economic foundations. Third, the very discussion of feminine discourse will raise hackles among some feminists—even among those with whose intentions and goals I agree. Let me explain.

Our culture has made a habit of relegating women to supposedly cozy corners by means of essentialist texts, that is, texts which assume an innate difference between masculinity and femininity. Because soap opera dramatizes an innate gender distinction, it automatically sets off some feminist alarm bells. There is a wariness that essentialist texts willy-nilly perpetuate the conventional male-female division that has historically involved masculine domination of the feminine and the foreclosing of a possible female subject position. The current popularity of some reactionary theorists has intensified feminist anxiety that unless we discuss masculinity and femininity in terms that transcend historical conditioning, we will remain "always ready" to slip into undesirable old sexist patterns.[3]

However, a desire for purity in these matters may, in fact, work against thoughtful exploration. Susan Bordo speaks of the limitlessness of the task of even imagining texts that will not create problematic patterns: "the dynamics of inclusion and exclusion . . . are played out on multiple and shifting fronts, and all ideas (no matter how 'liberatory' in some contexts or for some purposes) are condemned to be haunted by a voice from the margins already speaking (or perhaps muted but awaiting the conditions for speech), awakening us to what has been excluded, effaced, damaged."[4] Others have pointed out that the single-minded determination to avoid the concept of essence may be self-contradictory. As Diana Fuss points out, all thought entails some use of universals; indeed, to reject essentialism for constructionism—the theory that gender is socially created—is to polarize the two, "to buy into essentialism in the very act of making the charge; to act as if essentialism has an essence."[5] I do not fear essentialism, but rather those kinds of "good intentions" that keep us from examining the way it influences culture.

Of course, it is impossible to assert categorically that gender is or is not in any way innately determined. We simply are not scientifically equipped to decide between essentialism and constructionism. In fact, this project has made me sensitive to a nonscientific difficulty which complicates that decision: the inability to make a clear conceptual distinction between the two. Those who emphasize their anti-essentialist orientation frequently use quotation marks around the words "masculine" and "feminine" to indicate that these are supposed distinctions. Nevertheless, the very necessity for the device also indicates that, whether for historical or cosmic reasons, conceptions of masculinity and femininity seem inevitable. For this reason, exploration of those discourses that predicate innate differences between the sexes seems to me invaluable for understanding how we operate in society as it exists today. Soap opera's contextualization of gender distinctions marks it as a text particularly worthy of study. By exploring its use of essential gender, we will discover a fascinating and only barely suspected truth about daytime serial. Soap opera is too often viewed as a cheap version of the most melodramatic and conventional movies. This derogation bespeaks not the real nature of soap opera but a combined denial or anxiety shared by otherwise unlikely allies: most power brokers, most academics, and some feminists.

To understand the reaction of the soap opera audience and the potential of television technology to influence gender, we must see soap opera as it really is: an ironic recovery of the feminine through a most unexpected means. Michel Foucault has written, "Discourse is a system of possibility. It is what allows us to produce statements which will either be true or false—it makes possible a field of knowledge."[6] Appreciation of the construction of femininity produced by soap opera discourse has been thwarted by our lack of clarity about its "system of possibility." The blockage is not a problem solely for the spectator.

Unfortunately, the people who make soap operas do not themselves have easy access to language that allows them to conceptualize what they are doing. This is a situation common to all marginalized endeavors and peoples. People who do not fit the mainstream categories are "stuck" trying to express their own desires and to organize their experience with a set of classifications that pointedly exclude them. In the soap opera community, the result has been that the inordinate power of groundless mainstream ideas has riddled that community with cynicism and self-deprecation, obstructing self-knowledge among the majority of soap opera professionals, even those who are excellent at what they do.

In short, the industry is working in the conceptual dark concerning important aspects of the soap opera form. Technicians describe its technology; network administrators discuss ratings: dimmers and share numbers are perfectly congenial with the power structures that generate soap opera. What remains unsaid pertains to the tone of daytime fiction, which chooses for its protagonists not the conventional conquering heroes but instead women who regard the will to power and domination with a real sense of distrust. My method in this study is to articulate soap opera's silent reality as a gendered screen fiction with its own aesthetics and narrative and visual technologies. In doing so, I will follow the tradition of interpreting feminine discourse available in the criticism of Modleski and Doane, as well as in the work in related areas by Nancy Chodorow, Carol Gilligan, Mary Field Belenky, and Mary Daly.[7]

Soap opera fantasy, of course, includes a full array of human characteristics and conditions—religion, race, culture, sexual preference—in addition to gender. Granted, gender plays a more active role than these others in defining the soap opera fantasy; nevertheless, it should be recognized that the entire spectrum of difference is addressed—sometimes dazzlingly—in soap opera fiction. Thus, although the lioness's share of this study will be taken up with exploring what soap opera says about gender, in the last chapter I shall discuss in some detail its address to other social categories.

This study actively contests the reigning tautology that the soap opera form should not be taken seriously because it should not be taken seriously. Instead, I hope to bring to my reader an understanding of soap opera and the community that produces it, to suggest its narrative energy and the ways in which it is possessed of the same organic richness and complexity we recognize in texts and lives we have been given cultural carte blanche to value.

I am in a unique position to do this. In addition to my theoretical interests, I bring to this study my experience as a writer, a consultant, and an editor for five soap operas: *Ryan's Hope*, *Search for Tomorrow*, *Guiding Light*, *Loving*, and, most briefly, *Santa Barbara*. Thus, I can claim the sympathetic perspective of the participant, an advantage that has helped me to avoid simply imposing film theory, psychology, linguistics, and philosophy in the service of dominant cultural assumptions. By extension, all of my readings assume that good soap opera provides a cultural experience for the spectator as valid as that provided by any good production of any art form.

In *All That Hollywood Allows*, Jackie Byars emphatically cautions against unskeptical feminist critics who perceive and describe "ideas and documents as independent from the social, political, and economic conditions and people that produce them."[8] To provide some context for what is to follow, I should first offer some basic information about the production conditions of soap opera. Profiling the daytime production team will also partially explain how the patriarchal network hierarchy ironically authorizes the broadcast of resistant discourse.

In most ways, the destiny of a show is directed by its executive producer, whose job is to bring in the ratings so that sponsors can be billed for the maximum fee. How he or she interprets this charge determines the aesthetic of the soap opera, which is effected by line producers—producers responsible for the technical operations of the show—directors, writers, and the other professionals who realize the "look" of the show in costumes, makeup, hair design, and sets, and the actors and actresses. The executive producer, wielding command over a budget that supports a population almost the size of a village, exerts the most influence on the taste and the tone of a show. If the executive has a powerful vision, the show becomes an organic creation with a distinct and compelling identity; if her or she falters or is impeded by external authorities, the show itself falters, or, in the worst-case scenario, fails to acquire any identity.

However, at the same time that this theoretically well-articulated central authority sits in place, a subversive pattern of organization is also at work, one almost equally powerful. If centralized power is relentlessly applied in making daytime television, it is just as relentlessly eroded by the dailiness of soap opera production. There simply isn't time for those in charge to police the complex, interdependent soap opera community. An account of the process by which the script alone is generated may provide some insight into how impossible it is for hierarchy to operate with the kind of control possible when more production time is available.

Story ideas are thrashed out by one or more head writers and the executive producer, in consultation with network liaisons, who may include the vice president for daytime. Together they come up with the "long story." The head writer then delegates downward, assigning the pacing of events and character encounters to the breakdown writers, who work out daily outlines for scripts, which in turn serve to organize the show into acts. There are generally three acts, separated by commercials, in a half-hour soap opera and six acts in an hour-long one. The air time given to a separate story within an act is usually called a beat. In modern television soap opera, an act typically includes two or three beats, but may go as high as five or as low as one.

Each "breakdown," as these script outlines are called, is then assigned to one of as many as five scriptwriters, who fleshes it out with dialogue and dramatic structure. Each scriptwriter is responsible for an entire day's show. The writer's prerogatives in using the breakdown vary greatly from soap opera to soap opera. Some serials use highly developed breakdowns that mandate a great deal of what the scriptwriters will do; some go as far as to indicate crucial dialogue. Others assume that the breakdowns will serve as broad guidelines, thus leaving room for a writer to exercise a good deal of discretion. In such cases, although scriptwriters are never permitted to change a location or the general outcome and direction of a character's destiny, some writers have the option to omit scenes and replace them with others that are compatible but give a more subtle or interesting spin to character motivation than was suggested in the breakdowns. Upon completion, all draft scripts are edited for continuity and emotional focus by the head writer, the editor, or both. At any point, too, those higher in the pecking order—the executive producer or the network officials—may edit further.

The theoretical traffic pattern is neat; in practice, however, the lines of flow become random. Under the time pressures of producing the daily episode, anyone may wind up doing any of these chores. Further, the soap opera script, for all its supposed fixity in a hierarchical chain, is in a fluid state until it is taped, being always subject to change by the executive producer, the editor, the head writer, or the actors. Even when a script is not amended, its force may be totally transformed by the vision of the director and the interpretations of the players, who often uncover nuances that become the basis of new plot vectors in future scripts. Indeed, some of the most exciting characters and stories have evolved through administratively unplanned influences. In the formative years of *The Young and The Restless*, for example, the maverick character of Jack Abbott was at least in part the invention of Terry Lester, who acted the part. Noting the freedom to create character and tone accorded to Tony Geary on *General Hospital*, Lester played with Jack's dialogue according to his intuitions about the character and soon became aware that his take on Jack's nature was being picked up by the writers.[9] The resistance of an actor to plans that have come down from the top can also change the course of a show. In the late eighties, when *Santa Barbara* was the standard of creative invention in daytime serial, Nancy Grahn, who plays Julia Wainwright, often debated with the writers and producers Julia's direction on the show. When her understanding of Julia was baffled by an intended plot line, she struggled to guard her version of the character's integrity by refusing to play it out. More than once, she contributed to the definition of her character by rewriting dialogue both with and for her acting partner.[10] Similarly, during the early eighties, the period of greatest creativity on *Days of Our Lives*, Patsy Pease and Charles Shaughnessy (Kimberly Brady and Shane Donovan) approached the writers when they thought Kimberly and Shane had not fully explored certain issues, notably Shane's reaction to Kimberly's past as a prostitute.[11] And scores of other actors have contributed to the show by involving themselves in story planning.

Thus, the multiple viewpoints characteristic of the multiplot soap opera text are also characteristic of the creative process of soap opera at its best. In speaking about their work, soap opera professionals are clear about the interdependence and fluidity of their teams. One evocative word they use about their organization is "organic." Despite the privileged place of the executive producer in the hierarchy, the daily schedule seldom allows time for her or him to exercise rigorous authority from the top. The best executive producer in soap opera is one who sets out a coherent set of general guidelines but can mobilize inspiration from any of the myriad possible points of operation. The ineffective executive producer, conversely, is one who wastes energy on a vision dominated by a need for control that compels him or her to try to block too many of the nerve paths of the organization. Because of the time constraints under which it is created, and unlike any other screen fiction, soap opera captures for the camera much of the immediacy of an improvisational group, working within a coherent text and a coherent aesthetic.

The above influences far outweigh any that may come from the network divisions of standards and practices, which can order that a scene be censored. Many spectators wonder just how powerful network censors are; I certainly did before I worked in the industry. In my experience, the intervention of the station sponsors was rare and never of a social or political nature. I am personally aware only of instances in which the censors objected to a particular kind of physical contact between acting partners in love scenes. For example, during the taping of my first script for *Ryan's Hope*, the Office of Standards and Practices called directly to the studio floor to tell the director that Frank Ryan could not spank his wife in jest, even though she would shortly get her own back. In another instance, on *Santa Barbara*, a bathtub scene between Nancy Grahn and Terry Lester, already on tape, was deemed too sexually explicit and edited out. In raising such objections, however, the Office of Standards and Practices does not take orders directly from the sponsors but instead reproduces preceived social norms. Indeed, I have never had first- or even second-hand knowledge of the power of the sponsor that most of us imagine to be so pervasive in television.

Radio was a different story. The correspondence between Irna Phillips, a pioneer radio soap opera writer, and her sponsors makes it clear that the hand of the sponsor lay heavy upon radio soap opera.[12] Many letters and memos, discussing plans for new soap operas and those already on the air, explicitly limit Phillips to material that demonstrates correct "Christian" attitudes and that does not mention another sponsor's products. In current television production, the network employees who deal with the sponsors are quite separate from the soap opera production unit: no direct line of communication exists between sponsor and producer, let alone writer. In my experience and that of my acquaintances in the industry, sponsors in daytime television remain shadowy people, who simply pay more when the ratings are higher.

In fact, although there are many unfounded pronoucements to the contrary, daytime serials are not homogenized by the networks, and they are strongly influences by the individual sensibilities of a large number of people who work on them. Different soap operas are far from interchangeable. Even within the fast-paced conditions of soap opera production, the producer is able to create a tone that will establish a serial's identity, typically by focusing the staff's attention on a particular emphasis. For example, in 1978, the watershed year of the existence of *General Hospital*, executive producer Gloria Monty made the hallmark of the show a rapid shift between the threads of the many multiplots. Under executive producer Jill Farren Phelps and her group of innovative writers and directors, humor, an assault on the "fourth wall," and self-contained fantasy episodes became the signature of *Santa Barbara*. The emotional bonding of the audience as participants in *Days of Our Lives* has been the trademark of the show under Al Rabin, supervising executive producer. Such factors will be further articulated in the chapters to follow.

When things are working well, the daily soap opera episode is a triumph of fresh and unorthodox narrative made possible by a marriage between technology and the spirit of the creative artist. My purpose in this book is to remove the veil from this exciting process and from the richness of the soap opera text. In the process, those who already enjoy the genre will likely find support for their engagement. Meanwhile, those who will never enjoy it may begin to understand the value it has for those who do. And those who have no experience of it may decide they would like to see what all the fuss is about.

CHAPTER ONE

No End to Her: The Place of Soap Opera as Screen Fiction

A narrative form associated primarily with women, soap opera tends to provoke the same mix of desire and disdain that femininity itself produces in our culture. As with women, so with soap opera: one cannot speak of desire without ambiguity, since both the enjoyment of soap opera and the comforts and delights of intimacy associated with women and celebrated by soap opera have been defined mainly by their detractors.

Not long ago, Freud synthesized science and Sophocles and came up with an address to men that assigns the Oedipal narrative a central place in understanding the role of the maternal: however alluring, closeness with women threatens the integrity of the adult ego, unless it is policed by the father—the patriarchal. But some two thousand years before Freud, classical literature had already provided masculine narrative contexts for riding herd on the attractions of femininity: the "heroic" mastery of Circe and Dido, for example. Contain the delights of the feminine, say the new and old wise men of the West, or be thrown into division and degradation. Soap opera, a discourse quite at home with the comforts and intimacy associated with women, must inevitably be a renegade discourse. Given the traditions of our culture, it would have been a miracle had soap opera met with easy acceptance.

Thus it is no wonder that soap opera, imbued with the very sense of feminine importance that culture warns against, has sometimes been defined as dangerous. For example, Dr. Louis Berg conducted a crusade to convince the public that radio soap opera was hazardous to the listener's health, of which more below. More often, however, soap opera has simply been discredited as trivial. People who watch soap opera are expected, in casual conversation, to defer in silence to those who hold forth confidently on its negligibility while proudly stating that they have never watched a full episode. Similarly, academics who enjoy soap opera are hesitant to enshrine their fascination in print. In so doing, they acquiesce to the prevailing opinion of critics, who view any extended discussion of the topic as unnecessary, preferring to register disdain in parenthetical asides. Molly Haskell's famous, if unfounded, dismissal of both the woman's picture and soap opera in one fell swoop (see below) is a good example of the "learned" way of vaporizing the daytime serial form.

Unfortunately, then, silence characterizes most of those partial to soap opera, whereas language belongs almost exclusively to its critics. This study is therefore dedicated to discovering a discourse capable of expressing the achievements of one of America's few original art forms, a form that has suffered from a persistent, a priori rejection by the intellectual and power establishments, even the establishment that produces soap opera.

Trivialization of the genre is built into the very term *soap opera*—a name the industry did not give itself: stories that sell soap—which supports the erroneous belief that the form is little more than an elaborate kind of broadcast advertising that uses narrative to entice the potential consumer. Historically, of course, soap opera did come into being at the same time that broadcast advertising began to experiment with the dramatic scenario. But the daytime serial is not about selling.

In 1923 Ivory soap initiated an entirely new concept of marketing in the form of a newspaper campaign designed by Mark Wiseman. Wiseman created, in comic strip format, a "selling drama" about the Jollyco family, composed of Mr. and Mrs. Jollyco and their three children, whose lives revolved around soap. Narrative conflict was provided by an Oedipal distrust of the sensual fascinations of a certain Mrs. Percival Billington Follderol, who used (adulterated) perfumed soap rather than pure Ivory. On the strength of marketing studies conducted by Proctor & Gamble which suggested that a broadcast campaign using narrative could be equally successful, a young woman named Irna Phillips was then asked to reproduce the Ivory success on radio. She accordingly created a serial narrative called *Painted Dreams*, a daily fifteen-minute episodic show that aired briefly in 1930. Like the Ivory campaign, it focused on a family, this time called the Suddses, in hopes of attracting the Super-Suds Company as the show's sponsor.[1]

Yet Phillips's *Painted Dreams* is not, as it is sometimes called, the first soap opera. The most that can be said is that it encouraged an existing belief that radio technology could produce such a thing as daily drama. The direct descendants of the Suddses and the Jollycos are dishwashing liquid's own Madge the Manicurist and Mrs. Butterworth, the talking pancake syrup bottle—figures who conform to the Western tradition that guards against feminine sexuality. Madge and Mrs. Butterworth, however, are a far cry from the Lords and the Woleks of Llanview on *One Life to Live*, or the Bradys and the Hortons of Salem on *Days of Our Lives*, or the Hugheses, the Stewarts, the Dixons of Oakdale on *As the World Turns*, or the Capwells and their friends on *Santa Barbara*. While these characters may have emerged from the same basic conditions as did narrative advertising, they were destined to inhabit a unique form of screen fiction that privileges a feminine perspective. The remainder of this chapter will explore the history and theory of how soap opera, as opposed to narrative advertisement, originated and evolved, a story that—although linked briefly at its beginning to the Jollycos and the Suddses—has its own particular twists and turns.

Soap Opera, Femininity, and Desire

Soap opera is about women and desire. If the earliest interpretation of that desire was the sponsor's narrative of women's purported passion for personal and domestic cleanliness, this masculine affront to feminine aspirations was soon forced aside by the heroines who emerged from the special conditions governing soap opera production. The chronicle of what worked and what did not in soap opera's development demonstrates that the concerns of the heroine, rather than those of the sponsor, evoked the greatest response in the audience that first listened to and then watched soap opera.

In the career of Irna Phillips, widely known as the mother of the genre, we see in microcosm how the commercial establishment came to fund the development of a narrative that, root and (especially) branch, challenges the social definition of femininity. In 1933 Phillips wrote a memo about her plans for *Today's Children*, the successor to the fleeting

Painted Dreams and an early precursor to soap opera in its own right. In this memo, which clearly indicates that at the time Phillips still saw herself not as dramatist but as advertiser, she details her strategy for embedding advertising for La France bluing, a washing product, into the script of *Today's Children*. Phillips had worked out a two-week "story build" to the climactic moment when Mother Moran, one of the show's characters, would appeal to the listeners to "help Terry," a character in distress. Mother Moran was then to be told by the announcer that the show's sponsor, La France, would come to Terry's rescue, thus motivating the audience to buy La France in gratitude—and also to take advantage of the special premium offer bound up with the story's plot line.[2]

Today's Children managed to remain on the air from 1933 to 1938, but it just barely survived. Although during that period it changed its address to the audience significantly, relegating contests and special offers that tied the sponsor to the characters to the periphery of the soap opera's emotional story, the series remained too close to its predecessor, the selling drama. Such advertising was doomed as a central feature of daytime serial.

Phillips's early collusion with the sponsors, then, was not rewarded by notable success. For several years, she was eclipsed by Frank and Ann Hummert, who dominated radio with the first daytime serials that were distinct from selling dramas, including *The Romance of Helen Trent*, *Mary Noble, Backstage Wife*, and *Our Gal Sunday*. The Hummerts had not only taken the ball from Phillips but run with it in a different direction. If there is a simple way to say what the Hummerts had done with soap opera, it is that they told stories about how women feel. But Phillips eventually caught up with the Hummerts. In 1936 she created *The Guiding Light*, her first major soap opera success. This serial, which established her new, purely emotional approach to daytime drama, marked the beginning of what was to become the longest-running soap opera of all time. Phillips was no longer confusing marketing strategies with daytime serial.[3]

Indeed, Phillips's changing priorities are documented in her own voice. In 1941, when Phillips proposed a soap opera based on the successful film *Kitty Foyle* to a potential sponsor, Lady Esther cosmetics, toward the end of her memo she belatedly assures the sponsor of revenues. However, at no time in the memo does Phillips suggest any subordination of story to product. Instead, Phillips's approach to Lady Esther soars on the wings of emotional rhetoric: Kitty's story, she says, gives a name and a narrative to the invisible woman who "attends to those hundred and one details you don't even know exist." Phillips in fact insists that the movie for which Ginger Rogers won her Academy Award does not fully tell Kitty's story. Only the endless soap opera format can do Kitty justice. All we women, she says, "have something of the Kitty Foyle in us. We go on living, and why shouldn't she? Not only between book ends—not only on the silver screen—but on the greatest of all vehicles for human drama . . . the air waves. Why shouldn't she?"[4]

In this proposal we see Phillips's dedication to soap opera as a unique form for talking about the unspoken lives of women. By 1941 she was well beyond Mother Moran and her putative emotional relationship to La France bluing. Rather, Phillips was intrigued by the figure of the career woman, and by her ambiguous social position as both extraordinary and anonymous. And she saw soap opera as the best dramatic form for putting that narrative on record. Of course, the career woman in question, Kitty Foyle, was already a cultural fact, with a Hollywood story behind her. It is significant, however, that Phillips chose Kitty over the standard "woman alone," a character purveyed by Hollywood in movies such as *Back Street*. *Back Street* portrayed a long-suffering woman who, having set her heart on a socially prominent married man, dutifully remained his mistress, refraining from committing to plans or relationships that would give *her* social standing in order to accommodate his passions and needs. In short, feminine desire was painted as irretrievably marginal to morally upstanding society. By rejecting a similar proposal, however, Kitty gallantly affirmed a place in society for her desire, even if it was not as fashionable as that of the socially prominent man who wanted her at his beck and call. In short, Phillips had developed not only a commitment to daytime serial but one that had great affinity with feminine resistance to social definitions of the woman's place. Nevertheless, Phillips had not yet gone as far as she would.

In 1956 Phillips created *As the World Turns* for television. Indeed, we may say that with it she created television soap opera. Where previous attempts at television soap operas had merely thrust the fifteen-minute radio-designed format in front of a camera, Phillips's *As the World Turns* was conceived specifically for television and, revolutionary for soap opera, for a half-hour time slot. Homing in on the possibilities of the new medium, Phillips altered dramatic conventions of time and space to create the now old-fashioned but then radical soap opera style, employing thoughtful, elongated moments and a multitude of close-ups.[5]

It was on this show in 1973—some thirty years after she had taken on the task of preventing society from excluding the Kitty Foyles of the world—that Phillips pushed her commitment past what her sponsor, and the public, were ready for. She had begun to develop a narrative for *As the World Turns* about a new character, Kim Reynolds, an independent and aggressive young woman. All was going well until Reynolds went Kitty Foyle a few better. Whereas the innocent Kitty had been wooed by a philandering suitor, Reynolds herself seduced Dr. Bob Hughes, one of the serial's "ideal" husbands. The audience reacted with shock and surprise—not to Reynolds's manipulativeness (she was, after all, an "independent" young woman) but to her success. Phillips, however, was determined that the liaison remain intact and that Reynolds be given the life denied Kitty Foyle—that is, sole possession of the man she wanted, and on her own terms. Proctor & Gamble viewed Phillips's story as public sanction for immorality; Reynolds, they said, must be punished and the affair terminated. Phillips refused to accommodate the demand, and she was fired.

Phillips died shortly after the termination of her contract, and some commentators believe that losing her battle played some part in her death, although this cannot be documented. The relationship between biography and creation is always a source of curiosity. Irna Phillips dying of a broken heart because her fictional alter ego was as thwarted in desire as Phillips was in life makes a "good story." Yet there is reliable evidence that Phillips *did* contribute to the form she worked in by imbuing it with the truth of *her* desire.

Agnes Nixon, initially Irna's protégée and ultimately a major force in determining the direction of soap opera, was also Phillips's good friend (fig. 1). She recalls her mentor's idealization of family life and her belief that, had she married, she would have been a happy woman. Nixon doubts that Phillips would really have gained by trading her professional success for family life, suggesting that imagination overruled experience in Phillips. Phillips had not grown up in a happy family. Indeed, Nixon asserts that Phillips created the idealized Dr. Bob Hughes of *As the World Turns*, together with Chris and Nancy Hughes, his ever-solicitous parents, in the spirit of Emily Dickinson's insight that success is always sweetest to those who ne'er succeed.[6] Seen in this light, the fantasy of the erotic intruder Kim Reynolds insuating herself into Bob Hughes's life as his rightful love might be credibly construed as Phillips's fantasy of herself looking in on the idealized Hughes tribe and acquiring a place at the patriarchal table by imagining a world of gratified female desire.

Only in hindsight can we see the real meaning of the controversy generated by Phillips's bold authorial stroke. Kim Reynolds wanted a

Fig. 1. Agnes Nixon, pro-
tégée of Irna Phillips. In
creating *One Life to Live* and
All My Children, Nixon led
daytime serial writing into
the modern era.

man but was not content to be contained by social conventions, including marriage. Like Reynolds, Phillips construed that desire to be at
least as authentic as the socially sanctioned sexual involvement of Bob
Hughes. In contrast, the production executives enforced the venerable
prohibition on female desire when they insisted that Bob Hughes be
contrite about allowing an "enchantress" to lure him from the straight
and narrow. Phillips's clash with the network was not just an anecdote
about selling floor wax.

Mother Moran to Kitty Foyle to Kim Reynolds: these transitions in a
sense encapsulate what happened to feminine desire in soap opera narrative during its formative years. Even though feminine desire had always
driven the soap opera form, it was increasingly articulated in terms of the
resistance it met from social constraints. Hindsight suggests that had
Proctor & Gamble permitted Phillips to proceed as she wanted to with
the character of Kim Reynolds on *As the World Turns*, she would have
continued to be the most innovative force in daytime serial.

Indeed, in that moment of defiance in 1973, when she infuriated fans and hurt ratings by championing Kim Reynolds's seduction of Bob Hughes, Phillips was also, for whatever motives, pushing soap opera toward its destiny. No more "Ms. Nice Girl." Soap opera heroines were now on their way to redefining proper feminine comportment. True, for the time being, a serious encounter between the desires of soap opera heroines and public definitions of feminine propriety had been averted. But it could not be put off indefinitely: the soap opera heroine could not be forever denied. In this first major skirmish, the Kim Reynolds saga, the woman only *seemed* to be vanquished. As a generic figure, the soap opera heroine was about to seize the reins of her destiny with a dramatic flourish. Years later, even Kim Reynolds finally got what she wanted—as we shall see.

The fight over the Kim Reynolds story line heralded a major transition for the soap opera heroine that finally took place in the 1970s. As a result, the soap opera heroine no longer had to bear the guilt for any conflict between her wishes and the institution of marriage. In the late seventies, on ABC's *General Hospital*, the character of Laura Webber made a reality of the story of active feminine desire that Phillips almost told. With Laura, the soap opera heroine stepped forward as part of a media form that was becoming increasingly emphatic in its feminine challenge to the entrenched masculine narrative perspective.[7] Now marriage—a ritual ordinarily defined by the transfer of woman from father to husband—might be considered guilty of transgressing female desire.

Between 1978 and 1980, *General Hospital* focused on Laura Webber, a young woman with a determination to discover her own desires and pursue them. She captured the national imagination, quickly passing the point of expressed desire at which Kim Reynolds was stopped. Moreover, Laura's fidelity to her passion, rather than to her conventionally perfect marriage, inspired public approval, not outrage. The enthusiasm aroused by Laura's defiance of the bonds of marriage meant that the moment had finally come for soap opera to keep an appointment with the American public, one it had had from the beginning. It was permitted the open display of female fantasies about feminine erotic energy.

In 1978 Laura was brought to full bloom by Douglas Marland, who, having become head writer for *General Hospital*, terminated plans for a projected story line that he insisted would violate all credible emotional reality. The plan was that Laura's mother, Leslie Webber—recently married and thoroughly committed to her husband—be "storied" into an affair with David Hamilton, whose introduction into the *General*

Fig. 2. Douglas Marland, protégé of Harding Lemay, who was a leading light at Proctor & Gamble. By rewriting the direction of a love affair on *General Hospital*, Marland made soap opera history.

Hospital community was intended as a routine device to keep the plot moving. Unable to imagine such a chain of events, Marland was challenged to invent an alternate story that would give the characters something to do for the next days, weeks, months—years, if possible. Marland realized that, while the idea of desire incubating in the otherwise passionately committed Leslie was highly implausible, Leslie's vulnerable teenage daughter, Laura, might be just the ticket. Despite a reigning industry prejudice against foregrounding teenage romances, *General Hospital* went with Marland's story (fig. 2).[8]

Marland's story called for fourteen-year-old Laura to be initiated into sex by Hamilton, a man she would later come to understand had used her as a substitute for the actual object of his desire, her mother. When it became clear to Laura that her seducer had no intention either of loving her or of relinquishing his claim to her, she protested against further sexual involvement. Hamilton, however, thoroughly insensitive to the gravity of Laura's feelings and completely intent on using Laura for his own pleasure, sought to override her resistance with a violent sexual assault. Laura defended herself by killing him.

This story, which Marland deemed emotionally valid and which the audience enthusiastically embraced, has not been adequately recognized for its distinctiveness in mainstream screen narrative, a form of mass entertainment notable for its justification, indeed romanticizing, of the use of force against women in sex. The millions of girls who claimed that they loved Laura's story because she was "just like them" were not all upper-middle-class blondes who had been seduced and humiliated by suave sophisticates who were really lusting after their mothers.

Laura was a character in what initially looked like a conventional narrative, but in her case that narrative was recontextualized. Instead of being turned into an object, as would have happened in a typical Hollywood movie, Laura rejected that culturally sanctioned role and in so doing validated the desires of her spectators. Through the power of displacement, Laura's seducer, David Hamilton, could, moreover, occupy the position of father, brother, or boyfriend. Watching Laura's "no in thunder" to Hamilton's violent attempt to appropriate her, the audience was thus allowed to experience, in fantasy, long-submerged objections for which there was virtually no public sanction. It gave permission to rage, at least in private, against the gender implications of Hollywood's master narrative. By her response to Hamilton, Laura— though not yet a fully active subject—struck out against the classical role of the screen heroine.

Laura became a more complete subject in 1980. That is, she became the locus of the organizing intelligence of what is seen and of the organizing energy behind what is done. As her story evolved, Laura again rejected being relegated to the status of an object, this time not by a seducer of young girls but by her new husband, Scotty Baldwin, a model young man in the community. In this arc of her story line, Laura became aware that although she was no longer playing second fiddle to her mother, she was still an object. Her "good husband," Scotty, was kinder and gentler toward her than David Hamilton had been; nevertheless, she was fast becoming the major "thing" in his collection. Her insistence on a truth even more basic to her needs than the marriage vows she had taken would require her to deviate from social norms and expectations. Thus, when Laura ran off with the socially unacceptable Luke Spencer, soap opera heroines everywhere embarked on an active dialogue with social norms.

Soap Opera, Mainstream
Critical Discourse, and Desire

The line from Kim Reynolds to Laura Webber could have provoked serious critical interest in the soap opera form, especially with regard to its definition of female desire. The existence of Kim and Laura could also have raised questions about the early years of soap opera, and about the traditions out of which such characters emerged. But that did not happen. In its earliest years, and until recently, soap opera has been systematically misperceived. Consider the 1942 claim of psychiatrist Louis Berg that he had data to *prove* that listening to soap operas caused an "acute anxiety state, tachycardia, arrhythmias, increase in blood pressure, profuse perspiration, tremors, vasomotor instability, nocturnal frights, vertigo, and gastro-intestinal disturbances."[9] Berg soon became the center of a serious crusade to remove soap operas from the air—serious because here at last was scientific evidence to support the vague uneasiness that soap operas caused some cultural observers.

As it turns out, Berg's use of the scientific method was both desperate and illegitimate, for the data on which he based his attack were gathered solely from the measurement of *his own* physical responses while he listened to the radio.[10] The unfortunate Dr. Berg appears to have been thrown into a state of extreme bodily terror, even hysteria, by the soap opera experience—a fair conclusion, given that in presenting one individual's reaction as statistically reliable, he essentially suspended his entire professional training.

The likely cause of Berg's panic, not surprisingly missing from his account, surfaces when we read Molly Haskell's more recent, purportedly feminist dismissal of daytime serial. From her comments we can deduce that Berg became hysterical because listening to soap opera made him "feel like a woman." In *From Reverence to Rape*, Haskell accurately identifies the feminine priority on feeling and empathy in both soap operas and the "woman's film." Yet she views this priority in a very negative light, making it the basis of her harsh criticism of these two mass media forms.

In the thirties and forties, the heyday of the "woman's film," it was as regular an item in studio production as the crime melodrama or the Western. Like any routine genre, it was subject to its highs and lows, and ranged from films that adhered safely to the formulae of escapist fantasy, films that were subversive only "between the lines" and in retrospect, and the rare few that used the conventions to undermine them. At the lowest level, as soap opera, the "woman's film" fills a masturbatory need; it is soft-core emotional porn for the frustrated housewife. The weepies are founded on a mock-Aristotelian and politically conservative aesthetic whereby women spectators are moved, not by pity and fear but by self-pity and tears, to accept, rather than reject, their lot.[11]

The "woman's film" that Haskell here brackets with soap opera refers to a large body of motion pictures produced during the 1940s, although the term may be used loosely to describe any film centrally concerned with areas that are stereotypically women's domains: the family, children, clothes, the love story, and also stories of illness and madness. Women's films of the 1940s such as *Kitty Foyle, Rebecca, The Spiral Staircase, Beyond the Forest, Lady in the Dark, Possessed, A Stolen Life, Stella Dallas*, and *Gaslight* created vehicles for a generation of powerful actresses: Bette Davis, Barbara Stanwyck, and Joan Crawford, among others. Yet with her damning words, Haskell seems to identify these films as the nadir, but one—soap opera—of cultural expression. She then surprises with a lurking ambivalence about the so-called weepies a few paragraphs later, when we learn that she is not as fully committed to the contempt for women's pictures as the above words would suggest.

Haskell's presentation of her ideas about women's films thus reveals some disconcerting shifts in attitude. However, although her opinion of daytime serial is clear—she is so indisputably dismissive that the form does not even rate its own sentence—her contempt for soap opera is more unsettling from the standpoint of logic. Haskell clearly conflates soap opera and the woman's picture: "At the lowest level, as soap opera, the 'woman's film' . . ." Both are then deemed mock-Aristotelian, moving women "to accept, rather than reject, their lot." But there are obvious structural distinctions between television soap opera and women's films—critical distinctions with regard to Aristotle's theory of drama, which demands closure. While the structure of women's films does resemble Aristotelian dramatic structure closely enough to warrant the comparison, the open-ended structure of daily soap opera bears no relation to it at all. Moreover, Haskell's writing is problematic here. Is Haskell actually implying that soap opera is another mock-Aristotelian form, like the woman's picture? Or is she using the phrase "as soap opera" loosely to connote maudlin emotionalism? Whether Haskell imagined soap opera within the Aristotelian framework, or whether she failed to imagine it in any way whatsoever, in this widely quoted pronouncement she rendered a grave disservice to the feminist study of screen fiction. And like Berg's "experiment," Haskell's conflation suggests a hysterical subtext. These hostile critics appear to react defensively against a narrative in which, as they perceive it, emotions are out of control, a narrative form that refuses to acquiesce in the conventional elevation of reason over emotion. They react, in short, with hysteria—a hysteria produced by a system of education that creates meaning through repression.

Conventional theories of education in one way or another assume a need for reason to control the energy of passion. The roots of this assumption are deep and tenacious. Plato's image of the charioteer and his horses—reason the charioteer, instinct and feeling the horses—has furnished the defining Western metaphor for the relationship among these basic human faculties. Many current thinkers, however, reject the domination/subordination image of reason and passion, arguing instead that emotion forms a meaningful part of feminine discourse and has been wrongly dismissed by classical learning theory as a mode of making meaning. As Carol Gilligan, Jean Baker Miller, Mary Field Belenky and her colleagues, and researchers at the Stone Center at Wellesley have demonstrated, cultural pressure to achieve mature identity by learning to crack the whip over feeling and empathy is not likely to be healthy or productive for anyone, and historically has been positively damaging for women.[12] The theories of these scholars make it easier to imagine the integrity of soap opera narrative as a form of feminine discourse in which the energy of the protagonist comes from expressing feeling, not controlling it.

In the seventies, feminists began pointing out that almost all our understanding of maturation had historically been based on studies of boys, and that no studies included young girls without imposing male standards on them. In 1982 Carol Gilligan published *In a Different Voice*, in which she introduced a new perspective on human development. The studies that served as a basis for that book and others that followed have begun to illuminate the confusion and humiliation young women feel as they first make serious decisions about their roles in the adult world. At that point in their lives, their desire to found such decisions on emotion as well as reason is defined by both the academic and workplace hierarchies as second-rate in comparison to the "logical" way young men make decisions. The priority young men give to abstraction over human connection is traditionally imitated by ambitious young women in order to gain praise and rewards from power brokers. Some feminists contend that this self-destructive message to young women can only be countered by social recognition that the emotional priorities of feminine discourse are of equal value. From this point of view, it follows that the previously dismissed "emotionalism" of soap opera must, at least, be reconsidered.

Even feminists who do not accept the concept of gendered discourse lay the groundwork for such a reconsideration. Constructionists like Elizabeth Spelman, for instance, would say that while the reevaluation of feeling is necessary, we ought to be thinking in terms of androgyny and a nongendered discourse that will not order human faculties in terms of sexual politics.[13] Constructionists believe that it is only historical conditioning that has led us to conceptualize thought and feeling as gendered constructs—and at women's expense. For that reason, constructionists advocate that those who would revise our conditioning seek to uncouple human traits from such associations, rather than trying to understand discourse as either masculine or feminine. Although my reading of soap opera assumes the existence of a feminine discourse, it is not entirely unrelated to the constructionist school of thinking. For despite the deep divisions between the two positions, both sides oppose the devaluation of the emotional. From a feminist point of view, we are no longer justified in restricting our notions about intellect and feelings in screen narrative to the ones honored by Hollywood.

Character in movies tends to follow the Freudian model of human development, an interpretation congenial with classical Western thinking about and conditioning with regard to emotion. The Hollywood hero or subject is constructed such that the repression of the tender passions and the control of emotional expression define the mature individual. By contrast, the emotional priorities of the soap opera heroine (and sometimes its heroes as well) have appeared "soppy." We are constrained critically to debase such texts in much the same way that traditional academic and professional standards humiliate maturing girls. As we have seen, feminists who explore feminine discourse have provided an intellectual framework for second thoughts about such judgments, and, as we will see, soap opera narrative dramatizes a kind of self in many ways congruent with current feminist psychological theory.

If psychologists had looked accurately at soap opera at any point in its sixty-year history, they would have seen that women and girls were already challenging social gender definitions through devotion to their favorite heroines. Although early soap opera heroines did not openly challenge *their* heroes, their narratives were to a large extent concerned with the problematic nature of masculine identity (see chapter 2). Later heroines actively countered the adverse way traditional masculinity affected their lives. Kim Reynolds and Laura Webber were part of the transition to a second generation of daytime heroines. In the character of Reynolds, Irna Phillips tried to realize a heroine whose feelings would successfully challenge the logic by which society defines a woman's place, a goal she was not permitted to reach. By the time the character of Laura was developing on *General Hospital*, however, something had changed. Now Laura's feelings could be coded by a feminine narrative; now it was acceptable to applaud her for breaking the constraints of society in favor of her own emotional priorities, and to commend society for permitting this release.

A number of critics have already begun to speculate that soap opera narrative is distinctly feminine. Robert Clyde Allen, in his thoughtful, innovative *Speaking of Soap Operas*, explores the economic history of soap opera and the formal consequences of industry conditions. Through an accurate assessment of soap opera's historical development, Allen raises important questions that focus attention on soap opera as a unique poetic, one that cannot be profitably evaluated in conventional terms. Similarly, in both "The Search for Tomorrow in Today's Soap Operas" and *Loving with a Vengeance*, Tania Modleski breaks important ground by relating the lack of closure in soap opera to its identity as a feminine narrative.[14]

Given these new attitudes toward psychology and soap opera, the lessons of psychoanalytic film criticism, which has examined the issue of gender and subject in screen fiction, become pertinent.[15] In combination, feminist psychological analysis and film criticism challenge us to think about the possible female subject that has been suppressed by mainstream social discourse, whether in film or in life.

Freudian Film Criticism, the Screen Subject, and Desire

When we speak of gender in screen fiction, we use the vocabulary of psychoanalytic film criticism. In such criticism, the desire of the screen subject was initially interpreted as unwaveringly male. Christian Metz's analogy between the film screen and the mirror, and thus between the cinematic experience and Jacques Lacan's mirror stage of human development and the text of male desire, provided the starting point for further psychological explorations of the screen subject.[16] In his essay "Identification, Mirror," Metz tells us that when we look at the cinema screen we regress temporarily to the mirror stage of development, the interval (between the ages of six and eighteen months) preparatory to the Oedipal period in which we formulate both our capacity for subjectivity and our sexual identity.[17] In other words, watching a movie throws us back to that key developmental moment when, in Lacan's terms, the experience of looking into a mirror and seeing one's full reflection presages the formation of the ego and the possibility of bodily unity and control of the (then) uncontrollable bodily functions.

The mirror phase thus anticipates the formation of conventional sexual identity. During that time, according to Lacan, the mother's body—once experienced as continuous with that of the baby—becomes an object viewed at a distance. This development paves the way for the later, shattering discovery of a particular absence: the mother does not have a penis. The mirror image is consequently necessary for the later moment when the possibility of castration occurs to us and the mother becomes the threat to the self: the terrible gap, the dreadful lack, the horrible absence, provoking the Oedipal resolution that severs intimate connection with her. In theory, denial of her power and importance is supposed to lead to wholeness of self, sexual identity, and our entrance into symbolic logic and formal language.

Theories that confirm subjectivity as male, however, tend to betray the flaw in their reasoning by their one-sidedness. The patriarchal coding of subjectivity as the climax of a process in which femininity is rejected vividly describes how boys become subjects, but grows murky when it comes to the process by which growing girls learn to assume the submissive, objectified, feminine role. Although no one has furnished serious evidence to corroborate the idea that girls are equally horrified by the mother's lack of a penis, traditional developmental theories have found various ways to defer to Freud's assumption. That horror, it was thought, caused girls to cut their ties to their mothers and groom themselves to become lovable to men like their fathers by accepting the role of the object, rather than the subject, of desire. In *The Reproduction of Mothering*, Nancy Chodorow draws on her clinical experience to suggest that young girls in fact experience no traumatic sense that something is missing from their mothers. Indeed, Chodorow comes to the conclusion that feminine submissiveness derives from a *male* lack: the absence of the father's involvement in early childhood care. The full story of women's familiar internalization of their own marginalization will remain unclear until enough of us have gained voices to tell our own stories.

Feminist film critics entered this debate when Laura Mulvey asserted that the Hollywood movie was a formidable obstacle to the creation of that liberating women's narrative. In "Visual Pleasure and Narrative Cinema," in which she draws on Metz's use of Freud and Lacan to interpret the spectator's cinematic experience, Mulvey created the dominant context for psychological *feminist* film criticism by arguing that the screen subject in narrative film is inexorably male and must be rejected.[18] Whereas Metz theorized that as film spectators we look into another mirror and thus are prey to the reawakening of old Oedipal anxieties, Mulvey argues that screen fiction recapitulates not only the mirror phase experience but *also* the Oedipal resolution, thereby offering a way to dominate and control the overwhelming female so that her appearance on the screen/mirror will not cause a developmental disruption on the part of the adult viewer. The visual technology and narrative structure of the Hollywood film in fact conspire toward a closure in which the powerful woman is brought under the hero's control, a closure that is truly gratifying only to the male spectator. As for the female spectator, Hollywood closure merely lures her, through the pleasure of the narrative and image, to identify with her own subjugation. Thus, in Mulvey's initial estimation, movies reawaken old fears about woman and reassert the consolation of male domination over her. Six years later, however, Mulvey presented a reconsidered, less monolithic understanding of the relationship between film and gender.[19] This second article left room for a temporary feminine subject and an altered glance, before closure; but it continued to contend that Hollywood film endangered feminine identity.

I am indebted to Mulvey for presenting the problem in this way. Unlike any criticism I had read before, it gave me a way of talking about what soap opera does: the position of the daytime heroine on the home screen was the virtual inverse of that of the cinematic woman as described by Mulvey. If, as Mulvey suggests, women reject film narrative as injurious to feminine identity, the opposite might also be true. Soap opera might be embraced as a narrative congenial to the feminine self-image. Indeed, as the Kim Reynolds uproar in 1973 and the major upheaval in the plot and characters on *General Hospital* between 1978 and 1980 demonstrate, soap opera narrative is at its most compelling when the female subject pursues her desires. The temporary restraining order on Kim Reynolds had to come from *outside* the soap opera text, from the administrative "text" of the television hierarchy. To really stop her, of course, it would have been necessary to remove her from the show entirely. Yet Reynolds was allowed to remain a character—and eventually she managed to play out her desire and marry Bob Hughes. When Laura appeared on *General Hospital*, however, there was virtually no time lag. The narrative immediately justified Laura's resistance to the definition that men and male society tried to impose on her, even though her rejection of conventional authorities involved murder and the breaking of marriage vows. Neither did Laura's narrative make her pay the price for emphatic resistance that Hollywood demands—even in a film as sympathetic to the plight of women in a male-dominated society as Callie Khouri and Ridley Scott's *Thelma and Louise*. Oddly, while such films often win praise as daringly "feminist," the only comments I have seen regarding the Luke and Laura story on *General Hospital* have consisted of cynical remarks about the manipulation of sexuality for ratings. Granted, ratings and opportunism were unquestionably involved; the same is abundantly true for the Hollywood movie. But so far no one has thought to ask whether ratings went as high as they did not because the audience was titillated but because they were thrilled to be given a story line unusually free from masculine perspectives on female character.

As we explore the evolution of soap operas in the next two chapters, we shall see that its female subject has become increasingly active. On *Days of Our Lives*, for example, the characters of Kimberly Brady and her sister Kayla go further than Laura did in resisting male objectification of the female. With them, the patriarchal marriage narrative—in which the hero acquires his ideal feminine possession through mastery of her energy—is reversed. Instead, these heroines are released to struggle with the hero toward a redefinition of marriage as the mutual interplay of masculine and feminine energies. Even more explicitly, Julia Wainwright, a character on *Santa Barbara*, presents the viewer with a confident new feminine energy, one free to investigate the problematic patriarchal conditioning not only of men but also of the "achieving" woman. She comes far closer than most mass media women to asking feminist Silvia Bovenschen's poignant question: How are women to act or think when the very syntax of language and logic may be a bit of "virile trickery" that subverts a woman from inside her own mind?[20]

If we can benefit from contrasting soap opera with Mulvey's prototypical Hollywood movie, we can also benefit from subsequent feminist criticism that discovered in certain films a kind of subversive feminine sensibility. These atypical films, a gray area between classical Hollywood and the screen fiction of soap opera, are missing links of a sort, for they clarify the structural issues involved in raising the suppressed feminine presence in the screen narrative.

Mary Ann Doane, in *The Desire to Desire*, and Tania Modleski, in *The Women Who Knew Too Much*, argue that certain films provide a narrative context in which the loss involved in society's refusal to allow the heroine to emerge as a fully realized subject can be felt. Doane discusses women's pictures, which halt the linear plot narrative with emotional interludes and, by focusing differently on women's faces and bodies than do action films, offer scope for the desires of their heroines. In reevaluating *Stella Dallas*, a film widely known as a standard "mother weeperoo," Doane encourages viewers to look beyond the surface bathos to a narrative that explicitly addresses the destructive impact of the film image on Stella's self-image. *Stella Dallas* shows how films cause women to degrade themselves in their own minds, leading them to abandon their own needs, as Stella does at the film's closure. At the beginning of the film, Stella is watching a movie, comparing her reality unfavorably with its fantasy. While this opening can be seen as a largely inconsequential comment on typical feminine behavior, it can also be read as demonstrating a latent awareness of what film does to women like Stella. For this and other reasons, the film can be read, in Doane's words, as a "ritualized mourning of the woman's losses in a patriarchal society."[21]

Modleski goes further still. Whereas in Doane's reading we catch only a glimpse of the male subjugation of women, Modleski is centrally concerned with the issue, arguing that the films of Alfred Hitchcock expose the dark underside of men whose mature male identity depends on the repression of femininity. As is the case in women's films, women in Hitchcock's films benefit by a disruption of the linear plot as it moves toward the customary closure. In women's films, these disruptions occur when feminine responses slow down the action; in Hitchcock, the disruptions are effected by striking cinematic imagery. In both circumstances, however, the story line is weakened and the ordinary male-centered definition of subject subverted. In Hitchcock's *Notorious*, for example, Alicia Huberman (Ingrid Bergman) is endowed with a capacity for subjectivity but stymied by guilt. To dull the pain of the self-loathing induced by her father's treason, Alicia drinks too much, an excess that undermines her chances for self-respect and self-determination. U.S. Agent Devlin (Cary Grant) offers her a way to regain her pride, although not her self-determination. To atone for her father's betrayal, she must put herself and her body under Devlin's control and at the disposal of the government in a spy mission against her father's comrades. Modleski points out that while Hitchcock encourages us to approve Alicia's acceptance of her assignment, he also makes us aware that despite her heroic service she is not given the respect routinely accorded a male agent. Hitchcock, Modleski says, makes us identify with Alicia by condemning Devlin's position as a "withdrawn, judgmental spectator." *Notorious* thus "draws us into an intimate identification with the vulnerable and increasingly helpless heroine: for example, insofar as the film uses point of view shots to convey Alicia's impaired vision it forces us all to share in her disablement."[22] Wherever the narrative is halted and we are shown Alicia's visual perspective, an identification emerges that promotes sympathy for the heroine's less-than-masterful position and, even more interesting, criticism of the will-to-power of the lady's master.

Is it a coincidence that women's films, in which the subjugation, devaluation, and distancing of women remain incomplete, are, as a cinematic genre, marked for contempt by mainstream discourse? Why does the misreading of Hitchcock as a misogynist persist, when Modleski has convincingly shown that he made a career of examining the difficulties involved in male desire for the complete control of women? Clearly, the screen becomes threatening to the status quo when no Oedipal devaluation of women occurs, with the result that such movies—and certain theses pertaining to them—must be either abused or denied. On this basis, we might do well to revise our understanding of soap opera.

Modleski's work in soap opera led her to conclude that the lack of closure characteristic of that genre gave women a chance to identify with a maternal point of view, although she did not specify how. Her work on Hitchcock, however, in which she demonstrates that director's partial identification with his would-be female subject, creates an interesting intellectual starting point, especially in combination with Doane's readings of women's pictures, for analyzing the great changes that have taken place in television soap opera. In fact, as screen fiction soap opera actually goes the woman's picture and the Hitchcock drama one better as far as gender issues are concerned. By opening up narrative linearity, soap opera does not merely give a potential female subject the chance to cut a wide swath or gain spectator identification; it actually insists that she be free.

Narrative Syntax and Desire

As Ellen Friedman and Miriam Fuchs point out in *Breaking the Sequence*, feminine literary expression is forced from the outset to negotiate the gender politics of the very syntax of language.[23] The key to feminine discourse in experimental narrative, they suggest, is the rupturing of the linear narrative sequence, the creation of gaps to fracture the familiar logic that gives subjectivity only to men. Intentional distortion of conventional sentence grammar, rupture of linear time, and the conscious use of oxymorons are simple literary devices for breaking sequence. In soap opera, sequences are broken for commercial and technological reasons. Narratives are cut off to make way for ads or other parallel narratives, or because the day's episode is over. But, by removing the obstacles found in ordinary Hollywood narrative syntax that hinder the expression of feminine desire, these mandated gaps also foster a kind of linguistic gender politics.

Just as intentional experimentation with discontinuous form creates ways of forming a differently gendered fictional subject, soap opera perforation affects subject formation. As we know, words are not the real language of film; there the syntax of images and of plot combine to produce organized expression. Nevertheless, all linear syntax draws on the same linguistic foundation. An important connection thus exists between the predominance of linear syntax in narrative and the male subject of Hollywood film.

Anyone who writes conventional movie scripts is familiar with the rigor of sticking to scenes that move the action forward—as opposed to "slow" scenes of emotional reflection on what has taken place. The writers who scripted the narrative of John Wayne's battles to bring cattle to market, for example, emphasized Wayne's heroism by reducing other characters to adjuncts or obstacles to his goals. Although most writers are aware of the imbalance involved in the imperative that a bare minimum of emotional scenes be allowed to grace a narrative, only the rare, resistant reader would ask why we are told almost nothing regarding the hero's feelings about his actions, and even less about those of his opponents, or why heroism is equated with severing connection with anyone who will not submit to one's will. Why must Hollywood writers create such scripts?

The obvious explanation is that's what the audience wants. A more probing response, one that accounts for *why* they want it, can be found by turning to linguistic analysis. As narrative, the John Wayne plot bears a striking resemblance to the linguistic model of the basic expository sentence, ruthlessly stripped of the ambiguity of metaphor or the complexities of modification—anything other than that absolutely necessary to the syntax of subject and predicate. As with the modern, streamlined sentence, so with the action plot: they omit that which is perceived as disruptive in our culture, where linearity has become associated with "clean" masculinity and nonlinearity with the murky feminine depths. Often an action plot will literally embody those disruptive elements in an actual woman who, knowingly or unknowingly, gets in the hero's way. Because the action stops whenever she appears, the Hollywood hero's role is to put some kind of end to her "intrusion," a classic example being the role of women in *The Plainsman*. Even contemporary Hollywood films that claim to include women usually only mask the problem of feminine disruptiveness. In *Aliens*, a film construed as evidence that Hollywood can provide a female subject, the plot is linear—and the "heroine," who has no trouble "fitting in with the guys," is almost totally masculinized. Current film production outside Hollywood has responded to the women's movement by producing less linear films that, inasmuch as they break with tradition, have proved threatening to many spectators. The "quirky" *La Femme Nikita*, for instance, used discontinuous narrative to speak with sympathy about the problems untutored women face when men decide to "treat them as equals," but its elliptical presentation of events was deemed confusing, and the public greeted the film with distrust. Linguistic structure is powerfully connected with our feelings about the roles of men and women: a "clean" linear plot is coded to receive the same approving response awarded masculinity, while resistance to linearity meets with the same suspicion that femininity attracts.

Two theoreticians, Roman Jakobson and Julia Kristeva, use linguistic models in particularly illuminating ways to clarify the relationship between gender and syntax. Discussing the relation between the linear and the nonlinear in language, Jakobson refers to two linguistic functions, which he calls the maternal and the paternal.[24] Freudian psychology regards formal language as part of the paternal order: language is defined as what happens to communication once the Oedipal choice to reject the feminine has been made. In this formulation, the child's mode of communication prior to that choice is defined as an antecedent to language, something related to the maternal rather than the paternal. Nevertheless, Jakobson identifies a subordinate maternal component in what we do call language, an element that is the residue of the rejected pre-Oedipal communication.

Jakobson posits two axes of language activity—that of selection (the maternal) and that of combination (the paternal). The subordinated axis of selection makes meaning by substituting one word or image for another, as in the creation of metaphor. It is nonlinear by emphasis, creating intelligibility by reminding us of gaps, of what is not there. For example, Shakespeare's Sonnet 73 opens with the lines "That time of year thou mayst in me behold, / When yellow leaves, or none, or few do hang / Upon the boughs which shake against the cold"—old age being the unspoken concept, evoked in its absence by the image of autumn. Substitution, the linguistic axis of the "poetic" and the feminine, is thought to be a less serious way of making meaning than the creation of logical sequence along the linear axis of combination. The more serious mode of organization, the scientific, is, conversely, associated with the axis of combination and with masculinity.

The axis of combination underlies the mind's ability to achieve reassuring linguistic closure. It is the linguistic principle of linearity that we see in the construction of a sentence, where nouns and verbs, prepositions and modifiers, are combined to form a meaningful, linear unit— the language of science and exposition. This axis of language also creates the linear construct of the plot and its closure. The establishment of a firmly linear sequence of events leading up to an appropriate and satisfying resolution is, as Mulvey suggested, a way of pacifying the Oedipal threat posed by the screen/mirror. Therefore, language dominated by the axis of combination is not only supposedly more serious, but also less frightening.

In "From One Identity to Another," Julia Kristeva describes how, owing to the gendered identifications of these two axes, pleasurable access to the poetic, nonlinear axis of substitution is converted into a guilty transgression of the patriarchal incest taboo in our male-dominated culture:

Language as symbolic function constitutes itself at the cost of repressing instinctual drive and continuous relation to the mother. On the contrary, the unsettled and questionable subject of poetic language (for whom the word is never uniquely sign) maintains itself at the cost of reactivating this repressed maternal element. If it is true that the prohibition of incest constitutes, at the same time, language as communicative code and women as exchanged objects in order for a society to be established, *poetic language would be* for its questionable subject-in-process the *equivalent of incest*.[25]

Kristeva theorizes that when poetic language "reactivates this repressed maternal element" it promotes a profoundly unsettling sense of regression. This is because the structure of our language both creates and reflects the way we make meaning in our lives. Thus, our patriarchal culture finds in its linguistic repression of the nonlinear axis the organizational pattern for the social domination of women. Just as the screen/mirror reproduces old anxieties about mother's lack and a possibility of resembling her (castration), so the poetic also makes us remember that danger of wanting to feel too close to mother. Hence Kristeva's reading of the poetic as the threat of incest. Kristeva's position on language suggests that indulging in the poetic, nonlinear syntax is equivalent in our culture as siding with mother against father: the poetic threat to linguistic coherence is interchangeable with the threat to the social structures created by linguistic syntax. I suggest that, similarly, the weakening of linearity in both soap opera and the women's picture entails a partial loss of the "reassurances" of the linear linguistic axis, namely, that emotion, femininity, imagination—everything born of intimacy with mother—is firmly under father's control. Kristeva and Jakobson together suggest a linguistic basis for my earlier point: in their oddly subjective—if not outright wild—reasoning about soap opera, critics such as Dr. Berg and Molly Haskell exhibit a hysteria founded on being forced to "feel like a woman," the man because education makes manhood dependent on avoiding such feelings, the woman because education makes women wary of what they are.

If Kristeva is correct, the linguistic syntax of women's entertainment, which is constantly breaking the action, challenges the intellectual as well as the psychological foundations of patriarchal culture, which emphasizes the need to suppress femininity in order to maintain a concept of order. Perhaps the severity of the linguistic assault on male domination in the structure of soap opera and women's movies explains why power establishments of all kinds would rather laugh at than cry about these two subgenres of screen fiction—and why, of the two, soap opera is more daring in its resistance to the linear syntax of conventional narrative. As we have noted, gaps abound: during commercial breaks, between the intercut segments of the many plots that make up a daily show, and at the end of each installment. Its defiance of ordinary (masculine) narrative syntax, its permanent disruption of the linear, suggests why soap opera is commonly the target of defensive ridicule on the part of an intrinsically masculine power establishment.

From a feminist perspective, however, those gaps are precisely what make soap opera exciting and revolutionary. The syntax of daytime serial, unfettered by linear action that demands a beginning, middle, and end, privileges the forbidden gap. Thus the daytime serial creates an opening through which the female subject, ordinarily repressed from the patriarchal narrative, can emerge.

Here I must distinguish between the *daily* daytime serial and those serial melodramas presented weekly, at night, and—inappropriately, in my view—often called nighttime soap operas. Although shows such as *Dallas*, *Dynasty*, or *Falcon's Crest* might seem to borrow their structure from soap opera, they are, in essence, only protracted Hollywood films. They do contain gaps in their structures, but closure remains desirable and is always achieved at the end of the thirteen-week television season. The gap, in essence, only creates an appetite for what is temporarily withheld—that is, closure. In daytime serial, however, gaps—both frequent and unending—decrease the significance of the linear; in nighttime serial melodrama the gap heightens our longing for the aesthetic of the linear. Moreover, even the multiple plots of the so-called nighttime soaps really only expand on the familiar main plot/subplot structure. On *Dallas*, for example, the J. R. story line soon superseded every other story line in importance. In soap opera, the dailiness of the gap insures a less hierarchical, less linear relationship among story lines, the crossovers between the stories thus affording the same kind of substitutive relationships as between terms of a metaphor. Nighttime melodrama is, by contrast, a relatively linear fiction. As such, it is much closer in structure to masculine power systems—no doubt one very important reason why nighttime serial melodrama does not draw the ridicule reserved for daytime serial.

Disruption as a structural norm in daytime serial narrative is emphasized in soap opera parodies, where a scene might be interrupted with an offhand reference to one of the multitude of other plots ("But what of Cynthia?"). In such spoofs, rupture is construed as ludicrous. Yet it is precisely those gaps that tell us how soap opera communicates with its audience, and how what it communicates is shaped and formed.

The gap structure of soap opera creates *dominatus interruptus*, permanently postponing the Hollywood mastery of the feminine. As perforated narrative, soap opera provides a syntactical structure capable of expressing a female subject of the type identified in the developmental patterns of feminist psychology. Because its syntax works against Oedipal repression, soap opera creates a new screen mirror; here, the image of woman is reassuring because she is the norm, not the difference. Indeed, in this context the linear pattern of the Oedipal hero, the protagonist who realizes his destiny as a repressive agent, becomes intrusive. In short, the syntax of soap opera narrative fosters a kind of "automatic writing" in which, regardless of what mainstream discourse might prefer, there can be no end to HER. She will become a subject, an agent. Her desire will become, as it is not in Hollywood, the fuel for soap opera's narrative thrust.

A Differently Gendered Screen, a Different Narrative Myth

Studies by Nancy Chodorow, Carol Gilligan, Jean Baker Miller, and others describe a feminine form of discourse that produces narrative about feminine bonding and a text for feminine desire.[26] Mary Ann Doane's examination of the women's picture and Tania Modleski's study of Hitchcock indicate that when the linearity of screen narrative is broken, feminine desire can surface. Roman Jakobson argues that an alteration in the power structure of the axes of language will alter the relationship between the linear and the nonlinear, which suggests the reverse: breaking linearity must alter the relationship between maternal and paternal power structures in a text. Together, these analyses of discourse point to the conclusions that disruptive narrative, as is found in soap opera, offers a cultural site in which the tragedy of Oedipus as the informing mythic ideal can be decentered.

By recognizing the gendered element in narrative discourse, we are released from imagining ourselves on the basis of a single primary myth of the self, that of Oedipus. Now there is room for another mythic ideal, one that does not equate masculinity with the norm and femininity with difference—and a terrifying difference at that. In my view, that alternative is summed up in the myth of Persephone.[27] In that tale, the heroine is faced with a situation initially defined in terms of absolute choice: What is her primary bond—with female or male, mother or husband? In the wake of Hades' abduction of Persephone, her mother, Demeter, threatens to render the world barren unless her daughter is returned; Hades refuses to surrender his bride. Ultimately, however, it becomes clear that drastic exclusions are not the solution. Instead, cosmic circumstance and personal choice together mandate an inclusive bonding to *both* mother and husband: Persephone will spend part of the year with Demeter, and part with Hades.

The Persephone myth thus dramatizes a developmental choice that would reorder the classical Freudian depiction of the relationship between masculinity and femininity. The Oedipal pattern demands rejection of the feminine in the service of masculine bonding—and as the result of a quintessentially masculine threat, that of castration. But in the myth of Persephone, no threat of castration appears, nor does the mother's proximity entail sexual incapacity and the dissolution of self and social order. Indeed, the opposite is the case: the mother's *alienation* suggests barrenness and dissolution. Such a myth clears the way for a female subject, who exercises influence not through control, subjugation, distancing, and exclusiveness, but through unity, cooperation, closeness, and inclusiveness.

Moreover, in its narrative outcome, Persephone's story offers an alternative to the norm implied in the Oedipus myth. The Oedipal hero faces an all-or-nothing situation; he must choose his allegiance. The Oedipus story is thus a model of linearity, depending for its meaning on a definitive either/or closure. In contrast, the quarrel between Demeter and Hades is resolved by alternation, an oscillation that can satisfy competing, but equally valid, claims. In other words, the Persephone myth privileges not the line, but the gap. What constitutes closure is Persephone's destiny to move back and forth perpetually across the gap between mother and husband.

Both Jean Baudrillard and E. Ann Kaplan have argued that television's fluidity, its undercutting of closure by immediately conveying another story as the preceding one is completed, alters the presentation of the subject.[28] However, they also suggest that this subversion of closure dissipates the subject position altogether. Perhaps so, at least in the context of linear narrative. But soap opera narrative seems instead to reconstitute the subject position. Like the myth of Persephone, it validates a lack of permanent resolution, it honors the gap. As a result, the patriarchal claim to agency assumed by linear narrative—the Hollywood film, for example—appears an invasive, and even illegitimate, exercise of power.

Conclusion: The Female
Subject of Soap Opera

How does a creative community in the mass media work with a narrative structure and mythic ideal that assault social taboos about gender and desire? The daring proposal that dissolved Irna Phillips's career and the emergence of Laura as a heroine on *General Hospital* are excellent places to begin talking about the way meaning is made in soap opera. As we saw, both Irna Phillips and Douglas Marland set in motion powerful stories of feminine desire—yet neither was finally free to exercise the control normally allowed authors in the shaping of their creations. Phillips was dismissed from *As the World Turns*, and in 1973 the affair between Bob Hughes and Kim Reynolds was terminated. Interestingly, though, over the next ten years—a period of latency possible only in soap opera—Kim and Bob drifted back into each other's orbit, to be reunited at long last in a story that inspired fierce audience devotion and boosted ratings.

Similarly, in Laura Webber Douglas Marland created a rich portrait of the young woman as desiring subject. But ultimately the development of this character was out of his hands. Marland conceived the story of Laura's seduction by and revenge on David Hamilton because the original story line, which called for an affair between Hamilton and Laura's mother, struck him as too emotionally implausible. He later opposed Laura's liaison with Luke and break with her husband, Scotty, for the same reason: at the time, Marland felt that the emotional bond between Laura and Scotty was so complete that viewers would not accept Laura's interest in another man. Rather, Marland planned to use Luke's desire for Laura as part of a "Great Gatsby" story, in which Luke, a small-time gangster and member of the lowliest social class, would aspire to win over the beautiful, privileged Laura, building a fortune to impress his love, as Gatsby did, and, like Gatsby, dying as a result of his underworld connections. Luke's attentions to Laura would jeopardize her marriage to Scotty but not rupture it: after Luke died in Laura's arms, time would reunite husband and wife. Marland now believes that, had he remained head writer for *General Hospital*, audience enthusiasm for Luke and Laura would eventually have caused him to alter his plans and allow Laura to sever her marriage bond and cleave to Luke.[29] But Marland was fired before he could shape the text of his vision.

The alliance between Luke and Laura was finally scripted into existence by the new head writer, Pat Falken Smith, at the insistence of Gloria Monty, the show's producer, and Jackie Smith, then vice president in charge of daytime programming for ABC-TV. There is every reason to believe that the decision to break up Laura Webber's marriage to Scotty Baldwin stemmed from the network's desire to enhance ratings. As we take a closer look at soap opera texts in the chapters that follow, however, we will see that the entire ratings question is bound up with audience desire, itself unconsciously stimulated by the syntax of feminine desire. Apparently the narrative energy that liberates the soap opera heroine so forcefully contradicts the way meaning is ordinarily created in our culture that it cannot receive open acknowledgment. Instead, the decisions made about soap opera stories are framed in terms of issues we recognize as "normal": ratings, sponsors, and money—all issues of power. Perhaps the disguise is necessary; after all, it has permitted daytime serial to exist in network television. But it has taken also its toll on soap opera's possibilities. The discontinuities built into the daytime serial format can take the soap opera form only to a certain point in creating fresh and exciting narrative. Its long-term success depends on awareness.

One critical question concerns soap opera's ability to create specific and complex male and female *identities*, as opposed to narrating global fantasies of masculine versus feminine desire. Thus far, soap opera has produced only a limited number of narratives that include culture, race, religion, and sexual preference in the construction of the narrative subject. Although the perforated soap opera narrative is by its very nature opposed to strategies of domination, it seldom explores power and hierarchy in terms of historical specificity. Here, in addition to the sensibility of individual creators, the permission of network structures comes into play. In fact, when this rare permission *has* been given, soap opera has made an imaginative contribution to the exploration of the subject positions of blacks, Jews, gays, and other minorities (see chapter 5). Although the British beat us to the punch in *Eastenders*, a show that demonstrates the power of the American-born soap opera genre to dramatize the full spectrum of social and sexual difference, American daytime serials have at times managed to address the historical influence on self, despite the prevailingly hostile network climate. For this, they deserve more credit than they have hitherto received. They will do more, however, once a proud sense of identity becomes possible for American soap opera.

Hollywood institutions glamorize the break from the mother and all that follows from it, a break that the horrors of the Oedipus myth warn us is necessary. E. Ann Kaplan has argued that we must not automatically assume the same to be true of television just because it is also a screen fiction.[30] Kaplan is wise to wonder about what television's often "unbounded" structuring, with its likely implications for gender issues, means for the television audience, especially the female spectator. In the next chapter we shall see how soap opera production conditions have mandated a kind of feminine discourse that privileges continuity with the maternal and is tailored to the dialogue of difference, such as informs the Persephone myth. Thus is soap opera distinguished from the Hollywood text that mandates, in Oedipal tradition, a subject who dominates his Other.

CHAPTER TWO

Persephone, Not Oedipus: Soap Opera and the Fantasy Female Subject before 1978

The classical subject of Freudian-based psychology, the Oedipal self—organized by the either/or choice that affirms the father and denies the mother—has been a useful construct in illuminating the gendered aspects of the Hollywood narrative. However, the myth of Oedipus will not be helpful in interpreting either the narrative or the subject of soap opera. A look at a representative Hollywood hero, James Bond, will show us why Hollywood's best boy fails to translate intact to daytime television. More important, we will see why the soap opera narrative represents a kind of menace to Bond, and by extension to conventional masculinity, such that Goldfinger, Dr. No, and even Rosa Klebb prove in the end less disconcerting than the soap opera heroine.

A James Bond plot makes a compelling James Bond film because everything about Bond's world emphasizes the priority on control and male bonding that is so fundamental to the gendered agenda of the Hollywood movie. James Bond plots deal with saving the world. Such an accomplishment in less than two hours gives us a protagonist bursting with mastery. The James Bond story assumes commitment to the symbolic father as the hero's primary relationship. Women exist for Bond only to cement that relationship. Bond, the distillation of the Oedipal consolations of Hollywood, uses his virtues in defense of the law of the symbolic father *by forcing* the heroine into her rightful place as object.

41

In *Goldfinger*, Bond gives one of his most convincing demonstrations of the creed of the dominant protagonist. At the beginning of the movie Bond understands that he is in conflict with Goldfinger, but he does not yet see how to defeat him. As soon as he (and the spectator) understand that Goldfinger's primary asset in his plan to dominate the world is Pussy Galore's energy, Bond's task is clear: he must capture and contain Pussy's energy. This he does through sexual possession, in a scene that graphically emphasizes hierarchy and dominance—a filmic pun on the dramatic climax. Immediately upon Bond's conquest of her, Pussy collaborates with the American government to neutralize the bombs she and her all-female task force were to drop on Fort Knox. As good and evil are here defined, Pussy can only join the forces for good by submitting to Bond's conquest of her. An elliptical gap in the plot immediately follows Bond's sexual penetration of the enemy's first line of defense; that is, thereafter we never see Pussy voluntarily emptying herself of energy; we only understand that she has. This suggests that her sacrifice of her power for him is so natural a consequence of her final acceptance of "normal" womanhood that it is not even worth mentioning, even though her surrender is the key to Bond's climactic victory.

The Bond movies may be less subtle than other films in their Oedipal design, but they are the "true north" of conventional Hollywood closure: classic films feature an infinite number of ways to illustrate the satisfactions (and even patriotism) involved in male domination and possession of a woman, or of some female surrogate, such as nature. The technology and politics featured in all the Bond films *further* offer relations with women that are satisfying because they are safely distanced. Bond's sexual conquest of Pussy provides the spectator a mechanized sex fantasy, rendered impersonal by its detached air of objective official business. As part of Bond's mission, sex is freed from the taint of erotic fantasy—that messy, confusing desire for intimacy associated with the mother. Erotic fantasy, rather, is the domain of the villain, the source of his plan for world conquest. This triple containment in the Bond films of the heroine and of the fantasy and the intimacy associated with the maternal is an accurate, if quasi-cartoonlike, example of closure's influence on the presentation of gender in the screen narrative.

There are characters like Bond—in principle—in soap operas, but when they appear, they soon become involved in narratives that question their modus operandi. Without the promise of closure to validate any form of domination, the soap opera character is not authorized to dominate an Other. Hollywood's all-pervasive masculine controlling subject is "off his turf" in the soap opera narrative. It is as though Oedipus was suddenly to wake up and find himself inside the Persephone myth, a narrative featuring movement away from the prerogatives of male bonding. In Persephone's story, Zeus and his brother Hades claim those rights, but they are forced to recognize the rights of the mother as an element in the destiny of the daughter. Hades begins the tug-of-war with an Oedipal flourish by abducting Persephone violently, even though Zeus has said she can be his wife. But Demeter refuses to accept this violation. When she and Hades stand before Zeus, each claiming Persephone, Zeus discovers that he cannot enforce his agreement with Hades, in which full control over daughter Persephone had been granted. When Persephone eats the pomegranate seeds in the underworld she binds herself to Hades. And Demeter still has the power to render the world barren if she is not heeded. In the end, therefore, Persephone belongs to no one but herself. She will move between husband and mother.

The great father-god Zeus becomes no more than a witness to this inclusive solution. But where, in this solution, is the sanctity of the male bond, assumed as normal by Zeus and Hades and in the narratives of Oedipus and James Bond? Where can Oedipus—or James Bond—situate himself in this picture? Persephone's story means culture shock for the mainstream conceptions of masculinity. Similarly, this is the effect of soap opera narrative on the hero as defined by Hollywood, and thus on all spectators who look to him to validate patriarchal conceptions of selfhood. Since women and the film heroines who reflect their lives have, by contrast, historically struggled within an essentially disabling narrative structure, turnabout is fair play.

Releasing the Screen Heroine from Bond-age

Many current feminist scholars—Mary Field Belenky, Jean Baker Miller, Nancy Chodorow, and Carol Gilligan, for example— imagine the Oedipal scenario as it applies to growing girls much as I have imagined the myth of Persephone with regard to the hero as ordinarily defined. They suggest, in other words, that women routinely wake up inside the Oedipus myth and find nowhere to place themselves that does not either endanger their belief in themselves or force them to adopt male models of agency. These writers conclude, therefore, that

that struggle to move away from Oedipal narrative *is* the feminine narrative.

Women's Ways of Knowing, by Mary Field Belenky et al., offers one possible model for this narrative. The numerous interviews that inform that study suggested to the authors that, in order to find her own story, a potential female subject must move from the silence of the object—as she is defined by the Oedipal narrative—by shedding all forms of passivity. The study's prototypical feminine narrative imagines the aspiring girl forcing a temporary break from all authority so that she can free herself from invasive conditioning, whereupon she reestablishes a relationship to conventional society. At her zenith, the heroine of such a feminine narrative would achieve not closure but dialogue. She would— in the style of what the book calls a *constructive knower*—mediate between her own developmental priorities on empathy and attachment, on the one hand, and the abstract, individualist priorities of mainstream society, on the other. While this proposed feminine narrative does not define the exact route of all possible female subjects, it does propose the model for *a* feminine text: maturation through the pursuit of desire by resisting the "normal" pattern of growth that is fueled by fear and rejection of the maternal and an insistence on the either/or choice between heritage of the mother and loyalty to husband.

If we imagine this heroine in a media presentation, we can see that she would not be a conventional Hollywood protagonist altered primarily by a smear of lipstick and a dab of mascara. She would not be a "Bond-in-a-bra" (Emma Peel, Wonder Woman, the "Hold it right there" policewoman). Instead she would represent a more profound divergence from the accepted model of heroism. Unlike Bond, she would not privilege the abstraction of the fatherland over feeling, nor would she require an Other to subjugate, as the Hollywood hero subjugates the female object. In her narrative, Bond would be either a villain or an adversary, not simply because he is male, but because he is the type of male who guarantees the dominance-subordination hierarchy that threatens her desire for horizontal mutuality among subjects. Her narrative would resist closure by guaranteeing the claims of all characters as possible subjects.

Such a fictional subject does in fact exist. Soap opera is a mass culture model of the conventionally "impossible" feminine narrative. As might be expected, this screen subject is not only impossible by conventional standards; she is also unsettling. The way society makes meaning, the soap opera heroine is translated into an attack on the assurances offered by James Bond and his brethren. Perhaps as a result of this threat, the feminine narrative of mutuality is culturally withheld as a choice for the developing girl, who is continually instructed to make choices within the gender-coded framework of possessor and possessed ordinarily defined as reality.[1] Put another way, the feminine narrative is discouraged because of an incompatibility between Oedipal fantasy and the fantasy required for subject identity in the growing girl. The discourse of society presents HIS fantasy as reality. However, HIS "reality" is the repression of HER desire. Mainstream male "reality" operates on the developing girl as malevolent fantasy and insists that she adjust to it. What, then, happens to her desire to see herself as central, important, competent? If she finds a way of expressing this desire, she confuses herself and angers others. The satisfactions involved in acknowledging her need for self-esteem threaten her place as a member of the "normal" group.

In movies, her story is presented as it is in society at large, as confusing and dangerous, and, because women are conditioned to accept a male view of reality, movie fantasy seems "real." One sees a cultural fit between mainstream "reality" and the way movies narrate woman's empowerment as a castrating menace that the hero must suppress in the name of the father.[2] Soap opera, in contrast, presents the fear of the heroine's power as a sort of misperception. Thus soap opera fantasy seems odd, and even vaguely recognizable as something we have always been told is bad for us.

As cultural feminine narrative, the soap opera is permitted to exist because it has commercial viability, but it is packaged with cultural instructions that define it as ludicrous, as something deserving of shame and contempt. For this reason, its reputation as nonsense—the result of distorted coverage by an unsympathetic mainstream press and academic establishment—partly denies the soap opera spectator the satisfaction of a fantasy that deviates from society's gendered (or other) norms. Yet this ridicule has many unexamined implications for our culture and its attitude about femininity. The soap opera heroine, if we listen to what she has to say, raises good questions about what is conventionally construed as masculine identity. She is, therefore, a daunting figure to the patriarchal mind.

Kim Reynolds, Laura Baldwin Spenser—frightening? The ordinary critic roars with laughter, and with good reason, for the soap opera heroine has been thoroughly and effectively libeled by her detractors. In our examination of the soap opera heroine and her narrative, however, we will find reason for mainstream culture to defend itself against her challenge to ordinary narrative, and we may wonder how long she will be permitted to mount that challenge. For the time being, although she is mocked by the networks that profit from her, she is considered too commercially valuable to destroy. But as audiences for the major networks shrink because of the growing allure of cable and revenues from the daytime serials drop, she has come into peril. The traditional television power structure does not value her as a model of feminine identity; if falling revenues mean that the industry power brokers will tighten the reigns of control, decisions insensitive to the special nature of soap opera and its heroines are to be expected.

Regardless of what the future holds, soap opera can claim a fascinating place in American culture from its inception in the early thirties through the crest of its second phase in the late eighties. Two major periods of development can be identified: 1933–78, and 1978–88. Before 1978, on radio and in early television, the soap opera heroine succeeded in problematizing ordinary male identity by expressing disenchantment with male attempts to dominate and control her. Yet although these first-stage narratives contain occasional flashes of brilliance, more often they are characterized by uninspired chunks of dialogue and a story insignificant except for the unusual appearance of a heroine frustrated by the hero's inability to recognize her value. That early dreariness was more than repaid during the second stage, however. Now the heroine's struggle extended well beyond a mere survey of the gender situation; rather, she took on the task of unraveling (or, in the current jargon, deconstructing) the hero's power narrative to make room for herself and her desires. However, to appreciate the soap opera heroine's difference even before these changes, we must take a second look at the early female protagonist.

The Radio Heroine

In the radio soap opera, the heroine attended to her unclosed, nonvisual narrative as if a special dispensation had liberated her from the conventions of ordinary narrative and ordinary life. Under the names of Mary Noble, Helen Trent, Sunday Brinthrope (*Our Gal Sunday*), radio soap opera's female subject gave public permission to her audience to acknowledge their own reservations about the way men dominate social structures. Mary, Helen, and Sunday brought consolation to the many undervalued women who were tyrannized by a received opinion that they were "unrealistic" if they thought they could function competently in the hard world of day-to-day life. The soap opera heroine's story persistently undermined the belief that this is a man's world by presenting us with heroes who were neither as effective nor as aware as the heroines. In violating the conventions her audience was subject to, the early female soap opera subject was a fantasy in a double sense. First, she defied the ordinary patriarchal assumptions about woman's place: she was neither an object securely under male control nor dangerous. Second, she did not seem to need to fight for her right to deviate from the way the audience *knew* most women were forced to behave. She was a euphoric fantasy, the incarnation of the powerful female subject that Hollywood could only glimpse, for example in the persons of Bette Davis and Joan Crawford, before the plot well and truly chastened their uppity ways. Certainly radio soap opera did suffer from tedium—although reacquaintance with the original tapes and scripts reveals a much better quality of dramatic production than cultural memory recalls. But whatever tedium might have been present was more than compensated for by the excitement of a female freedom that was never revoked by either a hero or a plot.

Mary Noble, the subject of *Mary Noble, Backstage Wife*, a radio daytime serial that aired between 1935 and 1959, exemplifies early soap opera's fantasy denial of male prerogatives, a denial that cleared the way for the female agency necessary for daytime serial. Mary operated "backstage" for her husband, Larry Noble: she was the business manager, he the leading actor and playwright, of a little theater company. The situation, though real enough in theory, was dramatized with almost total lack of concern for the power relations that would operate in a real theater company. Rather, *Mary Noble, Backstage Wife* used the theater setting to explore, in metaphor, the hierarchy of male-female relationships. Larry, as star, was the focus of public attention and interest, while Mary, taking care of business, was behind the scenes, serving the needs of the theater company. Clearly to Larry, her status was inferior to his *because she was in a supportive role behind the scenes.*

It is a social norm that superiors delegate to subordinates the function of caring for others.[3] In *Backstage Wife*, taking care of business is a fantasy code for that function. The mom-and-pop organization of the theater setting, though somewhat improbable, allows the domination-subordination roles of men and women to be presented from a feminine perspective—a perspective that is all but impossible both in ordinary patriarchal discourse and in linear, closure-bound mainstream screen fiction. The world of *Mary Noble, Backstage Wife* was one both completely familiar and completely strange. It dealt relentlessly in every day issues but at the same time made the radio audience look critically at Larry's pedestrian obliviousness to Mary's value and effectiveness. While "taking care of business" so that Larry can project the image society wants to see, Mary secretly *does* have the power—in the world of the serial. She also provides the dominant perspective on the day-to-day trials and tribulations of the little theater company, one in which the affiliations among members of the group are of primary importance. On behalf of the claims of connection, and despite her mild voice and self-effacing style, she is able to experiment with a multitude of solutions to problems, solutions that preserve a balance between abstraction and feeling, individuation and connection. Larry, although valued by society, in the context of this serial is relatively dysfunctional. His individualism, certainty, and tendency to make either-or dualistic choices render him unable to see beyond his ego's limitations; this invariably makes Mary's job harder, and causes her to incur hurtful behavior from him while she is putting things to right.

In one particular post–World War II series of shows, the theater company is threatened by the greed of the enigmatic Ken Page, both a famous high-society portrait artist and the owner of the dingy little playhouse that they lease. The lease is about to expire, and Page's agent threatens the company with either expulsion or an unmanageable rent increase, an increase that contradicts a previous understanding. This dilemma is basically Mary's responsibility, as she is the business manager. Larry—who in Oedipal fashion requires an immediate, complete solution that will not threaten his sense of control—only confuses and exacerbates the situation when he concludes that there is no alternative but to accept the help of socialite Katherine Monroe. This woman, a wealthy potential patroness, has a clear personal interest in Larry. And although Larry, equally clearly, loves Mary and not Katherine, he does believe Katherine to be more powerful than Mary and much wiser in the ways of the world. In opting for Katherine's help, Larry acts out the Oedipal priority on individuation and power, thus threatening his personal life.

Katherine has all the accoutrements of power as it is culturally defined. She has money, and she uses it to dominate and control. She is valuable because she presents herself in terms a man can understand; she understands and emulates masculine patterns of action. Mary is devalued because her priority on attachment causes her to move in ways that privilege not control, but complex negotiations that will not threaten her marriage. Mary is not powerless, but she does not see power in conventional terms; instead she embodies a feminine attitude that defines power as "the capacity to implement."[4] Larry tells Mary it is not her fault that the theater is in financial trouble, but in his supposed consideration for her feelings he undermines Mary by implying that she cannot be blamed for not having the stuff to cope with the real problems of the world—the attitude of mainstream culture.

In the world of this serial, though, Larry is wrong about Katherine and about Mary. Katherine, for all her social advantages, cannot make contact with Ken Page. She takes Larry to a supper club Ken frequents, but fails to get anywhere near him. Mary, however, simply goes to Page's home. Perhaps her approach reads in a certain sense as "getting to the powers that be where they live."

In confronting the establishment on its home ground, Mary has already discovered an important secret about Page's concept of power: he augments himself and his control at others' expense. Page has a sister, Sandra, whom he treats as an invalid, making the girl a prisoner in her own home. Mary also learns that all of Ken Page's wealth is based on the suffering of the poor who live in his rental properties. Mary's blossoming friendship with Sandra reveals to Sandra (and to the audience) that she need not be silently confined to what ordinary male narrative defines as a woman's place. In encouraging Sandra to come out of her shell, Mary inspires Sandra's discovery that her life of privileged comfort as a silent invalid has been purchased at the price of her own freedom and the suffering of the poor. Once she discovers a perspective of her own, Sandra immediately realizes that she is in no way sympathetic to the life of power and domination that her brother finds so natural. Thus Sandra recapitulates the voyage of the silent women described by Belenky in *Women's Ways of Knowing*. And Mary, in her approach to the problems of both the theater and Sandra Page, performs as Belenky's constructivist thinker. She goes beyond Larry's dualism and Ken Page's hierarchical authority, combining her subjective voice and knowledge of others to arrive at fresh and liberating insight.

When Mary finally meets Ken Page to discuss the lease, the sails of Ken's wrath are fully unfurled. He chooses the Oedipal approach to conflict, with extreme either/or choices prevailing. He later storms into Mary's office to accuse her of subversion of his home, only to be won over when Mary stands up to him in defense of Sandra's right to her own life and of the poor whom he exploits. Most impressive to Page is Mary's forthright declaration that he is wasting his talents as an artist with his society portraits. Mary makes the voice of woman heard by the establishment—and more. She enters into an arrangement with Page that allows her—potentially—to change circumstances to fit her perspective. Ken Page, in defense of his art and his privileged position, makes a bet with Mary: he will paint her portrait. If he succeeds in winning a prize with it in an upcoming art show, she and Larry lose their lease on the theater; if he loses, she can write her own ticket.

This arc of action on *Backstage Wife* contains some interesting reversals of the norm of male possession of women. Certainly, the metaphor of sight is present: the hero does not see as much as the heroine, and the villain sees nothing but possession. Perhaps most startling in terms of psychologically based film criticism about male control of the woman through the gaze is the bet Page makes with Mary: if he cannot win a prize by painting her portrait, he cannot control her life. The failure of the powers that be to possess the image of the woman is equated with the woman's freedom, and that of the man she loves.

Mary flies in the face of all established values and is the more effective for it. Katherine Monroe, wanting to be the financial power behind Larry's company, competes with Mary, but Mary does not compete with Katherine. Her refusal to fight is not presented as a function of "feminine" fragility; rather, Mary demonstrates an alternate set of values. She thinks Katherine a fool (and so did the audience), even though Katherine mirrors the prevailing attitudes about money and conflict. Further, when Larry's behavior causes Mary to ask for a separation, she is portrayed as admirable for taking this initiative, despite the general belief that a woman is nothing without her man. Indeed, Mary has some interesting things to say about what makes a marriage viable, and about her supposed rival, Katherine. Larry insists on reassuring Mary that Katherine "meant nothing," but Mary brushes away the entire issue of Katherine. She, focusing on the lack of mutuality in their relationship, sees Larry as the big stumbling block to the marriage. Larry accepts the separation, but does not credit Mary's insight. The narrative voice, however, supports Mary by reiterating that she is indeed not separating from Larry because of Katherine but out of "Mary's desire to be a person in her own right, not only a shadow of her famous [read: valued] husband."

Mary Noble, then, improbably exhibited all the traits of the fully realized female subject in a milieu permeated by improbability. Without benefit of a narrative that would permit her to negotiate with and free herself from the subordinated position in which the ordinary woman is held, Mary simply assumed the subject position and then spent the rest of her network life shedding light on how oblivious her man was to who she really was. But she was effective for the needs of the soap opera, and she provided a feminine point of view on the communal power structure. Similarly, Ken Page's favorable response to Mary's assertiveness in the face of his rage, though highly improbable, did make the continuity of the serial possible, and at the same time opened up the issue of the real, if submerged, desire men have for the empathy and affiliation that Mary represents. Mary and her success with Page are both fantastic. This does not, however, invalidate the value of this story as a corrective in a society that negatively judges women's way of knowing. The narrative endorsement of Mary consoled millions of women who may have had no other public, or even private, confirmation of feminine values.

In hindsight, Mary may also be seen as a starting point for the evolution of a far more probable female subject yet to come. The fantastic heroine in early soap opera created a vantage point from which to view traditional masculine priorities, opening up a distance from the norms within which the feminine perspective found room to maneuver. Such a vantage point was to be found equally in the other early female subjects. Both *The Romance of Helen Trent* and *Our Gal Sunday*, for example, although they modified the main character's improbability, maintained the constancy of fantasy by presenting a heroine in unusual circumstances. Helen Trent was a fashion designer who owned her own fashion shop and designed for a major motion picture studio, whereas Sunday Brinthrope was a woman whose humble origins contained a mystery. Sunday, left as a baby at the cabin of two old miners, was raised by two men instead of her mother; she then married a member of the English nobility, Lord Henry Brinthrope. Where Mary was relentlessly ordinary, Helen was extraordinarily talented, and Sunday was a fabulous foundling with possibly exalted origins.

Helen and Sunday are both women whose ability to function as fully developed subjects might be accounted for by their unique qualities. Helen, the more probable character of the two, is also the more interesting in terms of the way male Oedipal control is exerted through the controlling look (a topic that will be explored in detail when we reach television). Helen, as a fashion designer—indeed, a designer for films— was a woman engaged in controlling how the look, the image, was presented. Nevertheless, she was not a dominatrix, but a figure of tenderness, intimacy, and community, in a setting that serves as a principal metaphor for cutthroat struggle for hierarchical prominence. Such a woman would have had little chance in the real Hollywood: the combination of her success and her values was a fantasy—and thus she had an interesting perspective as subject. In a conventional narrative screen fiction, Helen's feminized values would have required her subordination to the man who, proficient at conquest, was her rightful possessor. As subject of this serial, however, Helen Trent redefined the struggle for power around her.

Helen is a talented woman whose success is based on the feminine definition of power, that is, the "capacity to implement." In her narrative, all those who define power as control and dominance appear self-destructive and foolish when contrasted with her. For example, there is Doris Harper, the conniving daughter of an executive at Continental Studios, Helen's employer, who attempts to use Helen for her own underhanded purposes. Helen displays vulnerability to Doris's manipulations because of her value system: at one time Doris's father, Karl Harper, protected Helen from a studio attempt to render her totally dependent on them, and she feels disposed to return the kindness. Although he has stressed that she owes him no obligation, Doris capitalizes on Helen's natural feelings of gratitude, maneuvering for a job in Helen's shop. Helen understands that Doris is not qualified for the job and also that Doris is not really interested in the work. Doris simply hopes to ensnare Chris, Helen's handsome young assistant. Chris wants nothing to do with Doris and tells Helen that the girl will only cause trouble. Despite all this, Helen hires Doris in gratitude to Karl, believing that in time "Doris'll realize she's wasting her time." The audience is given to understand that Helen is making a judgment call based on appropriate values, but one that is naive about the operation of power-obsessed people.

Helen's obliviousness to the implications of Doris's heavyhanded villainy is fantasy code for the very real confusion about patriarchal power relationships that is common in women. Nevertheless, if, in the context of the serial, Helen is wrong about the virulence of Doris's destructive capabilities, she is right in the larger sense. Doris *is* wasting her time, and everyone else's. In seeing Doris's plans from a feminine perspective, Helen is wiser than Chris; she is also much superior to Doris, who, like Katherine Monroe, is found wanting in her unsuitability for the context of the daily narrative. Helen is viable as a subject for daytime serial precisely because she is too warm and generous by nature to understand how cutthroat competition can bend people toward self-destructive and stupid behavior. Even as she allowed the Dorises of the world to gain a toehold, and thereby set up story after story, she also continued to see extreme individualism, competition, and dominance as the symptoms of a pernicious disease.

Sunday Brinthrope, on *Our Gal Sunday*, was in much the same position as Helen Trent. She, too, valued intimacy, tenderness, and community over and above her exalted position in a structured hierarchy that viewed power, individuality, and possession as the main goals. Raised to the top of the social scale by her marriage, she was neither seduced by the perquisites of rank nor tolerant of oppression based on that rank. In the serial, the powerful social position of her husband—on which, the prologue reminded the audience daily, Sunday depended—was decentered by *her* values. In fact, Lord Henry Brinthrope's supposed power caused all the problems she had to cope with: women competing for Henry, women competing for other men who were attracted to Sunday, her brother-in-law Arthur's jealousy of Henry's position in the family and the world, and so forth. *Our Gal Sunday* inverted the conventional image of the wife's possession by the husband. He was the ruler of his realm "in name only." Rather, Sunday kept the serial going with her ability to see beyond the rigid value systems of the troublemakers. Before each episode, the announcer asked the same question: "Can this girl from a mining town in the West find happiness as the wife of a wealthy and titled Englishman?" Taken out of context, the question might imply a dependence on him for value. In context, it seemed to raise the possibility that the values of the power structure Henry represented would be enough to do in a saint.

The radio-serial female subject was extraordinarily free to make meaning of her own; she only *seemed* to be subordinated by the figure of male power within the diegesis. This apparent bracketing was also true of that standard element of the radio serial, the extra-diegetic voice of the male announcer. Each radio serial was "supervised" by one or more male voices that intoned a ritual prologue at the beginning of each show, set the scene, and provided omniscient commentary on the events of the story. The prologue to *The Romance of Helen Trent*, presented with particularly ornate flourishes, gives a good idea of the tone of these prologues. First a rich male voice sang a cappella:

Just a little love a little kiss
Just a love that holds a world of bliss
Eyes that tremble like the stars above me
And the little words that say you love me.

Then another rich male voice recited the prologue, which identified the show as the ongoing story of Helen Trent, told briefly who she was, and finished by intoning: "Helen sets out to prove for herself what so many women long to prove. That because a woman is thirty-five or more romance in life need not be over. That romance can live in life at thirty-five and after."

All the radio soap opera prologues served to distance and subjugate the show's heroine by suggesting the male as the boundary and even gatekeeper of the fantasy in the show. To some extent, the encapsulation of Mary, Helen, and Sunday was real; mostly, however, it was superficial. The male voices, though deep in tone, were also emotional, suggesting fantastic, non-Oedipal men who were both richly masculine and embodying the passion associated with the mother. More important, the male announcer was less a presence of power than he was part of the heroine's retinue, her herald. He was part of a world of which she seemed a true matrix. The heroine's desire to act on her insights involved her in an endless series of tableaux with a range of characters, including many nonthreatening asexual men, like the announcer and the confidant, or the supportive, pre-Oedipal papa. The heroine's relationship with these people contrasted with her involvement with the (sexual) hero who, in combination with the Oedipal idea of woman (Katherine Monroe, Doris Harper), gave the heroine a chance to show her stuff in a struggle with intractable patriarchal culture.

However, had soap opera disappeared with radio daytime serial, it would have endured in memory as a topic of minor curiosity for trivia enthusiasts. The Marys, Helens, and Sundays are of more than passing significance only as part of the history of the development of the more intrepid television soap opera subject.

The Early Television Heroine

The radio soap opera subject was distinguished by three characteristics, all of which disappeared as soap opera made its transition to television. Most obviously, she lost her facelessness, but her improbable immunities from process and male violence were slowly eroded away as well. The transition to television, however, marked the birth of a new and greater power for her. Whereas the narrative of radio soap opera involved a subject position that concealed a good deal more than it revealed, the addition of the television camera introduced into the soap opera serial the issue of "the look."

Theoretically speaking, just as the male announcer should have placed the radio subject under his control, "the look"—the power of the camera—should have opened the way to scopophilia: voyeuristic erotic pleasure gained from control over the object of the glance, historically the prerogative of the male. This is the Oedipal stance of male toward the female, in which he can experience erotic pleasure from the woman at a safe distance, her allure made less threatening because under the full control of his look. At a distance, female glamor begets a fetishistic denial of the terror experienced with that early, furtive glance in the mirror stage—that shock of recognition that mother has no penis, which in turn poses the threat of castration. The substitution of some other visual image for that one is the denial that protects the maturing boy from the awful lack.

Psychological feminist film criticism assumes that the Hollywood movie reiterates that initial denial by controlling the female body. As Mulvey explains, "The man controls the film phantasy and also emerges as the representative of power in a further sense: as the bearer of the look of the spectator. . . . A male movie star's glamorous characteristics are thus not those of the erotic object of the gaze, but those of the more perfect, more complete, more powerful ideal ego conceived in the original moment of recognition in front of the mirror."[5] If Mulvey is correct, the requirements of the male ego ideal dominate presentation of the image of woman—the only image that threatens him with mutilation of his wholeness—on screen.

If the look were as critical as Mulvey's early thinking suggested, the television soap opera heroine would have become a passive and fetishized spectacle. That she did not gives credence to the significance of the narrative structure in determining the gender of agency. Certainly, the heroine's evasion of the camera depended to some extent on the primitive quality of early television direction and the medium's inability to replicate the glamorizing technology of Hollywood cinema. More important, this naive camera glance of early television soap opera was coupled with a narrative form that was inimical to the Oedipal resolution. As a result, the camera in pre-1978 soap opera became a partner to, rather than the captor of, a new and evolving female subject.

Among the cinematic methods effective in demobilizing the female body through the camera glance and making her into a possessed object, three have been emphasized: lighting, the so-called shot-reverse-shot, and continuity editing. In the chaotic days of early television soap opera, of course, none of this technology was in operation; but as the medium developed, cinematic techniques were evaluated and, where appropriate, adapted to the situation at hand.

Lighting is a critical element in cinema for coloring mood and shaping impressions. Backlighting has long been used to create a halo effect around the female head and torso, to glamorize the female body, and recreate the female as a glittering fetish. In early soap opera, by contrast, there was little more to say about the lights but that they were on. All bodies, both male and female, achieved an equally matter-of-fact presence.

In cinema, the shot-reverse-shot is a series of alternating "bust" shots of the male and female characters in a two-person interchange. This pattern tracks the direction of the glance, establishing who is looking and who is being looked at. Whether the pattern employs a male-female-male, or female-male-female alternation, it shows the male looking and the female receiving his look. This is not to say that the female always averts her eyes, but that her expression is one of a desire to be pleasing rather than of "looking at" the male. In early television soap opera, the shot-reverse-shot was not used; rather two-person interchanges were visualized by a two-shot, which gave equal bodily emphasis to both parties. An alternate pattern, called for during an embrace, alternated male-female-male or the reverse, shot over the shoulder, with neither one the beholder and no dominance-subordination imbalance implied. When alternating close-ups were used during a two-person interchange, the pattern tended to be in units of four (sometimes referred to as "take-him, take-her; take-him, take-her") and similarly evened out the emphasis. In all cases, the television shot patterns moved away from dominance and even suggested mutuality.

Continuity editing is a mainstream practice of creating narrative flow by splicing together scenes, thus concealing the fragmentary nature of the filmic enterprise. In Mulvey's view, this illusion of seamlessness supports the entrapment of the female who has already been dominated by the plot line and the camera glance. Yet early soap opera was shown live; thus there was no editing of any kind. In addition, the gaps at the end of the show and between plot lines, as well as the pauses for commercial breaks, only emphasized the fragmentary reality of the narrative's construction.

All this inversion of mainstream narrative film technique and the lack of agency for bringing the plot to closure made for a screen fiction without the Oedipally possessive image; instead an image was created that conveyed its support of the female subject by replacing the domination patterns of cinema with visual patterns of mutuality. Nevertheless, the first impulse on television was to replace the heroine with a male figure. Irna Phillips's *The Guiding Light*, the only radio soap opera to make a successful transition to television, featured a male character in the subject position: the wise grandfather, Papa Bauer. This early example would seem to confirm Mulvey's thesis about the controlling effect of screen technology on the heroine. But the situation is not so simple.

It is difficult to call Papa Bauer a male subject, at least in Mulvey's terms. A figure as improbable as Mary Noble herself, Papa Bauer calmly spoke on behalf of filiation, emotion, and empathy, as she did. Nor was Papa, once the show reached television, in visual possession of the other characters. The inverse of the active, dominating figure discussed by Mulvey with regard to male agency, Papa was less active than Mary, Helen, Sunday—any female radio subject—since he had no stake in the situations over which he spread his enlightening perspective. A male, but not an Oedipal male, he was as complete a denial of Hollywood's Bond-like male agency as can be imagined. Moreover, as *The Guiding Light* developed, he faded in importance until finally he disappeared altogether.

The movement on television, rather, was toward a female subject-in-process, one whose narrative acknowledged the obstacles that patriarchal discourse mounted against her desire for identity. Papa's atrophy was the first step in this development. After all, his presence called for the kind of heroine who could only learn how to be a woman from a man, and so Papa, a feminized patriarch, took the role of man as mother: his job was to instruct women on the rules of feminine identity. In 1952, the year *The Guiding Light* moved to television, when the audience first met Papa Bauer (Theo Getz), his difficult daughter-in-law, Berta (Charita Bauer), and his confused and frustrated son, Bill (Lyle Sudrow), they also encountered a male definition of the female point of view. They saw Berta Bauer, upset with her husband's frequent business trips, complaining about their disruptive effect on family life. Mary, Helen, and Sunday would never have nagged; and if they had had a Papa who knew the best way to handle the situation, he would have been little more than a shadow of their wisdom. On the early *Guiding Light*, it was Papa's sensitivity that drew Bill out and got him to talk about those long business trips, whereupon Papa then defended the priority of the family as Berta *should have done it*—with tact and gentleness (7/10/52).

Papa's maternal rapport with his son suggests a validation of the mother-son relationship in complex disguise. It may also represent an attempt to inoculate the soap opera narrative with a subject that would preserve the dominance of patriarchy. But Papa didn't take. Considering the subsequent direction of soap opera development, I contend that he simply did not offer enough energy to the form. He lost his job to the only character type having the kind of energy the soap opera narrative can use productively, a new form of female subject who would ultimately lead soap opera adventurously beyond even the appearance of patriarchal conventions.

The time frame of television soap opera, and the opening of the camera eye made it necessary to fill the screen by multiplying the number of plots and subjects. Because the visual component of television made it desirable to change locations as well, interest was stimulated in alternating segments of different stories. When Irna Phillips moved television soap opera to the half-hour format in 1956, the stress of filling that much time five days a week mandated multiple plots, and effectively eliminated the single subject typical of the mainstream film. A number of young women became heroines in these various multiple plots. They put Bertha in her place, though not by means of pontification. Their very existence simply made Berta look so bad that ultimately she had to become a sort of Helen Trent to stay on the show.

Even on the early fifteen-minute *Guiding Light*, multiple stories had already become part of the structure. A second subject, for example, was necessary for a story line involving Berta and Bill's son, Michael, and a third was required for a subplot about another core family on the show, the Grants. Papa gave advice in all these story lines, but little by little he became more peripheral, and the women became the subjects of their own stories. Although these characters were not yet as well acted or as brilliantly drawn as later heroines would be, they provided a foundation on which later improvements would be built.

In one story, Robin Lang, the pathetic, sweet young woman with whom Michael was in love, began to emerge tentatively as a new kind of heroine. When Berta expressed disapproval of their relationship and used manipulative means to break them up, Robin Lang's suffering became a focus of audience identification. Robin, deprived of the possibility of mutual love by Berta's interference, found herself forced into marriage with Alex Bowden, a villainous character who, generally obsessed with a passion for control, needs to possess his wife body and soul (6/4/52). Robin's struggle to assert her desires against the power ploys aimed at controlling her, first by Berta and then by Alex, became the spectator's focus. Robin was no Mary Noble; she started from a position of vulnerability and was not given to the audience as a figure of feminine power. But her story opened up the possibility that she might grow into such a figure. Struggling against the social manipulation of the growing girl's identity, Robin was, hence, more believable than previous female subjects had been.

Another embryonic heroine on the early *Guiding Light* was Marie Wallace. Although her conflict with Mrs. Grant, the mother of her good friend, Dr. Dick Grant, is neither compelling nor particularly well drawn, her character is a good example of a new soap opera subject that would one day be fascinating. At first, Marie, confused by Mrs. Grant's attempt to use her to control her son's life, agreed not to dispute what she knew to be the older woman's lies aimed at disrupting Dick's marriage plans. But as Marie blundered through the situation, she clarified her thinking. When Dick realized what his mother was up to, Mrs. Grant, afraid of losing her son, sought Marie's help again. This time, Marie angrily refused. In an important scene, Mrs. Grant tries to persuade Marie to change her mind: "Is it wrong to try to save a person you love?" she asks. Marie's answer: "When it stops them from being a person, yes" (6/4/52). She goes on to tell Mrs. Grant that even though she is Dick's mother, she has never really known him or respected his wishes. Although from the point of view of conventional dramatic structure Mrs. Grant should have been the focus of this scene, since she was the character on the attack, the one who wanted something, Marie was the true subject—even despite being in the receptive position (where dramatists are warned not to place their protagonists). Her priority on mutuality organized the field of action.

We see several developments in the earliest television soap operas. First, the camera replaced the announcer in assuming the male position of control over the women in the show. This male bracketing of the female was weak in both instances, however: the male announcer always seemed to privilege feeling and empathy, and the camera in early daytime serial broadcasting made the visual field neutral or mutual instead of reproducing the cinematic field of dominance-subordination. Second, there was intensified need for a subject who would not bring closure as television increased the number of gaps in soap opera narrative by proliferating plots and subjects. Third, and most important, the new heroines tended to be younger than the heroines in radio had been. These girls exhibited a sense of confusion and, in struggling against

being overwhelmed by pressures they did not fully understand, constituted a new kind of female subject. These subjects reflected the difficult *process* of dealing with dominant values.

Marie Wallace and Robin Lang tentatively indicated a new direction
for female agency; lacking energy and real interest, they were place
markers for future development. A more vital and challenging new
female subject was Penny Hughes (Rosemary Prinz) on *As the World
Turns*, the first soap opera created by Irna Phillips for television. Unlike
the early radio soap opera subject, Penny was not a mature woman
through whose eyes the values of control and domination in husband,
friends, and acquaintances were defamiliarized. Instead she was portrayed as a warm, strong, courageous young woman with a need to
assert herself owing to a lack of "fit" between her desires and the values
of her loving father and mother, Nancy and Chris Hughes (Helen
Wagner and Don McLaughlin). Although Nancy and Chris were de-
picted as kind and concerned, like Papa Bauer, they remained on the
sidelines of Penny's story, which took center stage. However, Penny's
most significant difference from her predecessors lay in her relationship
with her lover, and potential husband.

Radio soap opera as precursor to the screen fiction of television soap
opera had begun to reposition the female character from object to
subject. In doing so, it also repositioned the male character. But it did
not merely reverse the hierarchy and create a female subject and a male
object. Instead it created an open invitation by the female subject—one
never accepted by the radio heroes—to mutuality. In television soap
opera before 1978, the invitation only began to provoke a response.
This pattern entailed the appearance of a new kind of male character, a
kind of consort for the Persephone figure. Like Hades, this consort
maintained his masculine priority on individuation, competition, and
conquest. Also like Hades, he was modified by the exigencies of the
narrative structure to accept Persephone's continuity with the world of
her mother.

Penny's consort was Jeff Baker (Mark Rydell). Jeff, like Penny, was
young and evolving. Most important, he was both a conventional,
attractive, mainstream masculine agent and a hero uncertain about his
Oedipal priorities. These chinks in his Oedipal armor opened up the
possibility, not for a conquering female, but for a new kind of couple. In
conventional screen fiction, Jeff's uncertain grip on the role of masculine
domination would have served the narrative structure only if he eventually overcame that uncertainty and contained the heroine, thus effect-

ing plot closure. On *As the World Turns*, however, two other options arose. First, Jeff's character served the *serial* form precisely because his desire did not impel him toward closure. Second, he served the development of the female subject because, though an image of male desire, he did not objectify the beloved woman. Penny and Jeff's story was no mere fantasy criticism of the dominance-subordination mode, as that of Mary and Larry Noble had been. It was, rather, a probing of the fantasy possibility of love and marriage as the mutual desire of two subjects.

Penny Hughes and Jeff Baker were college students from "good" families in Oakdale, a small midwestern town. But whereas Penny was strong, vibrant, and steady, Jeff's vitality remained uncontrolled. Indeed, Jeff, with his wild streak and his problems with alcohol and a domineering mother, was the very boy Oedipus warned us about, the boy who cannot separate from women and dominate them. In *Psycho*, that boy felt compelled to destroy the feminine over and over again. On *As the World Turns*, by contrast, he provided the occasion for the female subject's voyage of discovery and growth. Through her love for Jeff, Penny acted out the possibility of taking an acknowledged role of strength in relation to a man.

At this stage of soap opera evolution, however, Penny as heroine was only slightly ahead of Mary Noble—a strong woman constantly failed by the beloved man, whose image as the dominant partner she must always protect. In Penny and Jeff's story, therefore, Penny's strength and Jeff's weakness, his constant disappointment of her expectations, formed a continuous thread with the earlier radio narratives. Yet whereas in Mary Noble's time the relation between female subject and feminized narrative structure involved no opportunities for the heroine's growth and change, Penny provided a prime example of the possibilities for a feminine discourse of the evolving self. In the Oedipal narrative, repression is required: the significant threat posed by women determines the direction of the hero's development. As a Persephone-type narrative evolved on soap opera, however, repression was increasingly defined as a threat to the *heroine's* development. Where Larry Noble embodied only the unfortunate blind spots in men, in the newer narrative men insensitive to women took on a more sinister aspect, threatening not only to neglect the heroine but to abuse her as well. The need to resist closure so that the show could remain on the air became ever more vividly incarnated in the heroine's struggle for identity.

Jeff did not directly abuse Penny, but he was frequently involved in violent situations that touched her obliquely. The spring of 1958 found

As the World Turns developing a plot line in which Jeff was accused of and put on trial for the murder of a fellow student. The scenes in the courtroom constitute a virtual tract exploring violence in men and in patriarchal systems. This capacity for assault is implied not only in Penny's beloved Jeff, who is, after all, suspected of murder, but also in the prosecuting attorney, who abuses Penny emotionally and psychologically in the name of correct legal proceedings. In addition, the narrative explores the resources of women confronted by that violence. The question is asked repeatedly whether Jeff is capable of committing murder, and whether Penny, being emotionally involved with him, is truly capable of judging his character. The scene in which the prosecutor tries to establish Penny as Jeff's helpless victim contains many visually ambivalent shots of Penny being physically trapped by the lawyer: he is ambulatory, free to move; she is bounded by the witness box. These perspectives could be used to possess Penny's body in the frame, but instead they are used to problematize the camera's possession of Penny, as analogues to the lawyer's violence in his approach to her, his violence against her truth and integrity through his logical interrogation. The interchange verbally and visually defamiliarizes the conventional presentation of the relationship between logic and women, suggesting a distortion by the prosecutor of Penny's truth. This suggestion is validated as Jeff's lawyer rises time and again to object to this treatment, and the judge sustains the objections (3/25/58).

Penny does not dissolve under the lawyer's attacks. Rather, she organizes the scene as a subject; in contrast to her integrity, the style of the juxtaposed lawyer appears abusive. Yet the prosecutor is only conducting the interrogation according to what has been called "the doubting game," conducted by those who espouse the dominant way of making meaning. That is, he questions the significance and value of emotions in doubting that Penny can testify for Jeff because she loves him. Penny, however, responds with "the believing game," an alternate route to knowledge rooted in connection and positing emotion as a way of making meaning, through empathy.[6] On *As the World Turns*, that Penny knows and loves Jeff is the best source of knowledge. And indeed, Jeff is innocent. Penny is right. The spectator sees, through her struggle, that the violence which passes for strength in the male renders questionable Penny's traditional feminine belief that she will find security in a male-dominated culture. Similarly, it provokes questions about how Penny will be defined, and who will do the defining.

Penny and Jeff negotiate a path different from the one typically followed in comparable screen fictions. Although their love story would seem to fit into the category of women's film that is well known and well populated, in major ways it does not. In conventional screen fiction, the activity of love may be central to the film, but it is usually somehow culturally marginalized. Perhaps the lover himself is marginalized because he is recognized by his society as a feminized man, frequently an artist of some sort (*Humoresque*), or perhaps the relationship as a whole is marginalized because the woman is the mistress of a married man (*Back Street*).[7] Similarly, when Hollywood presents a love story in which the woman struggles for subject status, the man must assume the feminine position, as in Hitchcock's *Rear Window*, where only the temporary passivity of the invalid hero gives the heroine a chance to enter actively into the murder mystery.[8] None of these devices figure in Penny and Jeff's story, however. Instead, Penny and Jeff depart together from the values of their community, which condemns him and frowns on their union. The two tentatively approach knowledge of her power—that is, her capacity to accomplish—and knowledge of the violence and anger in both him and society that would hinder their union.

Penny is an early transitional subject. Her romance with Jeff was allowed to culminate, but only in a doomed marriage. Their marriage was part of a romance fantasy that implied a non-Oedipal, yet adult, erotic relation; it did not play out the full implications inherent in the earlier stages of their liaison.[9] Although my interpretation of the problem with their narrative will surely surprise many readers, I argue that neither Jeff nor Penny was created with bold enough fantasy to permit the exploration of male-female mutuality. The elements of their narrative were too tied to the details of mainstream culture to encourage significant departure from ordinary gender definitions. The major role for fantasy in *As the World Turns* at this time took the form of an improbable number of car crashes, sundry accidents, and court cases, which were used to provoke and resolve dramatic situations; there simply was not a strong enough positive charge in Penny and Jeff to allow them to struggle head on with their problems. Fantasy is knowledge, for the daytime serial subject, and the further probing of male-female dynamics had to await a reenergizing of fantasy in soap opera. In order to progress toward a further development of the female subject, both the fantasy of mutuality and the fantasy that makes Oedipal control over women visible had yet to be more daringly imagined.

The Importance of Being Victoria Lord

In the late sixties, the creation of the character of Victoria Lord on a new show, *One Life to Live*, allowed soap opera's Persephone finally to approach her underworld. Soap opera fantasy, in a giant step, thus escalated the narrative of feminine identity through a bolder and more audacious depiction of the subterranean violence in and around women. In Viki's case, the underworld took the shape of the submerged aspects of herself and the invisible aspects of her father. Viki was characterized primarily as a woman who had lost touch with the assertive part of her personality; her search to find the cause of her loss led to a confrontation with her own anger and her knowledge of her father's violence and rage.

On June 15, 1968, *One Life to Live* came on the air for the first time, as blonde, ivory-complexioned Victoria Lord,[10] the clichéd American princess, walked through the French doors of her Philadelphia Main Line home, Llanfair, into a summer night, sighing up at the moon. Only on the surface did this narrative preserve the stereotype thus presented, however. Unlike her film counterpart Tracy Lord (in *The Philadelphia Story*), also an inhabitant of that Main Line, Viki Lord was not a princess positioned to be dominated by a plot that brings her back under the control of her father and of the man who will take his place as her husband.[11] The daughter of powerful Victor Lord (Ernest Graves), Viki was instead heir apparent to a communications empire and managing editor of the *Banner*, the major newspaper holding in the Lord business empire. But, mimicking the discourse of the adoring daughter and omnipotent father, the serial's masquerade covers a secret about Viki's father, repressed in the recesses of her memory—a secret not so easily managed as Tracy Lord's knowledge of her father's adultery.

About four years before Irna Phillips grappled unsuccessfully with Proctor & Gamble to give Kim Reynolds a new feminine energy, her protégée, Agnes Nixon, had better luck with the newer, more innovative administration of ABC-TV. Nixon made Viki acceptable by means of fantasy and an image of illness that seemed to place Viki in the realm that defines femininity as a kind of disease. As the narrative proceeded, however, it became clear that illness, in Viki's story, was a function of paternal violation.

The catalyst for Viki's narrative quest was the sudden occurrence of blackouts and memory lapses, peculiar disjunctions in the time frame of her life. Viki's story, then, is not only made discontinuous by gaps; it is a narrative about gaps in her awareness. Thus it is to the perforated structure of soap opera what the "mirror shot," or image of a looking-glass reflection, is to the cinematic enterprise, a story reference to the process by which it is created. Plots that feature gaps in character perception are a longstanding tradition in soap opera, indeed, a cliché. The most burlesqued device in these story lines is amnesia, the fissure in memory. Other routine gap-analogue plots include the discovery of long-lost relatives and lovers who emerge to resuscitate possibilities from past times thought closed off forever. The aesthetic fit between the structure of daytime serial and these conventions suggests once again that ridicule of soap opera derives basically from an obtuseness about the interesting elements of its narration.

In Viki's story, the gaps represent her initial perception of her alter ego, Niki, the raw female energy trapped inside the well-modulated Viki (figs. 3–4). As the story progresses, this energy slowly gathers enough momentum to endanger the primary personality. The possible absorption of Viki by Niki threatens not only the screen character, but also the conventional definition of the heroine. Challenging Viki, the classic blonde, dressed in tailored, asexual suits, and a physical and moral model of restraint, is a personality and style totally unacceptable as a screen heroine. Niki's energy, dramatized by her red wig, her flashy clothes, her uncultured squeal, her exuberant physical abandonment, is the precise threat to patriarchal organization that conventional narrative exists to contain.

Viki plays the conventional narrative role of the woman on the pedestal for upwardly mobile Joe Reilly (Lee Patterson), a prototypically charming Irish-American boy of working-class background. In short, she is headed for the middle-class destiny of being the property of her husband. Niki, however, develops a more challenging narrative by forming a separate, freewheeling relationship with Joe's best friend, Vince Wolak (Anthony Ponzini), a partner in a trucking firm. In many ways the split in Viki is dramatized by the responses of these two friends to the two fragments of her personality. Vince has the manners and mores of a working-class man, which distinguish him from his good friend, Joe, who has very much shed all traces of his origins. Part of Vince's unembarrassed fidelity to his roots lies in is his attraction to Viki's alter ego, Niki, whom he finds much more attractive than the ladylike heiress. Vince respects Viki, but doesn't consider her a "real woman." Joe, however, finds Niki unattractive and in some ways alarming.

Fig. 3. *One Life to Live*. Viki (Erika Slezak), conflicted princess of Llanview society—why is this woman smiling? Courtesy *Soap Opera Digest*.

Fig. 4. *One Life to Live*. Niki (Erika Slezak), Viki's alter ego—her buried life. Courtesy *Soap Opera Digest*.

In this first long story arc on *One Life to Live*, Vince and Joe help to clarify the options open to the heroine; but the major issue in Viki's story has to do with how the split came about. The cause is rooted in the relationship between Viki and her father; the cure is rooted in Viki herself.

Traditionally, the story of the divided identity is processed as an either/or issue: in the twin sister narrative, one sister must be rejected; in the case of an alter ego, the energized feminine identity must be excised (*The Snake Pit*). Often the divided woman dies (*The Cat People*) so that a more suitably repressed woman can be possessed by the hero. This was not the course of the double-identity story on *One Life to Live*.

The creators of *One Life to Live*, in particular Agnes Nixon and the head writers who succeeded her, principally Gordon Russell and Peggy

O'Shea, made a major contribution to the evolution of the female subject by establishing Viki's double-identity fantasy as a matter of integration rather than repression. Viki's "disease" was an ideal vehicle for exploring the disjunction between appearance and reality for women. Trapped between the obedient role Viki's father imposed on her and the forbidden energy bottled up by that imposition, Viki was forced to struggle to find and reclaim the lost part of herself.

This development pushed the boundaries of imaginative license in soap opera much further than they had ever been pushed before, distancing the genre even more from old cinematic conventions. Viki's divided personality infused an energy into the daytime serial that could never be created in Hollywood movies by a similar mechanism, because here no hero came to exorcise the woman's "undesirable" part. Free of closure, the heroine's double personality could do what fantasy does so well: free us from normal social limits. Fantasy, namely, imparts to us an imaginary scene "in which the subject is a protagonist, representing the fulfillment of a wish (in the last analysis, an unconscious wish) in a manner that is distorted to a greater or lesser extent by the defensive processes."[12] It permits us, in other words, to say what would be unspeakable in a "realistic" context. It lowers our guard. It provides a steam valve for the pressure built up by taboos. In soap opera, the fantasy of the divided woman made it possible to tell a story of the repression of feminine energy free of the social insistence that her division is but further proof of how flawed women are, free of the Hollywood necessity to re-repress or chasten the emerging energy in time for a logical closure.

Viki's fantasy illness allowed her and the spectator a feminine perspective on the father's relationship with his daughter. Searching for what divided her, Viki came face to face with the source of her problem: beneath her father's suavity and apparent concern for her raged violence and the need to control. In this respect, too, *One Life to Live* is quite different from comparable conventional screen fictions. In *The Philadelphia Story*, for example, closure makes Tracy Lord, also the daughter of a powerful father, accept that her husband's alcoholism was in fact a reaction to her audacious insistence on the prerogatives of subjecthood; similarly, she adopts a "men will be boys" attitude toward her adulterous father, accepting his diagnosis that if she had been a dutiful girl—instead of an independent woman—she would have provided the girlish adoration he was forced to find in his paramour! But if conventional film orders daughters to submit to fathers' incestuous demands, it chooses to calumniate the mother-daughter bond. *Sybil*, the true drama of a woman possessing a fragmented personality, is acceptable for nighttime television because it lays all the blame at the door of an abusive mother who sexually molested her daughter. In contrast, *One Life to Live* traces the split in Viki's personality to paternal abuse of the mother.[13]

Viki's personality disorder, she discovers, springs from the moment when, at age five, she witnessed her father and pregnant mother arguing at the top of a staircase. This heated exchange led to physical violence and her mother's fall down the stairs. Though an accident, this fall was caused by her father's overbearing attitude toward the mother, and it caused terrible damage to all the Lord women: Viki's mother died as a result of the fall, after giving birth to a baby girl, Viki's sister, whose health was irretrievably harmed in the accident. After this event, Viki repressed evidence of her own strength and accepted her father's complete control over her. When she finally remembers the scene of her father's violence, a gap in her memory is filled that clarifies a terrible fear she has of the destructive need of male rage to control the female. She can see that Niki is a defensive strategy to protect herself from her father by burying the reality of feminine energy in an independent identity. Her discovery that this form of defense only did her more harm is an important step forward. But it is no small matter to heal a division that has sent feminine competence and sexuality in opposite, seemingly irreconcilable directions.

Viki begins her journey toward wholeness and fully realized sexuality by regaining access to her suppressed memory. Rendered on screen from Viki's point of view (POV) during a flashback, the critical vision of her mother and father fighting and of her mother's fall makes for an extraordinary moment. Narratively, it established Viki as the authentic possessor of her own situation, and hence the one with the power to affect it. Visually, it added to daytime television the POV shot (here establishing female interiority) and the feminine way of experiencing meaning through image. As possessor of the image, Viki is enlightened, not subordinated. No longer is she in a passive position, viewing her childhood indirectly, enthralled by the distortions her father passed off as the truth. Once her memory returns, Viki's experience of Niki is not achieved only vicariously, from the accounts of other people who have witnessed the alter ego during Viki's blackouts. Ultimately, Viki goes beyond mere awareness of her buried personality fragment, and she and Niki are integrated (see chapter 5).

One Life to Live is remarkable not only for the positioning of Viki and her parents, but also for the active subjectivity of the heroine, who becomes absorbed in redefining her father's version of her history as part of her self-cure. Viki in her fantasy division is significantly different from the conventional "sick" woman of film, a fairly typical figure in women's entertainment. There, "the medical discourse," as Mary Ann Doane calls it, is usually but another way of forcing women to exist principally as the object of a male gaze. In the medical discourse, illness is metaphorically equated with femininity, health with masculinity, as a doctor, transformed into a lover, restores the woman to health by possessing her with his curative look (*The Dark Mirror*, *A Stolen Life*, and *Lady in the Dark*).[14] The cinematic gaze on the sick woman, in short, proceeds toward a closure that *re-represses* the disruptive feelings, as female desire is defined by Hollywood.

Viki's disease on *One Life to Live*, however, is not part of a story in which repression is appropriate, mainly because her illness concerns not her femininity, but the inappropriate behavior of her father. The men in Viki's life at first see the alter ego in terms of an evil *in her*, but their perspectives are presented in a negative light. Viki's lover, Joe Reilly, meets Niki before Viki comes to her understanding of what has happened, and therefore before he understands the woman he loves. He is irritated, even disgusted, by the coarse and irrepressible Niki. He wants to subtract Niki, to suppress her and have only the fine, elegant dream girl. Although Joe naturally sees Viki's fear of sexual love as a problem, he believes that he can "save her" once he possesses her as his bride. He does not realize, as Viki herself eventually does, that only by integrating Niki's energy and boldness can she respond to him as he desires. Similarly, Niki's lover, Vince, despite his friendship for both Joe and Viki, reluctantly arrives at the conclusion that he must have Niki to himself, even if that means that Viki would disappear. As for Viki's father, he is characteristically unsympathetic. His inability to understand the situation is presented as a refusal to take any responsibility for what he has done and an accompanying desire to re-repress Niki.

It is left to Viki to realize that in order to remain the capable and powerful woman she has grown to be, and to add full sexuality to her repertoire, she must work to incorporate Niki, not suppress her. The heroine is supported in her desire for integration by Dr. Marcus Polk, a psychiatrist who confirms Viki's intuitions. His shadowlike presence is devoid of the erotic possessiveness of the medical gaze; Polk is a fantasy of the ideal father, encouraging the daughter in her quest for self. He is faithful to the psychiatric ideal of "acting as a link between rationality and irrationality, between visibility and invisibility," as Doane puts it, instead of becoming "the figure of their absolute disjunction" (like the psychiatrist in *The Cat People*).[15] After Viki comes to self-knowledge, Joe, too, gains understanding of her father's role in the problem and no longer sees her problem in his originally narrow way. Part of Joe and Viki's forming mutuality entails their cooperative view of Mr. Lord's part in Viki's illness and their united opposition to his continuing refusal either to accept his responsibility or to cease his demand for total control over his daughter's life.

With this story line, Viki achieves fuller articulation as a female subject than had previously existed in daytime serial, coming very close to confronting the domination of men over women. Under cover of fantasy, the Viki/Niki story told some difficult truths about men and women. We see that before Viki's attempts at integration, her life was her father's invention. This is unusual enough as a media statement. Still more unusual is the complex exploration of Viki's first attempts at freedom, desperate measures also controlled by her father's attitudes.

Niki, too, is a patriarchal invention, a crude effort at self-determination that plays right into the value system that divided Viki in the first place. In trying to act out her own strength and freedom, Niki resorts to the patriarchal fantasy of the threat of feminine energy, and, like her oppressors, she also wants to dominate: she will accept nothing less than total control over the body she and Viki share. Coming to grips with Niki is only an interim attempt on Viki's part to establish her own definitions of who she is.

The earliest soap opera subjects rejected male domination by means of an improbable fantasy that denied anger and its place in the growth of the heroine. This anger, however, is acknowledged in the Viki/Niki split; indeed, it takes the heroine to a primitive stage in the development of the female subject, one in which the girl must assume the aggression and individualism of masculine behavior, the only model of free self-hood available to her. Niki is Viki's temporary rejection of all forms of authority. As is the case for the prototype in Belenky's *Women's Ways of Knowing*, Niki's anger is not an end in itself; rather, it produces for Viki a new sense of freedom and value that paves the way to a high level of development and a greater wholeness.[16]

If the new direction of fantasy in soap opera indicated by the Viki/Niki story opened up the issue of female anger, Viki's discovery of a repressed interest in sexual body display also significantly altered the soap opera perspective on female glamor. In early daytime serials, specular (visual) interest had been generated by predatory female adversaries for whom glamor was a weapon, thus replaying Hollywood's message that female allure must be kept under tight control. Before *One Life to Live*, the heroine was charged with the task of negotiating with the power of the sexually fascinating woman, but she was presented as "above" the impulse to display her own physical charms in an alluring way. Viki's story gave the heroine a body and a struggle with the perils of glamor that was defined as a struggle with her own intimidation by men.

Attention was thus drawn to the question of what happens to the female body when women have neither the freedom nor the language to create and define their own identities. In going underground to protect herself from her father's rage, Viki hid her active sexuality, a part of her identity that her father did not authorize, but she took her disguise in the form of female sexuality authorized by the male power structure in society, the tawdry glamorization that is the hallmark of Hollywood. Because Niki expresses Viki's wish for an energized body through the only language available to her—Hollywood's fetishized image of the sensual woman—that language becomes associated in this story with Viki's disturbance.

Niki's sexuality was a problem to Viki. However, the problem was not that a part of Viki wanted to be sexual. Rather, the dilemma was that she could *only* express her sexuality as fetish. At first appalled by the gap she discovered in her personality, Viki was frightened less by Niki's energy and boldness than by all the foolish paraphernalia that went along with her alter ego's sexuality. As the initially repressed Viki changed and grew, she learned to manifest her desire in a form that did not require Niki's awkward, tinseled parody of Hollywood movie queens.

With Viki, soap opera made a bold advance toward examination of the violence with which women are sundered from full personhood and the problems caused by their response to that violence. But *One Life to Live*, in this early stage, to a large extent diminished the shock of Viki's discovery about her father by displacing the violence onto Viki's mother in the safely contained past. (There is certainly an identification between Viki and her mother—in the scene of recall Viki's mother was even played by Gillian Spencer, the same actress who played Viki.) Moreover, although Viki was clearly the object of Victor Lord's lust for control, she was impelled to recognize violence only toward someone *like* her, not toward her specifically. This displacement weakened the serial's portrayal of the fear *of* women that the Oedipal resolution induces in men. Similarly, the discovery of Niki by the men in Viki's life displaced male agitation at perceiving female resistance to social definitions of their identity. Victor and Joe saw Niki as a threat to Viki, not themselves.

Feminist analysts, however, all point out that the will to self-definition in women is more than just vaguely irritating to men close to them. Modleski, for example, makes the compelling point that female self-definition is not simply a matter of disobedience.[17] Assertive women, rather, raise profound fears in men about their own identities, for such women suggest the possibility that men and women may identify with each other in certain ways; the great task of the Oedipal male, then, is to deny any such identification. Modleski demonstrates her point by means of Hitchcock's *Vertigo*. In this film, the hero requires the heroine to submit to his every demand in order to become an object that he can find lovable. But even after Madeleine/Judy (Kim Novak) quits her job and lets Scottie Ferguson (James Stewart) support her, and dress her, and dictate her hairstyle and her makeup, his control over her is not complete enough to assuage his anxiety. The awful intensity of his experience of intimacy with Judy causes him to drive her back to that well-known roof's edge and to her death.[18] Thus, without going so far as actually to create a female subject, Hitchcock probes male terror of the *possibility* of her emergence.

In contrast, although *One Life to Live* creates a female subject, its text continues, in part, the tradition of denial begun in radio soap opera. The darker side of masculine fear of feminine self-definition is restricted to Viki's father, and imaged only in terms of his past violence toward her dead mother. *One Life* avoids what Hitchcock reveals: the Oedipal structuring of male-female relations—most difficult to talk about and, therefore, most necessary *to* talk about. The Oedipal male believes that his ability to control "his" women will domesticate the terrible female power. In reality, there can never be enough control over the feminine to protect him from reexperiencing, in the pull toward intimacy, the very pre-Oedipal closeness with his mother that his passage into manhood has forced him to deny.[19] Niki, as the embodiment of Viki's hidden rage against her father's control over her, a rage that she permits only because she witnessed the violence he did to her mother, thus tells only half the story of female agency.

The other part, which we did not see on *One Life to Live*, concerns a probing narration of the response of the men in Viki's life to the emergence of a part of Viki that seriously threatens both their desires and the conventions of masculine identity. Victor Lord's need to control his daughter, which provoked Viki to covert rebellion, is a part of his definition of his manhood—as are Joe Reilly's desire to heroically champion Viki as a damsel in distress, and Vince's passion for the "sexy" fetish persona. Niki means the end to Victor's lock on Viki's will and the creation of a will in Viki that resembles Victor's. Viki's dealings with her alter ego mean she can dispense with Joe's services as a knight in shining armor and become, like him, a competent survivor. Viki's survival means that Niki can be only a temporary phase in her development; thus, when Viki's sexuality no longer depends on the "feminine" trash of the Hollywood seductress, Vince will not have his sex kitten, nor will Viki's sexuality be pictorially demarcated from Vince's. Viki's new identity, in short, will mean that she and the men are closer than they were before, in the sense of being more similar to each other, and that she will be less submissive to male desires. The Viki/Niki story remains incomplete if it does not include aggressive, even violent, male resistance to the thwarting of their desires and to the blurring of the conventional lines drawn between their male identities and hers.

This is not to say that in a narrative that fully depicts the struggles of the female subject all men must become homicidal when they feel the need to be close to a woman. But as long as boys are raised with traditional beliefs about manhood, the men they become will experience fear, as well as desire, about any form of femininity they do not feel they control. Therefore, a narrative will not be complete unless significant masculine resistance is raised to the emergence of feminine subject identity.

The narrative of the female subject is most fully articulated as some variant of Brünnhilde's story of isolation from the world by the ring of fire her father has placed around her. The female agent cannot sleep within that flaming ring, nor will the fire disappear on its own. It is especially impervious to male agency, despite Wagner's mistaken depiction of Brünnhilde's rescue from the flame by Siegfried, since that imprisoning flame *is* male agency viewed from the female perspective. The fully articulated portrayal of the female subject in screen fiction must include the heroine's trial by Oedipal fire—that is, the aggression of the masculine narrative and the forcing of closure by a potential Oedipal dyad—the father-son configuration Victor Lord and Joe Reilly might have been. As the myth of Persephone demonstrates, the female subject rises or falls depending on whether she finds the narrative strength to counter the Oedipal dyad of father and son and their ring of fire.

It is this confrontation with the full Oedipal dyad that is missing in the pre-1978 soap opera. Mary Noble was a fantasy that completely denied pervasive masculine power. And while in hindsight we can see that Viki prefigured the heroine who would actively confront that power, in fact she confronted only the father. Only after 1978 would a new subject encounter the fully articulated process of the conventional narrative that binds her to both father and husband.

Viki suggested the direction to take in order to achieve that full encounter: through the underworld. By means of buried realities, the heroine would obliquely encounter the kinds of problems with her identity and with her body that women in the sixties were beginning to explore. Under pressure from the evolving narrative of soap opera, the possessive glance of mainstream film was transformed. At first, in early television soap opera, that eye was neutral, but with Viki and her alter ego it began to be liberated. In post-1978 soap opera we shall see a strong alliance develop between the camera eye and the female subject— resulting in an exposure of some of the ways glamor works to constrain femininity.

Conclusion

In pre-1978 soap opera we find an embryonic female subject who derives not from the myth of Oedipus, whose continued closeness to his mother brought plague and famine, but from that of Persephone, who insured the fertility of the world by pursuing an inclusive closeness to both her mother, Demeter, and her husband, Hades. Early soap opera subjects in radio and television, thanks to the practical consequences of the soap opera gap structure, rooted the day-time heroine in fantasies about an ideal of mature selfhood that did not privilege domination and control. The evolution of this unique female subject brought the heroine ever closer to a confrontation with the power of masculine rage against potential feminine selfhood. The augmentation of the role of fantasy, a mode particularly appropriate for the gap structure of soap opera narrative, was an important factor in making possible the soap opera heroine's increasingly dynamic narrative role.

Ordinary narrative process—defined by our culture as "realistic"—is a quest for male identity. In post-1978 soap opera the realism of that narrative, which prevents the heroine from assuming a separate identity, was countered by a special and more vivid fantasy, as part of a new narrative of feminine maturation. In the next chapter we examine how greater fantasy meant greater clarity as the new subject became a quester who defined not only the position of feminine identity, but also the narrative journey through which the feminine self is created.

CHAPTER THREE

The Fantasy Female Subject after 1978

Not until the second period of soap opera development does daytime serial begin to fulfill the promise of its early heroines. The post-1978 female subject of soap opera is still not a conscious answer to Silvia Bovenschen's articulation of the dilemma of forming a feminine identity in "Is There a Feminine Aesthetic?": "We are in a terrible bind. How do we speak? In what categories do we think? Is even logic a bit of virile trickery? . . . Are our desires and notions of happiness so far removed from cultural traditions and models?"[1] The new subject, like her earlier counterpart, is the product of an electronically created possibility for telling stories without closure for daily commercial presentation. Yet as the seventies waned, the soap opera heroine rose to her historic moment, overtly confronting and transforming the "virile trickery" that the earlier soap opera heroine did well to perceive. As she did so, the mythic ideal informing soap opera narrative surged with renewed energy.

The narrative of the post-1978 soap opera heroine brings her ever closer to open identification with a narrative of feminine identity such as the one related in the story of Persephone. In the more evolved of these modern soap operas, new narrative refinements increasingly recall the myth's insistence that the spectator separate her- or himself from the usual sympathies—even identification—with male desire.

In the Persephone myth as it has been shaped by Homer's *Hymn to Demeter*, we learn only after the fact that the violent abduction of the girl is business as usual among the father-gods. As Hades sees things, his act is part of an agreement with his brother Zeus, who, as both patriarch of the gods and Persephone's father, is in a position of power over the girl. Yet most of the information about this complicity of Zeus and Hades emerges only *after* the reader has identified with the terror of Persephone and the suffering of Demeter. What has already been firmly established as a rape is only belatedly defined by Hades and Zeus as an ordinary contract. Unlike most monolithic Western narrative, the *Hymn to Demeter* refuses to support that definition.

In Persephone's polyphonic narrative, the women renegotiate the contract so that a number of desires are in play. As each woman pursues her desire, a new arrangement is created in which there is something for everyone. Both Demeter and Hades will have a relationship with Persephone. She will have relationships with each of them. Zeus gets to save face by enunciating the final compromise. This feminine management of events is a far cry from the original plan concocted by the men, in which their desires constructed sharp divisions between triumph and humiliation and restricted Persephone's role to that of object. Persephone's narrative begins with the heroine as a helpless girl in the grip of the asymmetries of male power, but, with the help of her mother, Persephone finishes as a woman whose expression of her desire for mutuality has matured her into feminine selfhood.

Modern soap opera's aggressive attention to the inequities imposed by conventional male narrative desire similarly permitted the post-1978 heroine to counter the tyrannical aspects of male bonding and achieve her identity by preventing masculine conquest of her, thus adding energy, interest, and a provocative new power to the daytime serial. The relatively wooden quality of the pre-1978 heroine resulted from her iconic assertion of feminine values in an episodic structure concerned almost completely with endless incident and barely with plot. The heroine's story became increasingly dynamic after 1978, for now that resistance was placed within a compelling matrix of events.

The mature period of soap opera begins with the 1978 restructuring of *General Hospital* (ABC-TV), until then an all but moribund daytime serial. *General Hospital*'s Laura Webber was indisputably the first soap opera heroine to effectively challenge the excesses of male bonding at the foundation of the patriarchal power structure. As we have seen, this could have happened in 1973 on *As the World Turns* (CBS-TV), but the story of Kim Reynolds's desire was postponed by the show's sponsor-producers (see chapter 1). And although a story of feminine desire had been partially told on ABC-TV, on *One Life to Live*, its success was circumscribed (see chapter 2).

The case of *One Life to Live* is instructive here. A character well ahead of her time, Viki is a tribute to the imaginative power of her creator, Agnes Nixon, who understood that in boldly portraying the shadow self of woman, soap opera was in sync with wider social developments. Nonetheless, there were important limits to Viki's story, both in terms of her ability to energize the soap opera form and in terms of her place as a female subject. Viki found her narrative in a premarital underworld; the significance of that buried reality only for Viki as daughter, never for Viki as wife, thus left *One Life to Live* no better equipped to deal with narrative in marriage than soap opera had ever been. From a feminist perspective, the subject identity of the wife remained in limbo. It was left to *General Hospital* to cast a new light on Hollywood's most potent barrier against feminine agency, one even more effective than James Bond: conventional marriage.

General Hospital: Crooks in the Crannies

After a few false starts and some plot vagaries, the 1978 innovations on *General Hospital* solved the problem that haunted Viki's story. A new pattern was established that virtually turned the Oedipal plot narrative of conventional cinema inside out to serve the purposes of the gap-structured soap opera context. Once again the industry, without intending to do so, found solutions to the problem of daily dramatic production—a problem that coincided with the way women make meaning—through the demystification of Oedipal fantasy. With the marriage of Laura and Scotty (see below, and chapter 1), *General Hospital* had the same problem that all marriage, which conventionally operates as a form of closure, causes for daytime television. Their union needed to be opened up, disrupted. To create a tomorrow for Laura, therefore, the *General Hospital* writers created a postmarital underworld for Laura, one quite different from the buried secrets of the *pre*marital life that Agnes Nixon imagined for Viki Lord.

Laura, at the point of her marriage to Scotty, had begun, like Viki befoɪe her on *One Life to Live*, to define herself in terms of resistance to traditional masculine prerogatives. The young, beautiful daughter of an upper-middle-class family in Port Charles, an average small town some-where in New York State, Laura Webber (Genie Francis) had rejected being used incestuously as an object. David Hamilton (Jerry Ayres), on being spurned by Laura's mother, had taken advantage of the fourteen-year-old girl to vent his frustrated desire. When the girl realized Hamil-ton was offering her only exploitation, not love, she refused Hamilton's advances, and killed him when he pressed his suit forcefully. To save Laura, her mother confessed to the crime, but she was unable to hide the truth from the court. Eventually, though, Laura was exonerated on the basis of self-defense. Having successfully resisted the first stage of the patriarchal assault on the feminine, Laura was now in Viki's position: free to define her own erotic choices. Laura expressed desire for Scotty Baldwin (Kin Shriner). But there were still some surprises left for Laura.

Before they married, Scotty and Laura appeared to conform to a feminine ideal of mutuality. But marriage transformed Scotty. Scotty, the "right" man, son of a prominent attorney, a member of her parents' social circle, belatedly, once he was a husband, became identified in terms of the conventional male narrative; well on his way to becoming like his socially correct father, he enrolled in law school to enable him to support his wife "as she deserved." Unlike Viki's involvement with Joe on *One Life to Live*, Laura's story tapped into the ironic truth that those qualities in men that serve the purposes of conventional narrative—both in life and in Hollywood—are wrong for soap opera. For various rea-sons, audience and network seemed to be ready for a narrative that took arms against the problems caused by conventional marriage to a conven-tional husband. When Laura eventually resisted Scotty, she did not meet the fate of Kim Reynolds. *General Hospital* invited the audience to identify with Laura when she attacked her baffled husband, despite his protests that he was the one behaving appropriately—and so he was, by conventional standards. And the audience did identify with her, even when Laura, against Scotty's wishes, took a job at the seedy Campus Disco. They stayed with her even though Scotty reflected the "right" attitude in objecting to Laura's association with Luke Spencer (Tony Geary), manager of the disco, a man with a reputation as a ne'er-do-well. Indeed, they stayed with her *even though they knew* that Luke was worse than Scotty suspected—for unbeknownst to the upright citizens of Port Charles, Luke was also the hireling of a big crime boss.

To deal with the threat of closure implicit in Laura's marriage to Scotty, the *General Hospital* writers turned to a conventional master narrative of the Flying Dutchman type, in which the outsider, at first seemingly unwholesome, tries to reform himself through love of the burgher's daughter. However, lacking closure, *General Hospital* also lacked the sexist agenda of the traditional tale. The standard version of this story renders the burgher's daughter an obligatory female object and imposes the will of the necessary Oedipal dyad over her in one of two ways. The upbeat alternative is exemplified by *On the Waterfront*. Here, Terry Malloy (Marlon Brando) dissolves his bond with the pseudo (corrupt) patriarchs who have sold him short ("I could have been a contender") by possessing the virtuous social worker (Eva Marie Saint). She gives him entrance into an authentic patriarchal dyad with a father of the church (Karl Malden), guaranteeing a victorious closure. The darker, more prevalent version insures damnation by the male subject's tragic attempt to bypass the male bonding chain: *The Flying Dutchman*, *Sweet Bird of Youth*, *The Draughtsman's Contract*, *A Place in the Sun*, *The Great Gatsby*.

As with all attempts to adapt conventional, closed plots for soap opera, the open-endedness of the form forced a shift. On *General Hospital*, the burgher's daughter became the subject of the tale when she turned out to be privy to unsuspected information concerning the community of burghers: the double identity of Luke's boss, Frank Smith (George Gaines), as both crime magnate and business magnate.

Luke Spencer, the answer to Laura's dilemma—and to the general dilemma of marriage in soap opera for years to come—is an unlikely consort when seen in the light of conventional screen discourse. An unimportant errand boy on the payroll of Frank Smith, the head of organized crime in Port Charles, he had none of the masterful qualities usually associated with the hero. Luke's major asset for this story was his troubled male bonding with Smith. In fact, the Oedipal dyad that Luke formed with the apparently respectable, but covertly criminal, Frank Smith turned out to be as narratively useful for soap opera as the heroic mastery of John Wayne, Sean Connery, and Charles Bronson all rolled into one would be for Hollywood. The connection between Luke and the supposedly respectable Smith became Laura's ticket to freedom and, incidentally, a metaphor for a problem that was invisible to the "good" citizens of Port Charles: a flaw in the operation of the male hierarchy. By implication, Frank Smith's double nature as crime boss and influential businessman made all male bonding a problem. Ironically, once Luke rejected crime for love of Laura, he also fell afoul of the supposedly respectable male power structure of Port Charles (of which Scotty was a part) because it, of course, was built on Smith's authority. In the context of this narrative, Laura (and Luke) could define themselves as being on the side of truth only if Laura separated herself from the conventions of her society, and that meant from her "good" husband, Scotty.

Once its relationship to the underworld was made visible to the viewer, the newly problematic Oedipal dyad offered *General Hospital* an effective new narrative opportunity for exciting soap opera. From a feminist perspective, it did that and more. It offered the spectator a new narrative of feminine identity unsuited to the Oedipal mold.

Frank Smith's doubling as a leading respectable citizen and a crime lord gave Laura's narrative somewhere to go in the daytime format and unintentionally rendered crime a metaphor for the global Oedipal agenda. Under those circumstances, Laura's interference in the Oedipal dyad, as an erotic alternative to Smith's patriarchal power, created an extraordinary reversal in the narrative role of female sexuality. Where female sexuality is the great threat to the coherence of the Hollywood narrative, here Laura's invitation to intimacy was Luke's salvation and, ultimately, the redemption of the community. Laura's erotic power emerges in "the rape scene," but the contextual positioning of the polarities of intimacy and violence in that scene defy any appropriate application of the term: *Luke and Laura make love while Luke is supposed to be carrying out a contract murder for Smith*. Luke and Laura's sexual involvement at that moment defies the destructive submission to patriarchy each has made: Laura preferring intimacy with Luke to the emptiness of marriage as she knows it, and Luke preferring intimacy with Laura to "wasting" another of Smith's minions, who, mirroring Luke's very position, foretells Luke's own future.

Perception of Laura's narrative as the exhaustion of dominance-subordination hierarchy may be more than a little surprising to those familiar with Luke and Laura's story, given that the sexual encounter that prevented Luke from carrying out the murder was referred to by Laura, and by the media commenting on the scene, as a rape. When correctly identified, of course, rape is the essence of the dominance-subordination configuration. As the reductio ad absurdum of patriarchal attitudes toward femininity, it hovers uncomfortably over the presentation of normal sexuality, even in classic cinema intended for family viewing. Fraught with violent undertones, the patriarchal vision of woman as subjugated possession means that, at the very least, many "love" scenes in mainstream films are little more than romanticized rape scenes. For example, in *The Quiet Man*, which trades on a supposedly good-humored tourist's view of quaint Irish customs, the character played by John Wayne is sexually correct when he breaks down the door behind which "his woman" (Maureen O'Hara) has hidden herself. "There'll be no doors between you and me, Mary Catherine," he bellows. The audience is clearly intended to believe this *is* what the lady has been waiting for.

On *General Hospital*, the dominator model of male possession of the female was confronted and rejected already in David Hamilton's attack on Laura. The so-called rape of Laura by Luke was not a rape at all, since it was almost completely free from association with dominance-subordination eroticism. The labeling of their sexual encounter as a rape originated with Laura's use of the term. But as we shall see, she described her lovemaking with Luke in this way *only because she initially did not have the appropriate language.* The failure of language was made quite clear on the show; nevertheless, the misnomer "rape" was taken up by the media, even after Laura had disavowed it in the narrative, because mainstream discourse remained unable or unwilling to discuss Laura's rejection of conventional marriage in any other terms. (Although Tony Geary reinforced the misnomer in public relations appearances, it must be remembered that publicity exists in the discourse of the network, not in the special discourse of the soap opera narrative.)

The scene of erotic encounter between Luke and Laura bears some superficial marks of conventional domination-subordination sexuality, but ultimately it is dramatized in terms of the mutual need of female and male subjects to recognize female desire if they are to resist the tyrannical aspects of patriarchy. Because the scene takes place in the Campus Disco, Luke's turf, a hierarchy is suggested in which he supersedes her, she being only a waitress. But numerous details of their story erode the possessor/possessed model. For example, their encounter takes place during a dance after hours, when male hierarchy is in abeyance. Laura's official obligation is to Scotty, but he is elsewhere, having coffee with another woman (a notorious seducer of married men) at the very time he is supposed to pick her up. Luke stays with Laura, despite his obligation to fulfill his murder contract, because of his desire for her. Dancing together takes them outside the destructive contexts in which they think each belongs (figs. 5–7).

This dance, ostensibly initiated by Luke's desire, raises some complex questions, since Laura is supposed to be afraid of that desire. The Luke and Laura story thus hovers on the edge of ambiguity about male force in eroticism. Nevertheless, what this scene, both narratively and visually, impresses on the viewer most strongly is Laura's struggle with *her* own

Figs. 5 and 6. *General Hospital*. The dance at the Campus Disco that made Luke (Tony Geary) and Laura (Genie Francis) a couple.

Fig. 7. *General Hospital*. Laura: a new generation of soap opera heroines begins here.

desire, and with her fear of shedding conventional limits. Equally important, the sight of her physical involvement with the music stimulates Luke's break with Smith. Even in the Persephone myth, Hades' original violent approach to the heroine is qualified by her allure. This is embodied in the image of Persephone picking narcissus: her own desire and the delight she takes in her own sensuality, it seems, are prerequisite to masculine desire. In the case of Persephone, the heroine's experience of her sensuality is coterminus with her abduction. Only in the long run is her erotic power transformed into a strength that causes an alteration of the prerogatives of the desiring male—prerogatives acquired through his bonding with the father. On *General Hospital*, Laura's emergent sensuality immediately releases her from the patriarchal constraints of a deadening, socially correct marriage and saves Luke from a disastrous obligation to a corrupt patriarch.

We do not see Luke and Laura making love, only the foreplay, when Laura's dancing renders her a spectacle. Yet in their foreplay, the emphasis is on the power that her dazzling visual display has to challenge undesirable Oedipal bonding. In stimulating Laura's narcissism, the dance brings out her own sense of her sexuality, as well as Luke's. Thus, as with Persephone, Laura's interior experience of desire precedes male desire for her. From the very first, Laura narratively discredits the Oedipal definition of "forbidden" intimacy with women. Having rejected the erotic politics of the David Hamiltons of the world, she embodies for Luke her own definition of eroticism. Laura defines woman's appeal for man as the consequence of her active experience of her own desire; indeed, in her lies the possibility that female sexuality saves men from the excesses of the problematic relationship between masculinity and power.[2]

However, this is soap opera, and the next day brings oscillation. Laura returns to Scotty. She avoids his anger at her overnight absence by claiming to have been raped, adding that she was so traumatized by the assault that she cannot remember the identity of her attacker. Out of context, Laura's misrepresentation of the facts could be construed as an antifeminist portrayal of how women claim rape when they have in fact participated willingly. In context, however, Laura's lie is nothing less than a failure of the discourse available to her. She and Luke resisted conventional authority because it was not as upstanding as it seemed, only to be stymied by a language that presents authentic desire as rape.

For a long time, Laura remains on the fringes of society without words to express her desires. Yet eventually she affirms her active engagement with Luke when Frank Smith and Scotty Baldwin both strike out at him, forcing upon Laura an either/or choice. Luke does not abduct Laura, but, like the Hades-Zeus bond in the myth of Persephone, the configuration of men in Laura's life forces her into a situation that means leaving her family, particularly her mother, with whom she had a close relationship. If Luke is to evade Frank Smith's homicidal anger at Luke's failure to perform the contract murder, he must leave Port Charles; he begs Laura for help. She agrees to go with him, but with a determination to restructure that choice so she can balance the claims of both mother and lover.

In any conventional narrative, Luke and Laura's flight from Port Charles would have been doomed, or they would at least have been forced to find a redeeming replacement male bond to validate their actions. Instead they search for and find the "left-handed boy" who can provide the evidence that will reveal the truth about Frank Smith. This "left-handed boy" turns out to be a transvestite. Thus, by confronting the undoing of the conventional gender divisions between male and female, Laura and Luke find a way to cleanse the polluted social structure. Only then can Laura return, having created the identity of a heroine to replace the identity given to her by her husband, that of a runaway wife who betrayed a good man.[3]

Defined by Hollywood as a blockage in the male narrative, a reminder of the fatal maternal intimacy, eroticism must be controlled by possession of the woman so that the male subject can get on with the big fight scene, which will bring appropriate closure.[4] In creating Laura's narrative, however, *General Hospital*'s executive producer, Gloria Monty, and head writer, Pat Falken Smith, changed the relation of the erotic to the narrative. Eroticism became a new way for daytime serial to thwart termination of narrative. The visual treatment of Laura exaggerated the role of woman as spectacle as no previous daytime serial had done.[5] With this revolution, the bodies and faces of Luke and Laura came into specifically erotic focus. For their love scenes, the camera moved in with unprecedented closeness on their lips, while the volume was raised sharply to project breathing and labial sounds. But these images, far from subjugating Laura, emphasized the magnitude of what she had to offer in place of murder, the means by which Frank Smith exerts his repressive form of power. In other words, the eroticism of the soap opera text now replaced the violence of the Hollywood text as the preferred way of making meaning—and a decidedly feminine one at that.

Violence and possession are central to the Oedipal pattern, both as a means of obtaining knowledge and for dealing with eroticism. There, a power relationship is established between a conquering knower and a conquered known. Knowers (such as traditional students are) "suppress the self, taking as impersonal a stance as possible toward the object."[6] The feminine style of learning and understanding, however, does not emphasize the subject-object division; rather, it sees learning as a *relationship* between two subjects. In the feminine mode, empathy, intuition, and mutuality replace violent conquest as ways of "knowing" the world. Thus, unlike the adversarial method of establishing meaning in Hollywood narrative, the erotic scene in soap opera is an image of connected knowing.

In a sense it is true that "sex sells," just as in traditional cinema "violence sells." But soap opera is not simply a matter of titillation. Sex and violence in fact satisfy their audiences by mirroring the way information is processed, the way the subject approaches the world in all matters. Violence is Hollywood's celebration of Oedipal modes of knowing. Equally, the eroticism of the post-1978 soap opera is a celebration of feminine modes of knowing. Unless handled crudely, sex on soap opera has far-reaching implications for the affirmation of feminine identity, starting with Laura's prevention of murder by the power of her allure and desire.

Once *General Hospital* became a success, the industry tended to replicate the eroticism and intensity of the Luke-and-Laura relationship as a practical means of competing for ratings. At the same time, however, soap opera, regardless of commercial intent, found a productive narrative for its female subject. The rapidly growing audiences were being drawn to narratives that overtly restructured the preoccupations of women's screen fiction with love and marriage and covertly reevaluated the subject position in its encounter with the world. While in conventional screen fiction love is a form of diminution for the female character, and marriage the closure that certifies her object status, the new narrative deconstructs that kind of marriage by celebrating both the power of female eroticism and marriage as a relationship that permits an ongoing and strengthening of female identity in the subject.

Laura became a model of the power of feminine eroticism. With her, too, a new approach to the interruption of the linear in the soap opera narrative became available: the couple's disruption of the community. On older soap operas in both radio and television, couples had always remained a part of the communal order. Now, the problematic couple became a new form of gap.

Older shows, such as *As the World Turns* and *Guiding Light* (CBS-TV), were little affected by the success of *General Hospital*. At most a tepid challenge was posed to the Oedipal dyad: female subjects were allowed tentatively to flirt with splitting that dyad, and the couple was mildly energized. These shows, thus, largely maintained the emblematic place of the Persephone figure. On newer shows, however, some exciting challenges to the masculine definition of women began to emerge. The following narratives drawn from *Days of Our Lives* and *Santa Barbara*, chosen for their daring and success, demonstrate the areas of progress in soap opera for the heroine's narrative as a ritual of feminine achievement of identity.

Days of Our Lives: Energizing the Narrative of the Couple

Days of Our Lives, like *General Hospital*, was on the brink of exhaustion when it was revitalized by the new developments in daytime serial. Central to this change was the work of Sheri Anderson, who had worked on the post-1978 *General Hospital*; Brian Frons, then vice president for daytime at NBC-TV; Leah Laiman; and Anne Schoettle. Although the series' writers disclaim purposeful imitation of *General Hospital*, a comparison of the two shows reveals the influence of the latter, if only as a matter of zeitgeist. In creating new heroines, for example, *Days* suggested, as *General Hospital* had done, that disruption of the communal structure by a couple was often the best way to protect conventional society. This was a new idea on daytime serial. The new narrative relationship between the heroine and the Oedipal dyad emphasized situations in which the community repressed the heroine's redeeming erotic energy.

Yet although *Days of Our Lives* benefited from the innovations on *General Hospital*, it improved on its model by introducing the mature woman into the place of erotic subject, which Laura had occupied as immature girl. Ironically, too, it set this woman the task of confronting the dominance-subordination patriarchal media hero par excellence, the Bond-like spy, and challenging his very way of ordering experience (fig. 8).

The story of Kimberly Brady and Shane Donovan was initiated as a "high-concept" fiction of "the prostitute and the spy." This narrative concept, of course, has been extensively exploited to speak of the female temptation of the male to intimacy as a betrayal of the patriarchal order (as in John Le Carré's complex Smiley series, where Ann, George Smiley's wife, is the primary weak link in a chain of personal, class, and national betrayals). The *Days* story suggests exactly the reverse: here we see how patriarchal structures in fact threaten and betray. For *Days*, the prostitute-and-spy concept was a way to probe the surprising similarity between the woman who sells her body and the spy who serves his country (not her connection with the traitor that we find in patriarchal spy stories). It provided a yoking of opposites between espionage community and social community that made possible a probing of family relationships: why do family members become secretive about their real lives in order to live up to impossible images?[7]

The Shane-Kimberly narrative utilized the surprisingly complementary quests for knowledge of the female gothic and male film noir, a combination that Tania Modleski describes as applying in Hitchcock's *Notorious* as well. As Modleski reminds us, in the film noir, the male—with ruthless logic—investigates feminine sexual guilt; in the female gothic, the woman intuitively explores male guilt.[8] If Hitchcock's film permits Alicia (Ingrid Bergman) more latitude than the ordinary film

Fig. 8. *Days of Our Lives.* Shane (Charles Shaughnessy) and Kimberly (Patsy Pease), friends *and* lovers. Courtesy *Soap Opera Digest.*

heroine to discover the sin of coldness in Devlin (Cary Grant), Hitchcock nevertheless accepts the conventions of film narrative by permitting Devlin to remain a masterful subject, whereas Alicia's stigma of sexual guilt results in a near fatal marriage with the evil Alex Sebastian (Claude Rains), thus reducing her from a "wannabe" subject-in-progress to a supine object in time for closure. In Kimberly's narrative, the guilt that is ascribed to feminine sexuality in film noir is redefined by her as a legitimate aspect of the desiring subject, which gives her the right to resist the Oedipal scenario that has been forced on her. Unlike Alicia's marriage, which is created by Devlin and the American government, Kimberly's marriage is *her* creation and emerges from her fabrication of her own narrative.

The oldest daughter of the Brady family, Kimberly (Patsy Pease)—called by her father, Shawn, his "best and brightest"—begins her story wanting to fulfill Daddy's glowing image of her but haunted by a humiliating secret. She first appears on the show as she is returning home to Salem, a small town probably located in New York State, from an extended stay in Europe. She says she has been a photographer; in fact, however, Kimberly made her living abroad as a high-priced prostitute. Like the good girl/bad girl of noir screen fiction, Kimberly derives from her sexual guilt both gratification and shame. But unlike her screen counterpart, whose sexuality is dangerous until the noir hero takes her in hand, Kimberly wields no real influence because of her sexuality.

A woman whose experience of herself places her in the lowest category of self-esteem and initiative in *Women's Ways of Knowing*, Kimberly experiences being female as a form of powerlessness, beginning with her secret shame of having been sexually abused as a young girl by her paternal uncle. As both child and woman, she lacks language either to formulate her anger and fear or to do anything about her situation. She is a silent prisoner of self-hatred. Her father's admiration only functions as a warning against freeing herself by accusing her uncle. How can she tell him what happened to her without losing his approval? Unlike Hollywood's sexual adventuresses, Kimberly is no threat to the male order. The male order has harmed her, and she believes the reasons lie in being desirable—something she cannot help. She is helplessly alone.

Her evolving narrative, however, offers not the Hollywood choice between self-destruction or redemption by a good man, but a process by which she breaks the Oedipal dyad and finds language and human connection, thus allowing her to celebrate desire and escape her solitude. Kimberly's healing process begins in a familiar way. Her secret is discovered by the typical noir hero, a man "on assignment," a man paradoxically isolated from and at the same time allied with patriarchal law. In conventional film, he is Sam Spade (Humphrey Bogart) in *The Maltese Falcon*, representing allegiance to the male partner, or Devlin in *Notorious*, representing the U.S. government. In Kimberly's narrative, he is Shane Donovan (Charles Shaughnessy), an English-born spy for the International Security Alliance (ISA). Conducting surveillance by telescope, Shane, who knows Kimberly only as Shawn Brady's bright daughter, accidentally spies her through a window as she entertains a john in an apartment she covertly maintains for business. Thus perceived at an anonymous distance, Kimberly is the object the Oedipal man requires; Shane, distracted by her from his mission, is in turn Hollywood's Oedipal man. However, the old story doesn't stay on track for long.

On *Days*, Shane's Bond-like mission bears a certain resemblance to

Kimberly's prostitution: he is a professional voyeur who possesses by the look, just as she is a professional object possessed by the look. Kimberly has a sexy secret, but Shane does too, and his voyeurism is even more covert than Kimberly's commodification of her sexuality. Prancing around in her sexy underwear, Kimberly openly reveals herself to the customers, whereas Shane hides his gratification from everyone, under cover of official responsibility. Like the noir hero, Shane believes that Kimberly needs to be rescued from degradation, and initially imagines himself in a thoroughly mentoring position. Yet as he helps her, she challenges his perspective. Her remarks about his cold detachment are repeatedly validated: in its detachment, he finds, the ISA—the institutionalization of his stance—continually violates human decencies in the name of a higher good. Because of Kimberly, Shane finds that he must question both those violations and his own personal distance from Kimberly.

Conveying the similarity between the prostitute and the spy was the intention of the writers and actors alike; through their efforts these two traditional figures of American screen fiction became compellingly untraditional metaphors for parallel masculine and feminine problems with intimacy.[9] Shane is patronizing toward Kimberly even as he helps her to liberate herself from prostitution by means of image control. (For example, he teaches her how to erase a videotape that a local madam is using to blackmail Kimberly into staying in her stable of working girls.) But Kimberly matches Shane image for image. Kimberly really is a photographer, as she has claimed, even though that occupation has taken second place to her unrevealed employment. Much is made of her love of photography, her desire to move to it and from her degradation, and the beauty of her work. She, too, holds power through the look, particularly in the form of a prize photograph of Shane's home, coincidentally taken by her in Europe, in which she can visualize his origins and roots. Nevertheless, he refuses to recognize either her validity or his desire to be close to her. He maintains the pose of detached toleration.

Ultimately, Kimberly's resistance to Shane's point of view forces him to confront two truths he would rather deny. First, when he makes Kimberly his partner in information gathering, he is in fact using her much as she was used by her former madam. Kimberly's beauty, namely, serves as a lure for the men from whom Shane wishes to get information. Although she does not have sex with his targets, the use he makes of her reminds him uncomfortably of her life as a prostitute. Second, he is increasingly annoyed at the ISA for its growing interest in this role of hers, since he is stirred by a desire to abandon his detachment and become close to her.

In Hitchcock's *Notorious*, Alicia is redeemed when she prostitutes herself, under Devlin's supervision, for the American government. This sexual servitude is validated not only at a superficial plot level, but also at the profound Oedipal level of all conventional film. In terms of content, Alicia is justified in whatever means she uses to gain intimacy with Alex, for her seduction of the enemy makes her the conduit through which the Americans get information about Nazis; her sexuality is exercised neither for her pleasure nor as evidence of her power, but *pro patria*. More profoundly, Alicia's quasi-prostitution uncovers and destroys the dreadful threat of incest with the mother. The unholy closeness between Alex Sebastian and his mother, indeed, is at the heart of the alien threat, and in the end Devlin must save Alicia from near death at its hands. It is true that Devlin somewhat anticipates Shane in his growing annoyance at the government's attitude toward Alicia; but his perturbation passes. Devlin and his superiors are reconciled when they allow him to rescue Alicia from the poisonous energy of the maternal, in the person of Madame Sebastian.

In *Days*, in contrast, Shane's control of Kimberly's erotic powers leads her into danger from *paternal* power from which he cannot save her; she must learn enough about patriarchy to save herself. Eventually, Shane and Kimberly make love, but his ISA role continues to threaten her identity and their intimacy. As the plot develops, Kimberly is drawn by Shane into the orbit of Victor Kiriakis (John Anniston). A variation on Frank Smith, a patriarch who is both legitimate and criminal, Kiriakis is the narrative vehicle that allows Kimberly to confront the Oedipal dyad that has reduced her to an object.[10] Shane, for his part, considers Kiriakis his enemy, but in fact Kiriakis is the criminal double of the ISA that Shane serves. Like the ISA, Victor is defined by his interest in power and control and his authoritarian detachment; he shares with the ISA that urge for closure that is the mortal enemy of the soap opera form, and his desire to possess Kimberly poses a threat similar to that posed by the ISA in the uses it wants to make of her. Kiriakis is a fantastic embodiment of that abstract, aloof coldness which lusts for the possession and closure that are Shane's own devils. As the proper subject of the endless soap opera form, then, Kimberly must face Kiriakis—and thereby find and learn to value her own power, metaphorically represented by her eroticism—so that Shane can release himself from the male bonding that his work with the ISA represents and that prevents fruitful union with Kimberly.

The narrative importance of Shane's mission lies only in the opportunity it contains for Kimberly; the actual matter of Shane's contest with
Kiriakis is peripheral to the decisions Kimberly must make. We see this
clearly when Kimberly takes over that story moment which in conventional screen fiction would be the hero's. Shane and Kimberly are finish-
ing Shane's assignment. He tells her to detain Kiriakis "any way she can"
while he attends to one final detail. In doing so, however, Kimberly
becomes aware that Shane is in more danger than he knows: Kiriakis has
anticipated Shane's strategy and has set in motion a plan to kill him.
Kiriakis's single-minded devotion to his plan, moreover, makes him
impervious to any stalling tactics that Kimberly can invent—except one.
Kiriakis wants to possess her sexually as much as Shane does.

This narrative moment is particularly significant in that it crystallizes
the similarity between Shane as spy and Kiriakis as criminal, as each
affects Kimberly's subjecthood. Quite apart from the morality of the
team each plays for, the structure of their battle forces Kimberly into a
win-or-lose position. The conventional alternatives offered to Kimberly
all suggest that Kiriakis has defeated Shane. She, however, restructures
the situation by making a more complex, contextual choice that takes her
beyond the role set for her by masculine rituals of identity.

Here, as in Laura's narrative, female sexuality is imagined as the only
counterforce to a potentially destructive Oedipal narrative. But Kimberly's narrative is more complicated than Laura's. At Kimberly's dark-
est moment, her sexuality is both potent and compromised. Alone with
Kiriakis, and knowing Shane's danger, she chooses to distract Kiriakis
by seducing him. The source of her vulnerability to her abusive uncle
when she was a little girl, Kimberly's sexuality is now, in some ways, a
strength—but only in some ways. Although her seduction of Kiriakis is
her choice, as a form of power it is constrained by the flaws in Shane's
narrative that led to this ambiguous situation. Nevertheless, even
though the ISA/Kiriakis power configuration dictates that she express
her power by once more becoming the unfortunate object of desire,
Kimberly's eroticism is a powerful means of expressing her desire for
Shane, both when she makes love to him in fact and when she saves him
by seducing Kiriakis.

Indeed, when we compare Kimberly's narrative with Alicia's in *Notorious*, we see that soap opera gives its heroines much more attractive
options than Hollywood does. Alicia almost dies as the consequence of
similar service, her threatened destruction coming in the form of incest,
the classical consequence of the exercise of feminine erotic power. Alex,
upon realizing that Alicia is an American agent, regrets defying his

mother to marry her, and mother and son, reunited again, plot to kill her. On *Days of Our Lives* only the *specter* of incest is raised by Kimberly's daring erotic act, which, unlike Alicia's, is committed on her own authority. The dispelling of that specter is part of Kimberly's retelling of the masculine power narrative from her own point of view.

Trying to accommodate Shane's desires, Kimberly finds herself in Kiriakis's narrative. Kiriakis, being thoroughly familiar with power games, understands Kimberly's pretense of sexual attraction to him. He enjoys Kimberly sexually, thus allowing Shane to escape his trap, but then uses Kimberly's act to humiliate her and enjoy his prerogatives. Kimberly is reduced to begging Kiriakis not to tell Shane what she has done—for when Oedipal conventions prevail, regardless of who wants whom, sexuality is always humiliating for women, and always another form of power for men. Shortly afterward, Kimberly discovers she is pregnant; knowledge that Shane is not necessarily the child's father only increases Kiriakis's leverage. In a further narrative twist, Kimberly's mother now reveals that she once had an affair with Kiriakis, from which a child ensued. Not knowing about Kimberly's dilemma, she refuses to say which of her children is Victor's: Kiriakis may also be Kimberly's own father as well.

It is important to understand that Kimberly's narrative only appears to define the role of pregnancy as Hollywood does. In Hollywood, the polarity between male and female is exerted against the female subject most forcefully in childbearing. Liberated women are sentenced by Hollywood to die from pregnancies incompatible with their liberty, or at least they are humiliated by the pregnancies ensuing from their unconventional behavior: *Christopher Smart*, *Beyond the Forest*, *Twist and Shout*, and *Grease* contain only a few of the many examples of censure by maternity. In soap opera, however, essential difference between masculinity and femininity does not mean that biology must ultimately defeat feminine desire. In Kimberly's story, the pregnancy is problematic only because Shane has placed it within the closure narrative of ISA business. Kimberly, releasing herself from the chimeras that afflict her when Shane and Kiriakis organize her life, discovers that Kiriakis is neither her father nor the father of her child. Shane is the father and all would be very well indeed, were it not for his attitude. In Kimberly's narrative, all the real danger is projected by the Oedipal narrative of the Donovan-Kiriakis action story, which transforms babies into kinds of closure and raises the fantasies of incest for the desiring female subject.

Upon discovering the means Kimberly used to hold Kiriakis's attention, Shane resumes the Oedipally correct distant stance, rejecting her and the child she carries. When she defends her action as partly his creation, he responds contemptuously: "I thought you would use your brains, not your b——." Shane never gets beyond the initial plosive, but whether he intended to say "body," "butt," or "bum," one thing is clear—Kimberly as subject has brought to the surface the great masculine nightmare: the fear of betrayal, and confusion from the female as desiring agent.

Shane's abandonment of Kimberly puts her at risk once more from Kiriakis. From Victor's point of view, a baby is a kind of closure of the erotic encounter, a commodity belonging to the father. In those conventional terms, it is the living icon of Kimberly's sin, the focus of Shane's rejection of her—and, because Kiriakis forges some test results to make the baby appear his, a new way for Kiriakis to reduce her to an object under his control. At the same time, the baby also holds within its tiny person the power to neutralize the issue of control. Kimberly must now assert her narrative point of view, which she does, utterly rejecting Kiriakis's domination. By internalizing neither Shane's rejection nor Kiriakis's claim of ownership, she thus succeeds in splitting the Oedipal dyad.

As Kimberly insists on being her own person, Shane departs increasingly from the Oedipal stance of condemnation. When the narrative isolates them together in a cabin for the birth of the baby, the sexuality that binds them is reawakened. Shane's participation with Kimberly in bringing the baby into the world is just as infused with eroticism as have been previous sexual encounters between them. Only within the degrading context of the Oedipal agenda is her erotic power a threat and her baby a mark of shame. Freed from his own action-story narrative, Shane distinguishes himself completely from Kiriakis by ceasing to regard Kimberly and the baby as property. After a long narrative struggle, Kimberly has moved quite a distance from her self-hatred induced by her uncle's violation of her. Kimberly marries Shane only after she has recreated her feminine identity, in the process giving Shane a more flexible way of imagining his masculinity.

The visual presentation of Shane and Kimberly functions as prefiguration and fulfillment of their mutual liberation. Shane's position as Peeping Tom at the beginning of their relationship raises the issue of the erotic possession of women by men who look at them, or scopophilia. The parallel visual positions of Shane and the john whom he sees exploiting Kimberly prefigure the narrative parallels between Kimberly's

Figs. 9, 10, 11, and 12. *Days of Our Lives*. Shane's controlling gaze is met by a resistant image series of Kimberly as a repository of subject consciousness.

exploitation by the madam, on the one hand, and by Shane and the ISA, on the other. This equation implies the severest criticism of Shane's initial attitude toward Kimberly. Even the visual shot patterns undercut Shane's justification of his ocular possession of Kimberly, when he is forced by circumstances to include her in his official surveillance. In his revelation to Kimberly that he has been violating her privacy, Shane admits that his actions were invasive but also declares with Bond-like pride that he is acting on behalf of national security. She does not buy into his rationale. The accompanying shot pattern, moreover, confirms not his stance, but hers. When he makes his announcement, the camera shows him appropriately forceful in his expression; but then, in a reverse shot, the focus moves to Kimberly and her turmoil about his behavior; moreover, rather than moving back to Shane to confirm his possession of her, the camera, in two succeeding shots, zooms closer in on Kimberly herself, thus suggesting her interiority, her subjecthood (figs. 9–12). Further, once Shane consciously acknowledges his interest in being intimate with Kimberly, the visual images of erotic encounter change drastically: dominance-subordination voyeuristic images grow increasingly infrequent, replaced by visual models of mutuality that parallel the narrative shift. In the love scenes, Shane and Kimberly are both blissful. Gazing and being beheld are not separated into hierarchical, gender-defined functions. When Shane whispers, "Beautiful, beautiful Kim," she replies, "Beautiful, beautiful Shane" (figs. 13–16).[11]

The erotic aspects of Kimberly's narrative are metaphors for the way her story makes meaning. Eroticism as the dialogue between male and female subjects embodies the female way of knowing by empathetic encounter. Nevertheless, the Shane-and-Kimberly narrative also contains a significant number of specular evocations of dominance-subordination eroticism. Shane periodically showers Kim with gifts: an ancestral cameo pin, furs, flowers, clothes. His most enthusiastic display of such dominance involves a vacation, planned completely by him, in a romantic hideaway where he will propose to Kimberly. In this instance, a limousine arrives at Kimberly's door in the morning and the driver, playfully refusing to tell her what is going on, whisks her from beauty shop to dress shop to flower shop to mountain retreat. At the climax of Shane's objectification of Kimberly, he presents her with that instantly recognized small velvet box, along with his proposal of marriage. Indisputably, this fantasy recapitulates the closure scene of a thousand and one films. Here, though, the entire display is juxtaposed against Kimberly's need to tell Shane about her seduction of Kiriakis and make him understand her point of view. At the same time, Shane's imposition of his erotic fantasies surely titillates spectators trained to thrill to such male displays, and also subverts the stock response by identifying his expensive gifts as a gag on her expressiveness. How can Kimberly speak her disturbing truth when Shane is so gratified by the scenario he has created? She is reduced by him to silence, buried alive in his candlelit, but problematic, fantasy.

Kimberly begins her narrative as the forced participant in a male

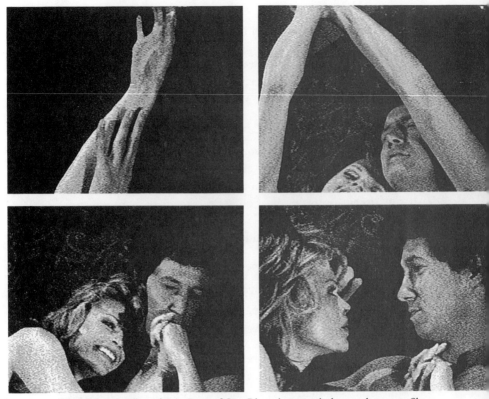

Figs. 13, 14, 15, and 16. *Days of Our Lives.* A postcoital scene between Shane and Kimberly emphasizes mutuality: parallel construction of "the spy and the prostitute."

fantasy structure she is desperate to escape; nevertheless, some complicity on her part, and on the part of the audience, is implied in her objectification. Although the narrative gives Kimberly her due when it implicates Shane as a detached voyeur who gets satisfaction from looking at her from a distance, and encourages spectator identification with Kimberly as she struggles against submitting to Shane's cold, distant, and patronizing attitude toward her, it remains tinged with female sexual guilt and somewhat dazzled by the feminine body as fetish object. For an intense narrative that fully questions the sexual guilt that patriarchy assigns to women, we must look at a slightly later narrative on *Days of Our Lives*—that of Kimberly's sister, Kayla. Kayla's story also deals with sexual guilt, but places it squarely on the way men impose their fantasies on women.

Unintentionally, in creating Kayla's story the series' writers adopted one of the rare traditional instances of a female subject: the Beauty who is paired with the Beast, a tradition fueled by the same transformative power of feminine desire available in the Persephone myth. In terms of screen narrative, Kayla's narrative inverts the medical discourse of the woman's picture, in which the heroine's sexuality is defined as a kind of disease. Here, the figure of the doctor *sees* with the aid of science the secret flaw in the Beauty and, through (Oedipal) reason, develops the erotic of the cure, making the woman suitable for life under patriarchy—and him (*Beyond the Forest, The Snake Pit, Johnny Belinda*).[12] The story of Beauty and the Beast competes with the medical discourse mode in that it defines sexual guilt as male and constructs the Beauty as the partner who *sees* and cures. Presented as a richly masculine grotesque, her Beast has imperfections that, although palpable, are ultimately superficial, illusory distortions, the result of the (mis)application of reason. Beauty rectifies the situation by replacing reason with empathetic knowing, thereby splitting the Oedipal dyad of the beast and her father, releasing the profound reality of the male from the patriarchal contract. Jean Cocteau understood this well, and in his *La Belle et le Bête* the tormented Beast makes the point explicit as he roars, "Don't look at me. Your eyes burn me." Beauty's eyes—the source of the Beast's terror and but also his salvation—represent the female power of the glance.

On *Days of Our Lives*, we become involved with Kayla Brady (Mary Beth Evans) shortly before she returns home from Ohio, where she has been a pediatric nurse. There, as we see, she is terrorized by Steve "Patch" Johnson (Steven Nichols), one of Kiriakis's henchmen, a savage one-eyed minor gangster who demonstrates a psychotic detachment from human feeling. Like Luke, Patch is a marginal member of the underworld, the minion of a crime boss with a quasi-legitimate role in the power establishment; unlike Luke, before he became involved with Kayla, Patch/Steve was fully established in acts of extreme sadism.[13] He begins their relationship by reducing Kayla to terror as he spies on her.

Here, there is no replication of patriarchal thrills of voyeurism and fetishism; Patch's clandestine observation of Kayla is decidedly nasty. Patch invades Kayla's apartment and, in its shadows, watches her undress. Her act of disrobing is portrayed as ordinary, normal, and non-seductive; she does not know he is there. His voyeurism reframes what he sees. The obscene phone calls in which he tells her of his observation of her body establish all the obscenity to be his. Scopophilia is a major element in the beginning of this couple's relationship, just as it was in

Fig. 17. *Days of Our Lives.* Patch/Steve Johnson (Stephen Nichols): the Beast. Courtesy *Soap Opera Digest.*

Kimberly and Shane's, with one thundering difference. While Shane is negatively portrayed as a type of voyeur, Kimberly *is* actively courting the Oedipal glance, albeit indirectly. Here, Patch is the only guilty party (figs. 17–19).

In her provocative essay "When the Woman Looks," Linda Williams demonstrates that in horror films, when heroine confronts monster what she sees is her own monstrousness in the eyes of patriarchal society.[14] In making her catalogue of fictions in which the woman beholds the monster, however, Williams leaves out the tradition of Beauty looking at the Beast, an act that releases the prince as well as herself. The Beast in fact goes through some specific change, the root of which is Persephone's transformative encounter with Hades, not Oedipus's destructive encounter with his mother. In Kayla's version of the tale, the symbolic change is a change in *his* name. Patch drops his nickname, which emphasizes his mutilation, and resumes his birthname, Steve Johnson. Steve's resumption of his original name suggests that he no longer feels alien to the human community because of his missing eye—rather an interesting

Fig. 18. *Days of Our Lives*. Patch/Steve
and Kayla (Mary Beth Evans): Beauty
and the Beast. Courtesy *Soap Opera
Digest*.

reversal on the Freudian relationship between the love of women and
mutilation. Kayla helps Steve to a sense of his wholeness by creating her
own strong feminine identity through a series of encounters with the
Oedipal dyad, beginning with her intervention in the Patch-Kiriakis
alliance.

Kayla is a successful professional woman, a nurse, when she joins *Days
of Our Lives*, but Patch's entrance into her life precipitates a descent to the
lowest level of feminine existence: powerlessness and silence. After Patch
terrorizes her, Kayla flees to the safety of her parental home. Her flight
home is regressive from a logical point of view and appears to fulfill
the patriarchal prediction about women's ineffectuality in dealing with
power. Yet that judgment is based on a model that values individual
isolation and detachment. Once at home, and in relation, Kayla is in a
strong position once more. Being in relation is in fact the power source
for the female glance. Now when Kayla meets Patch, on her home
ground, for the first time he becomes visible to her, although she learns
that he was her tormentor only after she cares enough for him to forgive
him. Because he continues to work for Victor Kiriakis and she has set up
a free clinic for the needy, they meet often in the same poor neighborhood. Their situational connection leads to Patch's experience of—and

Fig. 19. *Days of Our Lives*. Patch/Steve and Kayla: Beauty and the reformed Beast. Courtesy *Soap Opera Digest*.

resistance to—Kayla's definition of him as an emotional man underneath the criminal exterior. But as he begins to accept his desire for intimacy with Kayla, he comes to identify himself with a capacity for warmth and feeling. Encouraged by love, Patch no longer desires to remain a criminal; he severs relations with Kiriakis, readying himself for the vengeance Kiriakis will take on him, and worse, on Kayla for Patch's defection. Ironically, Kiriakis is fairly easily dealt with. The real danger to Kayla emerges when Patch reasserts his birth name Steve and moves into an Oedipal dyad rooted in legitimate society.

In the fairy tale, if there is anything wrong with Beauty it is in her initial submission to her father and her continued belief, his actions to the contrary, in his essential goodness and strength. Kayla exhibits a similar weakness. Once Patch resumes the name of Steve and leaves the criminal underworld, Kayla thinks all their troubles are over because she believes in the conventional pieties and sees a clearcut distinction between crime and the law. Patch likewise begins to see things her way as he gains perspective on his destructive relationship with Kiriakis. But once Patch is closer to Kayla than to "the man in charge," our sense of Kayla's reality is crucially altered by events in the narrative.

Kiriakis is *Days'* Frank Smith. Patch's separation from Kiriakis gives Kayla a chance to develop her own identity, just as Luke's separation from Smith gave Laura her chance. But here, the intervention of the heroine's allure between the legitimate/criminal power broker and his subordinate only reveals obstacles for the couple. As Kayla tries to move with Steve into the community she believes in, ordinary distinctions are blurred. Kayla's medical discourse is traduced by the "normal" communing, which permits her to be afflicted by a disease some call the "perfect" young man. Worse, Steve's attempt to please Kayla by entering "good" society as a "good" man ultimately—and inevitably—backfires.

As long as both Steve and Kayla believe in his reformation in ordinary terms, Steve's efforts lead only to disaster, for his "backstory" constantly catches up with him. His intimacy with Kayla is narratively coterminous with the return of his mother, who, he has always believed, abandoned him long ago to an orphanage. Now, though, he learns that she in fact put him up for adoption to protect him from his father, Duke, who routinely beat her up and, she feared, would soon get violent with Steve, perhaps even kill him. The age at which Patch was cut off from his mother was the Oedipal age, the violence of the father was the agency of the separation, and the threatening father bore the nickname of the paradigm of cinematic masculinity, John Wayne. Thus with the mother's return we discover that, paradoxically, if Steve's missing eye is a symbol for injuries he incurred because of his mother's desperate attempt to place him at a distance from his father, remaining within the confines of the patriarchal family would likely have produced in him less visible but more poisonous mutilations.

Steve's recovery of his mother brings with it the rediscovery of his younger brother, Billy, who, similarly placed in an orphanage, was adopted, as Steve was not, and by a wealthy, mainstream family. Billy, now known as Jack (Matthew Ashford), is unaware that Steve is his brother, and he too falls in love with Kayla. Jack is the kind of man conventionally regarded as "husband material." However, his handsome, successful, and clean-cut exterior hides the kind of vaguely defined debilitating illness that is reserved in the Hollywood film for women. In a reversal on cinematic medical discourse, Jack makes it clear that only Kayla's curative presence can save him. In Steve, reunion with his family brings about a kind of delirium, and without revealing to Jack that they are brothers, lest it rob Jack of the good things his adopted family provides, he buys into Jack's definition of Kayla's role and pretends not to love Kayla anymore so she will cure Jack. In this way he joins Jack in thwarting Kayla's desire and identity. Steve's sacrifice of his relationship with Kayla for his brother is a desperate act that defines a hysterical strain in the male bonding of "good" men.

If the Oedipal text frequently uses illness as a metaphor for femininity, in the Kayla-and-Steve narrative illness becomes a possible text of conventional masculinity. Kayla's entrapment between the Oedipal dyad of the Johnson brothers stifles her legitimately curative glance, which she used to deconstruct Steve's desperate, self-protective violence. When Steve and Jack redefine Kayla from their perspective, she is reduced to being a nurse to their desires. The marriage to Jack into which she allows herself to be bullied puts an end to Jack's physical disabilities but intensifies the spiritual aspect of his illness. Jack increasingly thinks of Kayla as his possession. By the time Steve is forced by the intensity of his feelings for Kayla to drop the pretense that he doesn't love her, they both must contend with the problems caused by the way her role has been defined for her. Kayla has been forced into the untenable, and distinctly uncharacteristic, position of a betrayer. She lives with Jack, lying constantly to avoid sex with him, and makes love to Steve surreptitiously. Kayla and Steve's self-deception about the "charity" marriage ends when Jack learns that Kayla has been giving Steve the sexual attention she has denied him. In retaliation, Jack rapes Kayla. In this narrative, women pay the price for the blind spots in bonding.

The secrets of the Oedipal dyad continue to unfold for Kayla until finally men appear as her enemy, and only Steve's clear emulation of her way of doing things can reconcile her to love. After the rape Kayla discovers that Steve opposes her plan to defend herself by accusing Jack publicly in a court of law. Surprised but undaunted by Steve's opposition, Kayla perseveres and succeeds in the courtroom. She thus wins Steve's approval belatedly, but she must also pay a price, for her victory brings about a covert eruption of patriarchal rage.

The decision in Kayla's favor destroys Jack's promising political career. And when, by association, the successful senate career of his adoptive father, Harper Deveraux, is threatened, the dark alter ego of the legitimate establishment surfaces. By night, Deveraux becomes the Salem Slasher. Under cover of darkness and a full face mask, he attacks and kills "loose" women, finally arriving at Kayla, the loosest of them all for having dared to resist the prerogatives of masculine possession of women.

The entrance of Jack's adoptive father into the narrative brings a baroque twist, much criticized for its violence toward women and its lurid melodrama. In *The Uses of Enchantment*, Bruno Bettelheim counters a similar opposition to the violence in fairy tales: the hero or heroine's triumph over violence, he says, is a great consolation to children because it both acknowledges what they know about the terrors of the real world and promises that these can be neutralized.[15] I suggest the same is true for the presentation of women in media. It is consoling to see violence against women acknowledged as long as the heroine herself is granted the power to deal with it.

In the context of the Salem Slasher story, Kayla is granted such effectiveness. Jack's adoptive father, a socially important but sexually impotent man, is another of those soap opera adversaries who blurs the line between crime and the male power establishment. In its violence his offense suggests a more direct criticism of the impact of male hierarchy on the heroine than was available in abuses committed by Smith and Kiriakis. Whereas Smith and Kiriakis are economic criminals, Deveraux victimizes women because of his failure with them. Hiding his face under a mask, he roams the streets at night attacking and killing prostitutes, patriarchally displacing all his sexual anxieties onto the "guilty" women; murder has become his metaphor for male dominance. The senator, disguised as the Salem Slasher, attacks Kayla on behalf of his son, another instance of the destructive nature of the Oedipal dyad. Kayla removes his mask during the attack and survives, but the trauma of the attack leaves her unable to recall the incident, as well as mute and deaf. Kayla has seen the monster: it is not her (as it is in the horror films analyzed by Linda Williams), but rather the power structure, and her glimpse into that realm paralyzes her.

Reduced to solitude, Kayla is simultaneously reduced to silence; she feels negated as a person and cancels plans for her wedding to Steve. (In soap opera, marriages are the opposite of the destruction of the female self: a damaged woman cannot create a good union.) Kayla, however, has prepared for this emergency by having opened Steve up to her. He now illustrates an altered definition of the good man when he imitates the attitude Kayla displayed toward him when he was an outcast. By learning sign language, Steve supplies Kayla with relationship, the source of feminine power and knowledge. Through connection, she regains her memory, her speech, her hearing, and her desire to wed. Like Persephone, Kayla's defense against becoming an object has been through the power of her way of making meaning: connection.

Soap opera narrative comments on, but is not informed by, the controlling, exclusive, and, at the extremes, sadistic and murderous narrative power of the Oedipal dyad. The feminine narrative of post-1978 soap opera proceeds through the subject's encounter with that dyad and marks the path of her progress toward the organization of her own narrative. Thus the narrative process itself is a part of identity. Laura tells the story of her turn toward Luke in patriarchal terms at first, calling her erotic encounter with him a rape. As she takes possession of her story she rejects, along with her old identity, that way of narratizing her emotional experience. Kimberly, too, at first narrates her seduction of Kiriakis within a framework of Oedipal guilt but later retells it from a feminine perspective. Kayla's inability to reveal the secret shames of a respected man in the power structure is an aberration in her narrative that she is able to correct by re-creating a hero for herself out of a man maimed by that same power structure.

In Hollywood, women's silence is the norm. We can see some representative examples of Hollywood's correlation between narrative and feminine identity in Doane's account of the women's picture of the forties. In mainstream cinema, she says, the glance at a female life is "subsidiary or complementary to the major scenarios of masculinity."[16] That is to say, the telling of a woman's story is possible only with permission of the male subject. It may be generated by means of male agency, as in *Possessed*, in which Louise (Joan Crawford) tells her tale of madness only after given an injection by a male doctor to help her remember. Alternatively, the story of Nancy (Laraine Day) in *The Locket* is related in flashback by two men and defines her as criminally unstable. Unaware that they speak of her, she is permitted only some silent image flashes of a past she has repressed, just before she loses consciousness and is taken in hand by a male doctor. Even when Hollywood focuses on a woman's story, it does so with a firm masculine hand on the camera and the microphone.

As we have seen in the stories of Laura, Kimberly, and Kayla, the narrative process by which the post-1978 soap opera heroine seeks the form of her desire, in contrast to the movie heroine, implicitly means an inversion of the Oedipal narrative—but not by design. Finding new stories is, admittedly, a preoccupation of the soap opera writer, but generally speaking, finding stories that criticize the male power structure is not. The critique of the impact of masculine identity on feminine identity has evolved naturally, by and large, as writers created stories for daytime's unorthodox form. One significant exception presents itself, however. Self-conscious critique of gender narratives has been the hallmark of *Santa Barbara*, a daytime serial created in 1984. When this show added conscious artistry to the process of dealing with daytime's special narrative, it demonstrated some of soap opera's potential for *explicit*, piercing insight about gender and identity. This show had its period of greatest creativity between 1986 and 1990.

Santa Barbara: Julia's New Frontier

For a time, *Santa Barbara* was the most innovative show on daytime, using humor, visual perspectives of intense style, and daring emotional relationships to take advantage of the possibilities of the soap opera structure. During this period, the show's writers were not interested in didactic exploration of either the feminist or the sexist agenda. They were, however, attentive to the drama of characters who had conscious questions about masculinity and femininity.[17] On *Santa Barbara*, more than one heroine has been articulate on the subject of men and women's stereotypical roles, intentionally seeking to construct a selfhood in defiance of what she thought was expected. Yet among the delightfully self-conscious heroines of *Santa Barbara*—or, for that matter, any soap opera—Julia Wainwright stands out as the most fully realized.

For a few years, Julia's bittersweet, comic, but also poignant narrative moved complexly between the culturally dominant Oedipal story and her own possible feminine story. The best of Julia's story lines brought soap opera as close as it has yet come to depicting the battle of the sexes as a battle between separate narratives that parody, mirror, and deconstruct each other.

Julia Wainwright (Nancy Lee Grahn) is a lawyer and a declared feminist. By temperament she is exuberant, witty, idealistic, generous, and assertive. She and her sister, Augusta Lockridge, a character already in progress when Julia was brought onto the show, are the children of a middle-class professional family; yet the two women represent distinctly different responses to their upbringing. Augusta defines the plight of the woman who accepts the "appropriate" feminine model. Constrained by the hierarchy of conventional masculine and feminine roles, deeply committed to conventional ideals of glamor, Augusta is forever enraged by the woman's lot in marriage. Although she is skilled at "being feminine," her deepest desires are forever thwarted. She does not entertain any alternatives to conventional sex roles and will always long for an intimacy that Lionel Lockridge, the love of her life, cannot give her.

Julia, in contrast, defines the plight of the woman who rejects the "appropriate" feminine model. Julia patterns herself after her father, following in his footsteps to become a lawyer. For a soap opera heroine, however, walking with the father does not solve the problem of creating herself as subject. Julia, in retelling her father's story, is less constrained than her sister, but she is equally baffled by love experiences with men. The satisfactions of intimacy also elude Julia, but for a different and more interesting reason.

Julia's sad comedy plays with the imposition of patriarchal fantasies on women, and with a major vehicle of that imposition: narrative structures. Julia's story concerns her determination to become a free woman by using a narrative such as men use to build their identities as free and effective agents. As she carries out her plan of constructing her own Oedipal narrative, Julia learns through comic and pathetic experience that a satisfying identity requires that she discover a feminine narrative discourse—one that bears little resemblance to a male definition of self or of women.[18]

As Julia learns, using a male identity ritual only *seems* clearcut and straightforward. In its repressiveness, however, such a structure surmounts a foundation that is a catacombed underworld unto itself, convoluted, producing strategies markedly vulnerable to boomeranging. Mulvey has remarked that the hero's mastery of the glamorized female object in conventional cinema is offered to hero and spectator as a reassuring, definitive testament to male control over women.[19] But Mulvey also talks about a residual fear in the spectator that the heroine might not be completely contained. In *The Women Who Knew Too Much*, Modleski shows how Hitchcock subverts the conventions of cinema by dramatizing the fact that the hero's desire to control the glamorous woman can never be satisfied. No matter how submissive the heroine is, she still reminds him of an element of femininity in himself which he fears intensely. In *Rear Window*, for instance, the Oedipal voyeur L. B. Jeffries (James Stewart) may betray some similarity to the wife murderer in his fascination with the scene across the courtyard, but there is more to his story. Bedridden himself, if only temporarily, Jeffries has for the moment an even more pointed resemblance to the murdered woman, and his fascination with what happens to her ultimately puts Jeffries in her position. Jeffries's fixation on the wife murderer visible through the rear window threatens forbidden acknowledgment of the femininity hidden in him. The forbidden knowledge is never quite his, but the intimations of femininity have two major consequences for him. First, his affinity with the feminine position provoked by his voyeurism almost does him in, but at the last minute he is saved, to be afflicted only by a second broken leg. The subversion of masculine distance by femininity thus turns out to be a fortunate fall with a second important consequence: Jeffries becomes more comfortable with showing affection to the woman he loves.[20]

Julia's narrative comically faces Julia with similar unexpected ricochets and benefits. Despairing of a decent relationship with a man, Julia attempts to evade submitting to domination in marriage by drafting a document that allows her to do the dominating. She decides to have a baby by legal agreement with a man who will fulfill his biological function as father and make no further claim on her or the baby. The patriarchal logic of Julia's premises leads her to attempt free womanhood by choosing for the father of *her* child Mason Capwell (played by Lane Davies at the time), a man with, to an absurd degree, the most problematic male identity that ever a feminist imagined. Mason Capwell is, in short, a consciously created Oedipal disaster.[21]

Santa Barbara's humor lies in the irony that Mason in fact *is* the perfect man for Julia to approach with her "feminist" contract. A contractual paternity appeals to him. Unable to relate to women emotionally because of his obsessive relationship with his father, C. C. Capwell (Jed Allan), Mason is typically involved in messy hysterical "love" affairs that appall him; he uses women as objects through which to discharge his rage against his father for withholding approval and as substitutes for the mother he wishes to punish for abandoning him as a child. From a prominent, powerful, mainstream family, Mason is in a central social position, but he is an alcoholic and an emotionally marginal person when Julia meets him. Thus, a contract is for him a much more reassuring prospect than the ordinary terms of his brand of personal relationship. In a very funny, inadvertent self-parody, Julia masterminds a scheme to draw both of them into the orbit of the very traits in the opposite sex that make them each most desperate. Feminist Julia and Mason, a most culpable womanizer, contract with each other to protect themselves from the horrors of marriage.

Julia, in rejecting masculine control, is Mason's Oedipal nightmare, as he, with his detached, sadistic emphasis on subjugation, is hers. The serio-comic, logical irrationality of their paternity contract is the narrative acknowledgment of these two characters' symmetry. Ironically, they are indeed made for each other. Julia is a torrent of the feminine energy that Mason has lost and needs but has been conditioned to reject. Mason, for his part, has the intelligence and sensitivity to appreciate Julia's qualities as no other man can. Her choice produces comedy that laughs at the difficulties which traditional masculine identity causes both for men and for women who use men as role models.

Julia's imitation of the male will to dominate creates a narrative that confuses the boundaries of premarital and postmarital, maternal and paternal. Just as in *Rear Window* Jeffries's self-protection, by means of voyeuristic distance, from the closeness associated with women perversely results in his sudden occupation of a female position, in *Santa Barbara* Julia's attempt to protect herself from male repressiveness plunges both herself and Mason into the very positions they have always dreaded. After her daughter is born, Julia falls madly in love with Mason; from that moment, she is confronted unceasingly by the various distresses that his Oedipal conditioning have caused him. Mason, too, admits a powerful need for both Julia and his daughter, which in turn sparks a persistent terror at the feelings these two women have reawakened in him. The no-strings-attached contract ties Mason and Julia up for over two years dealing with the very institution both avoided for their own reasons: marriage. They lurch into an ongoing dance, by turns erotic, pathetic, hilarious, and agonizing, in which they behave like magnets gone mad, thus demonstrating the power of Oedipal conditioning in the daytime serial narrative structure.

The main steps of their marriage dance concern Julia's identity. Throughout their on-again off-again courtship, both of them believe that Mason is the imperfect member of the couple. And indeed, he is an emotionally disturbed man. But theirs is a codependent relationship, and Julia's discovery of her complicity in their strife forms the major part of the story. Once Mason appears to have seriously committed himself to Julia, the Oedipal marriage narrative begins to subvert itself, making Mason a mirror for Julia. In being thus driven toward an understanding of Mason as a reflection of her own useless attempts at male agency, Julia learns that what she really wants is to create her own feminine agency.

The most intense part of Julia's narrative begins when Mason Capwell begins to suffer from blackouts, much as Viki Lord had done twenty years previously on *One Life to Live*. Like Viki, Mason also discovers an active alter ego who threatens to usurp his personality. Mason's is Sonny Sprocket, the name being a conscious pun on the macho Sonny Crockett of *Miami Vice*, but this Sonny appears in the form of another macho figure in American lore, the cowboy. Like Viki's personality split, Mason's is the result of early paternal violence. When Mason was five years old, his father threw his mother out of the house for sexual misconduct. Mason in his loneliness created an invisible cowboy playmate, Sonny, that has matured into a larger-than-life fantasy that now threatens to dominate him. In the Mason/Sonny split, the needs for intimacy with

Julia and his tenderness for their daughter, Samantha, adhere to Mason, who regrets the isolation imposed by his alcoholism and wishes to get it under control. Sonny assumes all the standard Oedipal traits: he is the fragment of Mason who sees the world in terms of dominance and subordination and perceives women solely as objects; he is, in fact, a degraded parody of Mason's manipulative power-broker father, C. C. Since Sonny can mimic Mason, and Mason is initially overwhelmed by Sonny's energy, Sonny quickly takes over Mason's personality and begins to live his life in the external world of *Santa Barbara*. Sonny keeps his hold on Mason's life by keeping those intimate with Mason at a distance, not letting them know of his existence.

If conventional film consistently permits the female narrative only if it is shaped by male authority for male purposes, on *Santa Barbara* the reverse is true. Mason/Sonny's narrative is bracketed by Julia's inquiry into her own situation. Mason/Sonny's duality is an image of the twin faces of the male authority figure, the establishment lawyer and the macho loner. But the combination of Mason and Sonny works for the heroine much as the dual identity of Frank Smith and Victor Kiriakis did: when the male identity is criminalized, in whatever manner, a heroine gets a chance to figure out her own priorities. The emergence of Sonny, then, and his exaggeration of the baseness in Mason, cause Julia to look at herself and to deal with what the alienating qualities in Mason mean for her. Sonny, a petty, uneducated, boorish crook, makes a sophisticated comedy out of the "criminal" element in the Oedipal agenda. This farce goes further in exploring the problematic male identity than any other soap opera succeeded in doing, by showing how it is tangled up in the relationship not only to the father but also to the woman the father has created: the male image of the desirably glamorized female fetish. Indeed, the glamorized male idea of woman is Sonny's only support in this narrative.

Sonny is given a story by Gina, a notorious woman who has twice tricked Mason's father into marrying her. She is best described by Julia: "I . . . don't need anyone to tell me that to Mason you're not a woman; you're more like a little wire terrier in spiked heels" (10/4/88). Gina Blake Capwell Capwell Timmons Capwell Timmons has spent her life knocking herself out to become glamorous enough to attract powerful, rich men. Most of all she wants the man with the largest fortune, C. C. Capwell—or to be more precise, she wants his large fortune. Yet each time C. C. marries her she loses her distance and charm for him and he divorces her, managing to cut her off without a penny. Gina, the only person who realizes that a Sonny fragment exists, teaches him to imitate Mason—her latest plan for gaining control over the elusive Capwell empire. Though much maligned because of her obnoxious conniving for social position through matrimony, even Gina benefits from the propensity of soap opera structure to create feminine subjectivity. Gina complexly exemplifies the double bind of the woman in patriarchy, who in Modleski's words is "first assigned to a restricted place in patriarchy and then condemned for occupying it."[22]

Gina is that kind of woman who instinctively understands the power relationships of men and women under the patriarchal system and plays the game with talent and relish. While everyone else is simply wondering about Mason's bizarre conduct, Gina has already figured out that Sonny occupies the blind space in Mason's personality. She has also devised a way to use the Sonny fragment to gain control of the Capwell wealth for herself. Working to keep the Oedipal Sonny stronger than Mason, and planning to use Sonny against C. C., Gina turns the conventional Oedipal narrative into a howling farce.[23]

Gina wants Sonny in disguise as Mason so that the man Julia marries will be under her control. In Gina's eyes, Julia is her way of gaining leverage with Mason's estranged father, since marriage to Julia will signal to C. C. that Mason has entered the social hierarchy that C. C. dominates. Unable to get the money directly from the father, Gina is now working on plan B, which operates on her tacit understanding that the flow of goods from father to son involves proof that the son, like the father, can hold women in their place. Gina's innovation will be that through control of the pseudo-Mason once he is in his father's good graces, she will be the one to take over C. C.'s millions. In other words, without knowing any of the theory, Gina has found a way to subvert the patriarchal practice of distributing women through marriage to gain power without submitting herself for subjugation. Gina will distribute Julia. Her narrative affirms the male dyad as the pressure point of Oedipal narrative power, but it also proposes the absurdity of any woman infiltrating that dyad behind a man. Gina's plot satirizes the conventional marriage story when, as a pseudo-male subject, Gina tries to make an object of another woman for her gain.

In Julia's narrative, the joke is on Oedipal conditioning. Julia will not get full possession of her baby by treating parenthood as a sterile power transaction. Neither will Gina make the male bonding practices that have failed for Mason work for her. Gina's absurd narrative constructed around Sonny is, in fact, a mirror for Julia. In this way, it is not Sonny, but Gina's use of him in a parody of Julia's attempt to make male methods work, that gives Julia her chance to gain her own, more valid and satisfying form of power.

Julia spends considerable time blind to Mason's reality and her own. But the audience is not encouraged to impute Julia's suffering to the effectiveness of her antagonists, Gina and Sonny. Sonny is hopelessly inept at turning Julia into an object because being with her stirs emotions in him, and he always returns to Gina with a desire for intimacy with Julia. Refusing to give up on making the Oedipal scenario work for her, Gina must continually recharge Sonny with a desire for dominance-subordination by playing hilarious sex games that "help" him to recall the kind of fantasies that Oedipal conditioning encourages men to project onto women. Dressing up like a cowgirl in short skirts, adorning her living room with fake cactus and country and western music, and filling Sonny with bourbon—thereby encouraging Mason's alcoholism—Gina tries in vain to gain control of scenarios calculated to bring out the beast in Mason.

These comic conspirators are not what really afflicts Julia. Rather, Julia is thwarted by her inability to see Sonny. She cannot see him because she has been co-opted by Oedipal narrative in a way other than that intended by Gina. The visual and narrative treatments of Julia's attachment to Mason at this stage of their relationship both show that, while Julia rejects the role of the glamorized object, and thus the peculiarities of the object position demonstrated by Augusta and Gina, she does not yet have a genuine female narrative of her own. In attempting to be one who loves as well as one who is loved, her imitation of men— though for much better purposes than Gina's—also makes her appear foolish. While Gina acts out men's fantasies, Julia projects her fantasies onto men the way men project theirs onto women. When Julia projects her fantasies onto Mason, the result is an undesirable form of symbiosis, not the mutuality Julia desires.

Confirmation of the unhealthy aspect of Julia's relationship with Mason appears even before the splintering off of the Sonny persona from Mason's identity, when Mason disappears after being caught in an explosion. During this time everyone but Julia logically presumes him dead. Refusing to accept the general consensus, Julia furiously refuses to resign herself to her loss, her intransigence a form of depression that underlies her determination to get Mason back again. In her obsession to recover what has been lost, Julia resembles Scottie Ferguson (James Stewart), the hero of Hitchcock's *Vertigo*, whose obsessive response to the "death" of Madeleine/Judy (Kim Novak) indicates, as Modleski points out, a melancholia based even more on damage to the ego than on the mourning of loss of the other.[24] Julia's obsessive response to Mason's "death" implies a similar loss of self.

In *Santa Barbara*, Julia's projection of part of herself onto Mason is reflected in use of the mirror image. When evidence surfaces that Mason is alive, Julia travels to Las Vegas, an unlikely place for the elegant Mason, but where a man answering to his description has been seen. It is, of course, the Sonny fragment. But although Julia is close to Mason's alter ego, she cannot find him. Alone in her dark hotel room, exhausted, she looks in the mirror and rubs her mouth, eyes empty of vitality. She turns from the mirror, sinking into the recesses of her imagination, and then "sees" the door open. Mason enters. They walk wordlessly to each other and, dark shapes against a bright nimbus of backlighting, embrace with the emotional intensity that signals the end of many a film. Mason then lifts her in his arms and carries her to the couch. Emotionally as well as physically supine, Julia numbly receives him on top of her, and seems to come to life only in response to his passionate lovemaking. The image dissipates. There is a real knock on the door. Another man enters and asks her a question. Julia turns from him without response.

Julia's fantasy scenario completely excludes the Sonny persona, about which the spectator is well aware. Julia's Mason is not Mason at all, but a fantasy stirred by Julia looking at herself. This Mason is part of *Julia's* identity. Her discovery of Mason in her mirror conveys a sense of symbiosis in their relationship, promoting confusion about individuation and causing Julia to misunderstand both herself and Mason by missing what makes him different from her, seeing in him only what she can project from within herself. Some weeks later, when Mason does return, Julia is in front of the mirror in her home. Again what she sees of Mason originates in her reflection. In the glass, she sees the door actually open in back of her, with Mason in the doorway. At this point Sonny is more of a threat than ever, but Julia is aware only of what her mirror shows. In addition, the dynamics of this scene contrast tellingly with her Las Vegas mirror fantasy. When Julia is actually before Mason, she is the source of vitality, he the receptor. Speaking his name, she moves toward him; he responds by approaching her in silence. Pulling him into her arms, she shrieks, emitting a primitive shriek of pain and triumph that affirms her recovery of herself in his presence. Mason receives this torrent of emotion silently. Smiling at her with satisfaction, he holds her, returns her kisses. He functions only in theory as the source of her energy; in fact he is its recipient.

In projecting her strength onto Mason, Julia denies the feminine source of that power. Unlike the feminine way of making meaning in which the self grows in relation, Julia's confusion reflects the symbiosis that Freud suggested was the major way in which women love. Freud's perception of confusion in the way women love is what justifies his belief that a normal male must distance himself from women. Yet in Julia's story, such confusion is the result of a female self denying its own capacity. Julia can grow and prosper only if she learns to use her mirror/imagination with a difference. Her narrative permits her to do exactly that. Consequently she learns that there is a powerful fragment of Mason that is Other, unassimilable into her self. And she confronts the reasons for her habit of projection.

The first major showdown between Julia's and Gina's competing narratives occurs when Julia and Mason are first supposed to get married, on November 22, 1988. As the wedding approaches, Gina changes Sonny's story, because Julia is proving not to be a cooperative object of exchange. The mere fact of Julia's presence has stimulated Mason's power to fight against the Sonny fragment, and, as the days elapse, Sonny finds that Mason's core personality is gaining strength. Gina then decides that she and Sonny can get C. C.'s money only if Julia and Mason do not marry.

When all of Gina and Sonny's attempts to shake Julia's faith fail, Gina arranges for Julia to see "Mason" and Gina, through the window of Gina's house, making love in front of a roaring fireplace the night before the wedding. Julia arrives on cue in the pouring rain to learn the awful truth, to the extradiegetic sound of the song "Crazy."[25] Julia, in the male voyeuristic position, embodies what Patsy Cline sings about: the impossibility of women's dreams about men and the "crazy" insistence with which women cling to those dreams. The cliché of the passive woman's face behind the rain-streaked pane of glass emerges as a visual image of the female possession of denied and forbidden knowledge. There is a shot of Julia's reaction as she watches, a reverse shot of "Mason" and Gina, and another shot of Julia.

Here the shot-reverse-shot, which is used more sparingly in daytime television than in Hollywood movies, makes Julia the possessor of the look and gives her ownership of knowledge about Mason she has denied until now. This is not the passive woman at the window waiting for

HIM to return and possess her once more. Julia watches a scene that oddly blends the narrative-within-a-narrative, in which she and Gina have been indulging, with the diegetic reality. Mason/Sonny and Gina are performing for Julia, but they are really making love. At the same time, Julia is watching a fantasy but seeing a reality about Mason that she can no longer deny by clinging to her fantasy of him. The blend of fantasy and reality in the scene Julia beholds may well stand for the entire enterprise of soap opera as beheld by the spectator.

After such "knowledge," what forgiveness? For the moment, Gina does tear Mason and Julia apart. Julia refuses to go through with the wedding. This rejection of Mason is a function of Julia's partial clarity about Mason, for she recognizes in him an irreparable confusion between the need to love and the sadistic urge to control. Sonny, now in firmer control of Mason than ever, confirms this partial truth by playing out that very urge: he tries to reclaim Julia once she refuses him, by intoning his love for her. Julia tells Mason/Sonny that he does not love her: "You like to hurt me. There's a subtle difference which I know escapes you" (11/22/88). Yet she fails to recognize her own role in the destruction of her dreams, for she sees the feminine dilemma only in terms of Gina, with whom she correctly does not identify: "I don't feel challenged by a woman who thinks the word love is spelled with a decimal point." Julia, also correctly, reserves her most emphatic blame for the father-son dyad. When C. C. Capwell demands that she explain what has happened between her and Mason, insisting that he must know if his name has been shamed, she replies:

I'm sorry, you're going to have to do without. I've had to. . . . Not everything can be judged by whether it stains the Capwell coat of arms. Why don't you ask yourself how you can raise a son who is constitutionally incapable of understanding anything but utter unhappiness? I should be the one demanding to know what the Hell went wrong. (11/22/88)

There is much truth to Julia's tirade, but there remains a great deal in her situation of which she is not yet aware.

As long as Julia is invested in a male form of agency, her life continues to confuse her. The plot turns with all the color and confusion of a Mardi Gras masquerade when Julia discovers the existence of Sonny, from Gina's housemate, a female impersonator. Bernardo Tagliatti—or Bunny, as he prefers to be called—is estranged from the Tagliatti crime family because he is a transvestite. Bunny—whom Gina (having been abandoned by Keith, the love of her life) has taken in as a lodger—is deeply in love with his housemate, whose energy and beauty he sees despite, not because of, her masquerade as a glamorized female. After all, he can do that act himself. Bunny knows about Sonny and tells Julia, jealously hoping that she will be able to reclaim Mason before Sonny marries Gina, so Gina can be free to marry him. But Julia can't help.

The marriage of Sonny and Gina is "annulled" by a bullet when the Tagliattis attack Sonny, believing that Gina is Bunny's last hope for manhood. Mason survives the attempted assassination because Bunny, innocent of this insanity (perhaps because he is both masculine and feminine?), figures out what is going on and pushes him out of the way; in the end, the bullet is fatal only to Sonny.

With Sonny gone, Mason and Julia try again, but the renewed specter of intimacy drives Mason back to alcohol. Julia is ready to give up on him, when, to save their relationship and his relationship with his daughter, Mason admits his alcoholism and joins Alcoholics Anonymous. His treatment includes Julia, who is prompted to examine her codependence in her lover's problem with drink and to explore her relationship with her late, similarly alcoholic, father. This self-analysis frees Julia from symbiotic attachment to Mason by splitting the pseudo-Oedipal dyad she has formed with her father, in which she figured as a pseudo-son.

Julia approaches her marriage liberated for the moment from the conventional marriage narrative; indeed, her soon-to-be mother-in-law locks Gina in the vestry closet, thus insuring that she and all she represents will not be at the wedding. Up until the very last moment, however, we are never really sure that the wedding will take place. Julia and Mason are anxious to the end, with Julia voicing to Mason's sister, Eden, a fear that she will "dwindle into a wife": she wanted to be the star, she says. Similarly, Mason tells his younger, unmarried brother of the agony of never again seeing a woman, aside from Julia, in "stockings and nothing else" (6/2/89). She fears his subordination-domination mode; he fears her qualification of it. Marriage, almost always a closure point in Hollywood, leaves Mason and Julia breathless with anticipation. The promise of mutuality inherent in their marriage is underscored by the shot sequence of their embrace after they have said their "I do"s. As they approach each other, they each hold equal place in the frame. As they move in for the kiss, despite the disparity in their heights, their faces are positioned so as to permit mutual gazing (figs. 20–22). However, the

Figs. 20, 21, and 22. *Santa Barbara*.
Mason (Lane Davies) and Julia
(Nancy Grahn) get married. Mutual
occupation of the frame—but what
price Oedipal conditioning?

problems that remain leave open the question of whether they have
really learned enough to make it work.

Julia's narrative uses many inversions on conventional shot patterns.
When she sees Sonny and Gina on the night before their intended
marriage, the glance belongs to her. Similarly, after a fight with Sonny
on another occasion, he leaves, and the shot-reverse-shot pattern suggests Julia in dialogue with herself. In a lighter vein, after Mason is free
to marry her, he plays a little trick on her about her wedding ring. At the
end of the episode, she replays the trick on him. The shot-reverse-shot
charmingly portrays Julia in possession of the mischievous glance (figs.
23–25). In another playful moment several months later, Mason (now
played by Terry Lester) took off all his clothes to disarm Julia during an
argument. Fully covered, Julia had the gaze (figs. 26–27). Erotically,
Sonny is always presented in a dominance-subordination configuration,

Figs. 23, 24, and 25. *Santa Barbara.*
Julia plays a little joke on Mason
about his wedding ring and gets the
glance.

but Mason and Julia, when at peace with each other, share the screen
frame equally. In one pattern they are seen, full body, to approach the
center of the frame at the same time and embrace, with neither in a
dominating position (figs. 28–31). In another more stylized pattern,
their heads enter an empty frame simultaneously and move toward the
center where they meet in a kiss (figs. 32–35).

Julia's narrative is the soap opera version of mainstream cinema's
"uppity woman" narrative, of which *Adam's Rib* is a prime example. In
that Hollywood film, however, by closure Amanda (Katharine Hepburn) has learned her place in a male-constructed system that compen-
sates for her lacks. Julia, who teaches men about their blind spots and
learns about her own, may be understood best as Amanda without
closure. Thus the needs of the soap opera form prompt it to do what the
movies have trouble doing: provide a forum for an elusive feminine ideal
of freedom in connection.

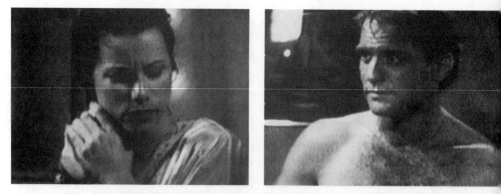

Figs. 26 and 27. *Santa Barbara*. Julia gets to gaze at a nakedly displayed
Mason (Terry Lester).

Conclusion

What has occurred in daytime serial since 1978 is a matter
of a sublime confluence of circumstances. In striving to find stories for
soap opera, the industry has resorted to a natural source of story:
narrative that has worked before for Hollywood, the theater, and novels.
Feeding conventional narratives into a form without closure, however,
required that changes be made to compensate for the difference between
soap opera and film narrative. Without closure to support the hero's
desire for control, the soap opera narrative became a reflection of the
heroine's desire to resist control. The second period of soap opera
development brought greater energy to daytime production and to the
heroine, for plots now promoted the value of her special erotic powers.
In this period, soap opera boosted its ratings by reversing the conventions in which male bonding contains the "potential chaos" of female
eroticism. The new soap opera heroine, faced with a community blind to
the criminal element in the male bond, increased her importance and
significance by bringing to bear a potent, and cleansing, eroticism.

The presentation of new truths requires that the conventional sense of
reality be opposed, since realism is defined as the view through, not in
opposition to, the prevailing idea structure. In splitting the narrative
Oedipal dyad, post-1978 soap opera mounted a serious challenge to
ordinary cultural reality, and so we should not be surprised to find a

Figs. 28, 29, 30, and 31. *Santa Barbara*. Mason (Lane Davies) and Julia: a technology of erotic mutuality—equally positioned bodies resolving to equally positioned heads.

proliferation of overt diegetic fantasy. Post-1978 plots burgeon with espionage labyrinths, crime kingdoms, and time-and-space warps.

Such fantasy has proven useful for narrative that resists ordinary discourse. Because the triumph of the Oedipal dyad is the natural culmination of what most people think of as narrative, the energy to split the dyad is more likely to occur in a defamiliarized context: one that is either overtly subversive (Brechtian theater, semiotic deconstruction) or subtly suggestive of other possibilities (science fiction, comedy, fantasy, cartoons). For this reason, the fantasy spirit of the feminine narrative of soap opera must be distinguished from the fiction of the cinematic narrative, which distorts institutional reality in order to facilitate closure. Such fictions, blatant examples of which are *The Dukes of Hazzard*,

Figs. 32, 33, 34, and 35. *Santa Barbara*. Mason and Julia: a technology of erotic mutuality—heads simultaneously entering the frame.

Miami Vice, and the "Dirty Harry" movies, use unbelievable coincidence, bodies magically impervious to physical abuse, and the like to aid the hero as he improbably cuts the Gordian knot of plot tangles. These improbable mass media Oedipal heroes pose an entirely different reality problem for cinematic narrative. They are only hack versions of what mainstream film accepts as reality. Soap opera fantasy presents a truly different kind of reality that, by rejecting solutions dependent on patterns of domination and submission, subverts the mainstream version of truth.

A character who promotes a femininity shared by women across time and cultures, the soap opera heroine has, since 1978, developed the potential to defy mainstream society's earnest image of itself. As a marginal discourse, soap opera, where it succeeds in presenting a kind of feminine text, renarrates the conventional patriarch as a kind of criminal, the conventional hero as an agent working for a paternal order that promotes isolation, alienation, and brutality, and the conventional marriage scenario as a sad comedy that mistakes human beings for material possessions. Its heroines achieve identity only by actively perceiving these situations and changing them to suit their needs.

We may now seriously challenge the conventional view of the bored, frustrated—above all, addicted—soap opera spectator. There is good reason to believe that daytime serial audiences, contemporary spectators in particular, respond to soap opera with joy and devotion because they are relieved to have an alternative to the dominance-subordination film narratives.

Increasingly, the audience also includes men. Indeed, the presence of an ever larger male audience of soap opera may be a litmus test for daytime serial's role as both a molder and a reflector of public desire: it would seem that unterrified male spectators watch both heroines who are subjects in their own right, and heroes who are in touch with the feminine components of masculine identity. Like the women who enjoy daytime serial, these men too would seem to require other fantasies than the ones that Hollywood provides. Soap opera, in sum, as it has evolved, now serves as an important corrective to the traditional portrayal of "normal" gender roles, a portrayal that has taken its toll on women—and men—throughout society.

CHAPTER FOUR

Persephone's Labyrinth: The Aesthetics of an Involuntary Feminine Discourse

The male subject's relationship to closure in mainstream film dominates not only the heroine but also the Hollywood aesthetic. Indeed, Hollywood has made an art of using the strength of the hero to satisfy, by aesthetically creating in the audience a need for relief from the "perilous" fascinations of the heroine, which only the hero can give. The uses of enchantment in Hollywood narrative involve an aesthetic through which anxiety is attached to whatever resists the hero's progress toward closure (that is, the feminine), and desire is attached to the hero's "reassuring" determination to deprive the audience of feminine energy.

Soap opera, in contrast, by resisting closure denudes repression of its glamor. The rhetoric of daytime serial requires an aesthetic that detaches desire from its accustomed Hollywood associations, that reshapes the spectator's experience so as to permeate with painful anxiety the assertion of those same male prerogatives that bring closure in conventional movies. Turning the conventions of Hollywood on their heads, soap opera's aesthetic, so hostile to anything that supports narrative termination, promises the audience relief *from the hero's "perilous" struggle for mastery* in the person of the questioning and questing soap opera heroine. In what follows, we will explore several of the artful strategies soap opera uses for presenting the *heroine* as a form of reassurance.

Suspense

In the Hollywood film, suspense is one of the prime aesthetic justifications for the hero's repressive creation of closure. Neutrally defined, suspense is the ordering of events to build anxious anticipation. Yet in conventional screen narrative, suspenseful anticipation almost always is used to evoke dread of the threatening power of the feminine. The classic suspense film engenders in the audience a longing for the hero to chasten his own fascination with "the woman" so that he may rid himself and the spectator of the awful anticipation of what she may do. In *The Maltese Falcon*, for example, Brigid O'Shaughnessy (Mary Astor) is the focus of the suspense; as Sam Spade (Humphrey Bogart) seeks knowledge of her true identity in the vortex of changing stories she tells him, he is distracted by her allure and wary of her ever-shifting presentation of reality. Spade acts out the hero's role in relationship to suspense when he discovers that Brigid has killed his partner—that is, she has broken the Oedipal dyad. At that point he achieves certainty: he must disregard his feelings and get this *femme fatale* under control. Sam tells Brigid that he's turning her over to the police *because* (not although) everything in him wants not to. The spectator cheers him on.

If suspense were restricted to the pervasive Oedipal form described in Freud's essay "The Uncanny," it would have no place in daytime serial whatsoever, since there the closure that suppresses the terrible mother plays no role.[1] That is, Freud is absolute in identifying suspense with a dread of the forbidden, long-repressed feeling of intimacy with the mother, experienced by the hero as "uncanny."

Because he deals with conventional cinema, Pascal Bonitzer, in his useful exploration of suspense in film "Partial Vision: Film and the Labyrinth," is equally absolute about the feminine character of the "blind space" that cinema manipulates to achieve suspense.[2] Bonitzer details the way suspense movies play with the spectator's field of vision, making us nervous enough to want to look behind the screen to see what is beyond the imposed limits of the projected image. The suspense film teases us by emphasizing our partial vision, reminding us that there is something we can't quite see, as if we were wandering in a labyrinth trying to see around corners. The kinds of images particularly conducive to conveying that suspenseful blind space are shots that emphasize how little we see: close-ups, depth-of-field shots, enclosed spaces, horizontal positioning of the camera, rather than the high angle down that suggests visual control. These are also the very images that characterize the visual texture of soap opera. And in a similar manner, soap opera creates suspense by playing with the screen's blind spaces.

Bonitzer's analysis, however, inevitably identifies suspense with the erotic chaos of the Oedipal mother—the hidden element in the cinematic labyrinth. Through its brilliant manipulation of suspense, the conventional film evokes the Freudian version of the uncanny and dazzles us into agreeing that at the heart of the labyrinth *always* lies the threat of feminine erotic power. Orson Welles's *Lady from Shanghai*, with its mazes and enclosed spaces that reveal the female threat to the hero's manhood, is the kind of cinematic suspense that dominates the moviegoing public's imagination. At the end of the film, when the hero (Welles) is caught in a labyrinthine funhouse that leads to a destabilizing tumble down a set of slides and the disorienting illusions of the hall of mirrors, there is a sense of inevitability about the "awful truth" he uncovers about "the woman" (Rita Hayworth).

While manipulation of the blind space to create suspense is shared by both Hollywood cinema and soap opera, the payoff in soap opera, because of the erotics of its extraordinary narrative shape, must differ. True, Hollywood suspense is not a simple, unequivocal business; conventional cinema permits temporary enjoyment of the power, the charisma, and even the quasi-validity of feminine desire. In fact, display of HER energy is part of what gives bite to the mainstream suspense thriller; but it is HIS obligatory containment of HER that satisfies the aesthetic conventions of Hollywood narrative in the end. Therefore, although the visual textures of soap opera create a suspenseful, labyrinthine sense reminiscent of that in the Hollywood film—that something unseen is about to spring out on us—since there is no end to HER in soap opera, HER containment cannot be what the spectator anticipates. Indeed, daytime serial does not deal in containment at all. What is the soap opera spectator awaiting?

Let us again use Persephone's myth as an explanatory aid. Where the aesthetic of suspense in the Oedipus myth frames feminine desire as a dirty, dangerous secret that can envelop us in confusion, in the Persephone myth feminine desire is, from the beginning, overt, innocent, and wholesome, part of the landscape of a flower-filled field. The secret threat in Persephone's narrative is the ineffable power of patriarchy, striking suddenly, appearing from nowhere, and depriving the heroine of choice. Narrative anticipation in her story concerns the struggle of Demeter to identify the assailant and then to restore the possibility of feminine connectedness. Suspense validates Demeter's search by building in intensity the reader's experience of the confusion and suffering caused by the aggressions of power as exercised by the father gods.

This model describes the experience of suspense in the soap opera narrative as well. The soap opera audience understands, in a profound but rarely conscious way, that its text anticipates with hope that which is forbidden by Hollywood: the heroine's splitting of the oppressive Oedipal dyad. In soap opera, suspense functions to intensify receptivity to the heroine's pursuit of her desire, inverting the conventional techniques of suspense that awaken a fierce need for the prohibition of that same desire.

In ascribing to soap opera an alternate arrangement of suspenseful anticipation, I am suggesting the presence in this genre of a feminine, non-Freudian version of the uncanny. The possibility of such a phenomenon is intrinsically present in the myth of Persephone, where Demeter and Persephone discover something unexpectedly appalling in the ordinary exercise of the husband and father's authority. The feminine uncanny is also present in recent feminist developmental theory. Some film criticism has even identified a suggestion of the feminized uncanny in the occasional Hollywood film.

If the Freudian uncanny involves a peculiar sense that there is something unsettlingly familiar about the terrifying (the intimacy with the maternal when we were completely helpless), the feminine version of the uncanny involves a presentiment that something horrible lurks beneath the surface of the familiar (the supposedly protective paternal). In the heroine's text, the uncanny produces the shock of recognition about the underside of mainstream "normality." In *Beyond God the Father*, Mary Daly all but expounds a feminine version of the uncanny when she states that feminist assertion of the self begins with a woman's disturbing discovery that the cornerstone of patriarchy's version of ordinary life is the assumption of her own nonbeing.[3]

Christine Gledhill, in an analysis of the film *Coma*, shows that Hollywood can flirt with a limited version of the feminine uncanny.[4] In that movie, when Dr. Susan Wheeler (Geneviève Bujold) searches for an explanation for the peculiar events at the hospital at which she works, she discovers that the conventional, fatherly head surgeon, Dr. George Harrison (Richard Widmark), is at the heart of a horrifying plan to induce comas in patients so that they can be stored and their body parts sold for huge profits. To protect himself from Susan, Harrison attempts to portray her the way the woman in the ordinary suspense thriller is portrayed: as dangerously out-of-control, insane, a threat. In this film, however, his attempts to "bring her under his control" evoke in the spectator not the usual relief, but anxiety. An alternate form of suspense is at work in *Coma*, one that generates hope that the heroine will see through the patriarchal threat and deal with it, as in the Persephone narrative. In the end, though, since *Coma* is a mainstream film, Mark Bellows (Michael Douglas), Susan's boyfriend, must recuperate a purged form of patriarchy in the closure. Miraculously, once Mark understands that Susan is right, he is able to validate her sanity—but by that time Susan is lying passive on an operating table, and he must save her. The hero can affirm her intuition and subordinate her at the same time.

In supporting the aesthetic needs of the soap opera genre, this alternate form of suspense is a major fact of the soap opera heroine's existence. Daily, the soap opera narrative shapes events to create anticipation about bewildering pressures on the heroine; her narrative validity, however, does not depend on affirmation by the hero.

Patrick Mulcahey (fig. 36), who has written for *Search for Tomorrow*, *Loving*, *Guiding Light*, and *Santa Barbara*, defines the craft of creating suspense in the soap opera episode by means of an analogy. He tells of driving in New England and seeing a roadside sign bearing two lone words: "Frost Heaves." The possibility in language for perverse opacity, captured for Mulcahey by the eruption of this ambiguous sign before the traveler, is, he implies, the essence of the daily soap opera scene.[5] Although this roadsign is somewhat more humorous, it also evokes the sense of Bonitzer's maze—claustrophobic and endless in potential involution. In soap opera, however, this maze creates an uncanny sensation, not about the sensual energy of the mother, but about the logic of "normal" social organization. The familiar words should reassure the wayfarer; one function of language, after all, is to create order. But the words on this sign, so syntactically peculiar, actually deny access to knowledge that is implied to be essential to passage along that particular route.

In the soap opera narrative, such imperviousness of logic to life awakens anxiety and creates anticipation that someone will relieve the dread. The anxiety is not fear of an onslaught by feminine desire, but instead a dread that feminine desire will be obstructed. The writers Leah Laiman (*General Hospital*, *Days of Our Lives*, *One Life to Live*) and Ann Schoettle (*Days of Our Lives*) speak of the centrality of erotic desire to soap opera suspense when they boil it down to one question: "When will they kiss?"[6] Highly compressed and seemingly simplistic, this formula-

Fig. 36. Patrick Mulcahey, standard-bearer for the *Santa Barbara* writing team, 1984–1989. Mulcahey set the pace for moving the spectatorial distance between emotional realism and irony.

tion reflects a crucial difference between soap opera suspense and suspense in the movies. In soap opera, the desire for intimacy propels the story line onward; it is not, as in Hollywood, a counterenergy requiring containment. Ultimately, in soap opera, the suspense issue evolves into the need to discover what is obstructing that kiss—the soap opera synecdoche for intimacy.

If in Hollywood suspense films the hero spends part of the narrative figuring out whether the feelings aroused by "the woman" portend some great evil he cannot quite foresee, the heroine in soap opera deals with a more patriarchal form of invisible threat. Agnes Nixon suggests that soap opera has two structures, which she likens to the intricate double form of the tornado: there is the large exoskeleton of forces flying about the periphery—the long-term story projection; and the more discreet internal movement, which, in fact, propels the story forward—the daily episode.[7] I read that exoskeleton as a force field of masculine priorities invisible to the heroines—the operations of the power-broker adversaries like Frank Smith, Victor Kiriakis, and C. C. Capwell. In the daily episode, as the characters pursue their desires, they receive, in the ineffable signs of which Mulcahey speaks, intimations of the obstacles placed in their paths by these men. Like Mulcahey confronted by that road sign, the soap opera heroine finds herself in the presence of what is at once familiar and strange, banal but oppressive. These signs shake her confidence in the normal and propel her toward a discovery of what is wrong—which leads invariably to a confrontation with the excesses of some form of male bonding.

Mulcahey has created hundreds of suspenseful encounters of this sort on *Santa Barbara*, some of his best being in the narrative of Julia Wainwright (see chapter 3). Julia is continually beset by anxiety over a blind spot in her relationship with Mason Capwell, which leads her down a suspenseful labyrinth in pursuit of intimacy. Julia's sense of the uncanny is the focus of the dramatic events in her scenes. Her evolving perception is physically evoked through a spatial organization that corresponds with those signs of the labyrinth recognized by Bonitzer: enclosure, close-ups, the convolutions of horizontal space.

Julia's desire for a mutual intimacy with Mason leads her through a rat's nest of enclosed spaces and features visual perspectives that emphasize depth and horizontality and tightly framed head shots that promote in the spectator a sense of eerie disconnectedness. One moment particularly evocative of suspense daytime serial style occurs when Julia, on the night before her wedding, is lured by a phone call to Gina's house where, through the window, she sees Mason/Sonny and Gina make love. Julia's perspective on this scene is framed in multiple ways, all of which suggest the partial vision of the labyrinth and the uncanniness of Oedipal repressions.

The staged love scene hits Julia as both familiar and bizarre. As a tableau it is the culmination of a long series of events calculated by Gina and Sonny to control Julia's understanding of Mason/Sonny's relationship to her. Its familiarity lies in the fact that it purportedly clarifies the relationship between Mason/Sonny and Gina, which has been playing on the periphery of Julia's vision for some time. But it is also bizarre because the trail that has led Julia to the staged tableau is entirely too clear, and, as Julia tells the man she thinks is Mason, he is far too intelligent for her to have caught him unless he wanted her to. The scene has the effect of "Frost Heaves." The spectator knows, however, that the secret at the heart of this labyrinth is not Gina's power as an erotic force;

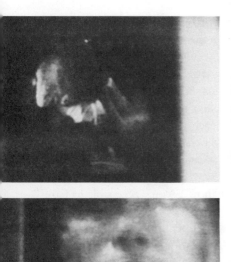

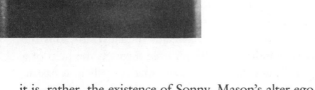

Figs. 37, 38, and 39. *Santa Barbara*.
Julia witnesses a charade staged by
Sonny (Lane Davies) and Gina
(Robin Mattson): feminine suspense.

it is, rather, the existence of Sonny, Mason's alter ego. What is hidden
from Julia by this partial vision is a secret about the damage of Oedipal
conditioning that has split Mason in two.

The way the window frames the scene emphasizes the limited vision
forced on Julia by this labyrinth. The sequence opens with a medium
shot of Julia gazing in from the outside through rain-streaked panes of
glass. The next shot reveals the object of her scrutiny, Sonny/Mason and
Gina beginning to make love. We then cut to a tight shot of Julia's face
through the windowpane, illuminated by a flash of lightning. The sequence of shots thereby constructs the spectator as a female subject,
producing the unique experience of suspense gendered from a feminine
perspective (figs. 37–39). For both Julia and the spectator, then, the
uncanny horrible in the familiar seems to hide a patriarchal threat to
mutuality, not the matriarchal threat to control common in conventional
suspense cinema. In a very real sense, this is Julia's version of the hall of
mirrors at the climax of the *Lady from Shanghai*. In Welles's film, though,
there is a bittersweet relief in the containment of the dangerous female,

symbolized by the image of Rita Hayworth's body doomed among the mirror shards, whereas in *Santa Barbara* the mixture of truth and distortion, in the image of Gina and Mason/Sonny making love, provides no such relief. Spectator identification is with Julia's desire, and the suspense involved in her encounter with this seeming obstacle to her desire lies in the anxious hope that it will somehow reveal to her that "Mason's" dismissal of their intense feelings for each other is really the work of Sonny, a negative fragment of Mason's personality born of his terrible relationship with his father. Generally speaking, the hope that Julia will make that discovery carries with it the encompassing feminine hope that the problematic Oedipal man can somehow become accessible to feminine desire.

In so presenting the labyrinth, soap opera is more faithful than conventional cinema to the mythology from which Bonitzer culls his defining image. Put another way, the myth of Theseus, which Bonitzer uses to explicate the Oedipal structure of cinematic suspense, is more compatible with the myth of Persephone than with the myth of Oedipus, as defined by Hollywood. The terrible Minotaur at the center of the labyrinth at Crete originates in the father-son connection—the Oedipal dyad—not in the mother-son connection. Indeed, it is the maternal that puts an end to that terror. Theseus navigates the labyrinth, kills the Minotaur, and, most wondrous of all, returns, through the help of a woman, Ariadne, the king's daughter. In the myth, her help is cast in images that powerfully summon up the agency of the mother. In all versions, Ariadne meets Theseus secretly at the opening of the maze and gives him a ball of string, the end of which she ties to a nail at the entrance so that he can find the way back. In some versions, she gives him the sword with which he kills the Minotaur too. A phallocentric interpretation would explain the sword as a masculine symbol, but the clear power of the feminine evident in the umbilical string suggests that, in giving him the connection that will see him through the maze, Ariadne also gives him the power to be separate. The myth of the labyrinth of Crete both endorses the connection to the maternal as nonthreatening to individuation and counters the paternal threat to the abundance of life. It is a companion to the myth of Persephone, which also warns us against the excesses of heroes, father gods, and kings. Unlike the Demeter-Persephone narrative, however, in Ariadne's myth Theseus abuses the offer of connection and individuation that she offers, by abandoning her to despair once she has helped him. Theseus's treatment of Ariadne can be interpreted as proof that she made a mistake in helping him to deal with the labyrinth; indeed, in some versions there is a suggestion that knowledge of the maze was given to Ariadne by Daedalus so that she could negotiate the convolutions herself.[8]

In soap opera, it *is* the heroine's task to negotiate the myriad turns and twists of the labyrinth, drawn ever onward by the fleeting glimpses of a lurking, uncanny father. The spectator is filled with anticipation that the heroine will finally identify him as the progenitor of her sorrow and frustration. Although the inexperienced often describe the daily soap opera episode as "pointless," lacking in direction, clearly it is not. But perhaps the sense of dramatic purpose has been culturally appropriated by the gendered aspect of conventional suspense, which limits meaningfulness to reenactment of the containment of femininity. Because soap opera does not reproduce the intention to subjugate the threatening female erotic, its structure seems to the uninitiated barely a structure at all. Yet even those who enjoy soap opera have been trained by conventional expectations to believe that it is fitting and proper to turn the woman over to the police *because* everything in the man wants not to. Can we then say that soap opera, which, in a manner of speaking, turns the police over to the woman, seems an illicit satisfaction? If the soap opera spectator enjoys her (or his) complicity with the heroine only by defying social norms, perhaps that is why she feels so guilty about her pleasure, submitting to the critic's negative labeling of her as an addict.

Since cultural definitions prevent critic and connoisseur alike from granting soap opera a valid aesthetic of its own, it seems useful to explore just how suspense works in the daily installment. For that purpose I have selected for analysis *Santa Barbara* #1053 (October 4, 1988; head writers Charles Pratt, Jr., and Anne Howard Bailey) as an instructive episode. Written by Patrick Mulcahey, it is both typical and superior. While exemplifying how soap opera deals with suspense in its customary intercutting of different story lines, #1053 has story lines that are above average in conception, as is the quality of the script, edited by Courtney Simon, a sensitive editor and an excellent scriptwriter herself.[9] The episode also included in its cast four of the most compelling performers in daytime television.

Ease in discussing the nature of soap opera suspense depends on where a heroine is in the arc of her long story. On any show, on any day, she may be so lost in the ambiguity of the signs around her that the relationship between her plight and the masculine power structure is difficult to glean without a long synopsis of previous action. *Santa Barbara* #1053 is ideal for analysis in this regard because it is an episode during which two of *Santa Barbara*'s long story arcs intersect, thus juxtaposing two of the series' most fascinating heroines in very clear relationship to the uncanny. In this episode, Julia Wainwright and Eden Castillo must both confront the sudden eruption of menace in the problematic male of daytime serial.

As is usual in the soap opera daily installment, #1053 begins with a teaser, the segment before the opening credits and the first commercial break, that is intended simply to tell the audience which of the many story strands will figure significantly in the day's presentation. But teasers that are sharply focused on an aspect of suspense in the multinarratives will do more: they set into bold relief the blind spaces in the serial's labyrinth.

The teaser of #1053 begins at the home of Gina (Robin Mattson). She and her husband, Keith Timmons (Justin Deas), the outrageously corrupt district attorney of Santa Barbara, are bending over the body of Mason/Sonny (Lane Davies), whom Keith has knocked unconscious. They are trying to decide what to do with him, but their decision is complicated by uncertainty as to which of Mason's personalities will be in control when he wakes up (fig. 40). The scene cuts to the home of Eden Capwell Castillo (Marcy Walker), Mason's sister and Julia's close friend. Eden is shaking with anxiety as she finishes a phone call. Eden has recently been raped by a masked assailant. She tells her husband, Cruz Castillo (A. Martinez), a police detective in charge of finding and identifying her attacker, that the caller was the rapist. Cruz wants to know what the man said. Eden does not respond; instead she wonders when this invisible man will stop tormenting her. The scene cuts to a dark room in the home of Philip Hamilton, a prosperous businessman who, however, is unmistakably marked by his experiences as a major in the Vietnam War. Hamilton silently hangs up the phone, a cryptic smile playing about his lips. In the final segment of the teaser, we return to Cruz and Eden. He again asks Eden to reveal the words of the rapist. She remains silent, preoccupied with anxiety.

In each segment, suspense clearly depends on a blind space: the illness of the Oedipally split Mason/Sonny; the unknown caller at the other end of Eden's phone; the ambiguous gesture and character of the war-damaged Major Hamilton. It is no accident that these elements all suggest the ineffability of masculinity. The positioning of the masculine as problematic suggests how vastly soap opera differs from Hollywood. In conventional screen suspense, the impairment of vision by the screen frame suggests that what is just beyond vision and control is the ambig-

Fig. 40. *Santa Barbara* (#1053, teaser). Gina, Keith (Justin Deas), and Mason/Sonny: masculinity as a blind spot.

uous female; on soap opera, that shadow just outside our sight is ambiguous patriarchy. The ordinarily reassuring logical masculine mode here seems uncannily sinister.

Julia's darkly comic narrative identifies an eerie blind space with Sonny—the wound inflicted on Mason by his father's tyrannous control of the Capwell home. Further, through the multiplication of lies around Sonny's hidden existence, Julia's narrative simultaneously mocks and problematizes the darker aspects of the Oedipal marriage narrative. The burlesque of the "logic" of that narrative is brought to the story by Julia's comic nemesis, Gina, whose misdirected desires find a modus operandi in the troubled relationship between Julia and the divided Mason/ Sonny. As a feminine imitator of masculine power, Gina spends much of her screen time struggling to force the logic of masculine negotiations to work for her. The way men do business, giving priority to domination, control, and closure, is always marginalized—made peripheral to an emotional plot by soap opera. *Santa Barbara*, however, during this creative period of its development disrupted male hierarchy in another way. Gina's attempted subversion of Julia places power front and center as part of the conventional marriage narrative, but Gina's wild obsession to hold power through rules she didn't invent, in a world she didn't make, renders the power structure of conventional, patriarchal marriage ludicrous.

In Julia's story, #1053 develops suspenseful comic anxiety about the same aspect of conventional marriage that made the audience sympathize with Laura's desertion of Scotty for Luke: the incompatibility of feminine desire with what male domination of society has made of marriage. Here *Santa Barbara*'s brash wit inflects the conflict between the way Julia (Nancy Grahn) and Gina interpret desire. Gina makes us look anew at the "ordinary" perspective on ordinary weddings, through her scheme to use Julia to gain wealth through marriage, as men traditionally use women. In trying to force her narrative onto Julia, Gina drops one clue after another about Sonny's existence—clues that Julia must learn to interpret. One such clue is Mason's disappearance in #1053.

Mason is missing in that episode because something has gone wrong with Gina's plan to control his and Julia's relationship. Something is always going wrong with Gina's plan, not least because the marriage Gina has in mind discredits the usual Hollywood pieties about marriage to a good woman—an unacceptable scenario for *Santa Barbara*. Gina's lunatic scheme, rather, reveals the sinister subtext of Hollywood marriage: the economic binding of the son into the father's hierarchy of power. Gina believes that Mason's marriage will reassure his father, C. C., that the elder Capwell's dynasty is in order; then, once the vows are said, C. C. will do what fathers always do when their sons are properly bonded to them through male hierarchy: give the son access to the Capwell coffers. Of course, Gina does not plan to permit the buck to stop with the son. She wants the coffers for herself, and she figures she can get them—by manipulating the son thanks to the unsuspected damage inflicted by the father.

Suspense in this context means our hopeful anticipation that Julia will be able to rewrite the prescribed marriage narrative, that her pursuit of her desire will make her see the situation as it really is, not as Gina wants her to see it. We count on Julia because, to her, marriage is not about stabilizing C. C.'s family or about getting in line for property distribution; it is about intimacy with Mason. As in the Luke-and-Laura story, what will satisfy her desire will also empower the son to escape the tyranny of the destructive patriarch. The spectator's sympathies are directed to Julia's struggle with a version of marriage that debilitates women by trapping them behind a white veil. Through Gina and Julia, *Santa Barbara* satirizes the ordinary marriage arrangement. Here is a fiction which reveals that the kind of marriage smiled on by the male power structure in fact depends on a virtually nonexistent parody of a man, a distortion of the son created by the tyranny of the father, a blind space that baffles real desire.

Significantly, Julia's solution of the mystery would benefit Gina too, since in #1053 we discover that her own real desires are as imperiled as Julia's when she imitates the money/power priorities of male hierarchy.

In the first act of the episode, Gina and her husband, Keith, plan to confuse Julia with a new lie, because their own passions have gotten in the way of their crazy scheme. Mason/Sonny has been knocked senseless by Keith in a fit of jealousy and is now draped over Gina's couch; as far as Julia is concerned, of course, he is missing. Keith, throughout Gina's sexual masquerade with Sonny, has pretended to be her brother so that they can get their hands on the Capwell money, but he is violently jealous of the time Gina spends playing erotic games with that fragment of Mason's personality. Now, because he has acted on his real feelings, he has opened up the possibility that Julia will discover their plan. Gina and Keith know that Julia is already worried about Mason's disappearance. If she discovers where he is and why, she will be more suspicious than ever and possibly discover both Sonny's existence and his collusion with Gina. Keith thinks up the ruse of sprinkling Sonny with cognac and returning him, still unconscious, to Julia's house. Since drinking is one of Mason's problems, Keith reasons that Julia will think he has been out on yet another drunken binge. This lie is not for Julia's benefit only. Sonny will want an explanation too: for why Gina's "brother" is acting like a jealous husband. Keith and Gina hope that Sonny, none too coherent on a good day, will also be baffled by the smell of liquor on his clothes and believe that drink, not Keith, is responsible for the bump on his head.

This lie—like all the lies Gina is forced to tell—is necessary because the machinery of Gina's plot must constantly contend with *Santa Barbara* reality, the reality of all soap opera: the need for intimacy. In this scene, reality means that Gina's idea of marriage makes Keith and Gina torture their actual feelings for each other, to satisfy their greed. Julia, in coping with their fabrications, builds anticipation in the spectator about whether she will see through them—and Sonny. In this narrative her desire is the seed not of illusion, as in Hollywood, but of hope that reality can extricate itself from the crazy power games that pass as business as usual in a patriarchally run world.

Gina begins Julia's journey in #1053 by calling her and lying about where "Mason" is. Lured to a local nightclub, The Lair, Julia finds Gina, who is there to detain her while Keith struggles to move Mason/Sonny to Julia's house (acts 2 and 3). The juxtaposition of head shots of the two women allows us to contrast Gina's "glamour masquerade" with Julia's naturalism, her ownership of her real body (figs. 41–42). Gina's diversionary tactics take the form of the tautological use of language.

Figs. 41 and 42. *Santa Barbara* (#1053). Gina and Julia at The Lair: feminine masquerade versus the authentic female body.

JULIA

Where is he?

GINA

Hello to you too. He left.

JULIA

I thought you said he was drunk.

GINA

I said drunk, not dismembered. Look, I'm not his keeper. That thrilling honor belongs to you.

JULIA

Where was he going?

GINA

How do I know?

JULIA

Did you tell him I was on my way?

GINA

How was I supposed to know if you were or you weren't?

(*Santa Barbara*, #1053, act 2, p. 18)

Gina's strategy affects even the language she uses, turning it into a maze that leads nowhere. If ever frost heaved, it is in Gina's drive to imitate male agency, to which Julia, heroically, refuses to capitulate.

Julia and Gina argue as Gina continues her efforts to keep Julia at The Lair. But while Gina works desperately to fool Julia, Julia pokes holes in Gina's absurd stories, and Gina keeps losing her cool. Gina initiates the lie, but Julia's earnest fidelity to her emotional truth hits home time after time with Gina, causing Gina to blurt out her real feelings, which she then must try to cover. Julia finally provokes Gina into losing control of her strategy utterly, just before she makes her exit and after telling Gina what she thinks of her.

JULIA

. . . . I also don't need anyone to tell me that to Mason you're not a woman; you're more like a little wire terrier in spike heels. You can bat your eyes at him from now till doomsday for all I care. But if you're the one responsible for starting him drinking again, I swear—

GINA

Me? Mason doesn't need a reason to drink, and if he did, he wouldn't have to look any farther than the other side of the bed! People don't like to be reformed, Julia; they like to be who they are. Which is why you're out chasing Mason around, and I—well, I'm two things you've never been and obviously never will be: happy and married.

(*Santa Barbara*, #1053, act 3, scene 2, pp. 29–30)

Gina, stung by Julia's understanding of her "female impersonations," has entirely forgotten that her whole plan hinges on Julia's marriage!

Gina's acceptance of the role of sexual object as a means to power would define her as the source of dread in the mainstream film, but in soap opera she becomes a comic purveyor of illusions, a pseudo-male that the heroine must understand rather than the essence of femininity that the hero must destroy. Indeed, on soap opera, such a woman as Gina is a danger more to herself than to anyone else, since she is destined to fall in with her own illusions. Gina's attack on Julia represents a loss of control, as she drops clue after clue that something is terribly wrong with the fragment of the picture of Mason that Julia sees. We may now hope that when the bright, passionate Julia gets home she will penetrate this maze through direct contact with Mason/Sonny.

In acts 4 and 5, Julia finds Mason/Sonny at home and tries to get past the lies Gina has told her. Mason/Sonny, who, comically, has as little knowledge as Julia of what has happened to him, blunderingly tries to fill in the details of Gina's story as Gina would want him to. The maze takes an even more absurd turn as Sonny tries to impose on Julia a false reality he barely understands himself. Yet in fact, and despite his swaggering, Sonny himself suffers from a strategy that afflicts the desire of the repressed core personality of Mason. As Sonny struggles to find a credible substitute for reality to present to Julia based on her recapitulation of a conversation with a liar, the sense that the uncanny is growing ever more vivid for Julia builds anticipation—suspense, in other words—that the patent lunacy of Sonny's remarks will rescue Julia from her present distress by providing insight into Mason's split personality.

Julia's desire to know what is happening to Mason, and Mason/Sonny's attempts to discover what he can say to placate Julia, add up to a moment of clarity in which Julia gets through his defenses; perhaps now she will discover his mystery, which lies at the heart of their dilemma.

JULIA

My God, Mason, will you stop talking like a cartoon character trying to get off on a technicality? Do you really think I'm so coarse that all I care about is whether you had sex with her?

SONNY

(UNATTUNED TO EMOTIONAL NUANCE, UNLIKE MASON)

Well, is that the question, or isn't it?

JULIA

What's happened to you?

SONNY

How do you mean?

JULIA

The Mason I knew wouldn't have to ask. Two weeks ago you asked me to marry you. Since then you've done nothing but get drunk and disappear and carry on God knows what kind of bizarre dalliance with Gina. And when I dare to point it out to you, you get indignant and claim you're observing the minimum standard of decency between men and women so what is my problem?
(SONNY CAN SEE SHE'S DEEPLY HURT AND HE FEELS ASHAMED BUT DOESN'T HAVE THE MATURITY OR SKILL TO KNOW HOW TO FIX IT)

SONNY

I'm sorry, Julia. I know I shouldn't have kissed her even once . . .

JULIA

I think drinking makes you stupid, Mason. It's not a matter of kissing or sleeping with or any of that. Being in love isn't like giving up candy for Lent. Do I really have to tell you this? I don't look at other men because I don't want to! I have what I want, or thought I did, and so it's easy for me to treat you with the respect and affection I—forget it. If I have to explain the fundamentals to you, it's no use. (SONNY FEELS TERRIBLE. NOW THAT IT'S BEEN EXPLAINED TO HIM HE UNDERSTANDS PERFECTLY)

(*Santa Barbara*, #1053, act 5, scene 1, pp. 48–49)

But the maze remains. Mason/Sonny's new understanding results only in another set of ineffectual lies. To cover, he pleads for Julia's love. What is remarkable about this interrupted succession of scenes is that the characters have so confused lies and reality that there remains no hard-and-fast line between Sonny's claim to want Julia's love as a part of Gina's plan and the breakthrough of Mason's real need for her. This ambiguity shapes viewer perception of events from Julia's point of view: the audience is made to experience, along with Julia, the mysteries of masculine ambivalence about emotion.

At the beginning of act 6, when Mason and Julia continue the conversation of the preceding two acts, the hopeful anticipation that Julia will resolve the complications of the maze is reawakened, but the interchange quickly turns into a final battle of the day. It concerns "Mason's" drinking—a real issue, to be sure, but framed here by Keith's falsification of evidence. Lost in a labyrinth of truth and illusion, Julia and Sonny fight over nothing—this particular incident was a fraud, Sonny was not really drunk; and over something—Sonny is inebriated often enough to warrant what Julia says to him. Counterpointed "dueling" close-ups of Sonny and Julia emphasize Julia's experience of desperately confronting an ominous sense of nothingness (figs. 43–44). She can only scream at the uncomprehending Sonny:

JULIA

Mason, I walked in and found you passed out on the floor! [changed in televised show to "couch"] How bad does it have to get? Do you have to have an accident with the car, or get in a fight, or set the house on fire some night when you're alone with the baby before you'll believe our life together is threatened by the fact you have a dependency problem?

(*Santa Barbara*, #1053, act 4, scene 2, p. 66)

Sonny leaves the house, angry and confused, and Julia ends the episode still beset by the uncanniness of what is supposed to be normal life.

Figs. 43 and 44. *Santa Barbara* (#1053). Mason and Julia in conflict: the male enigma and the female subject.

During this episode there has been some conventional, linear narrative motion. In the teaser, Mason/Sonny was at Gina's house, unconscious; in act 6 he walks out of Julia's house. Since Julia has been following him for the entire show, she would seem to be part of his narrative. But this semblance of male agency is an illusion, because Mason has nowhere to go. He stands at the center of nonbeing, a shifting mystery that Julia examines. In this episode, the predominant energy is in Julia's increasing engagement with Gina and Keith's pseudo-narrative.

The comic nightmare world of this labyrinth inverts the places of the hero and heroine in the Freudian form of suspense. Like the hero's experience of the Oedipal uncanny, the feminine experience of nothingness is a place where the distinction between opposites blurs; thus the comedy and the pathos of Mason and Julia's thwarted romance become one. The mystery of the Oedipal dyad, the debilitating bond between Mason and his father, has built this maze. Indeed, the C. C.–Mason bond is so destructive that it renders the world chaotic, turning even language, the gift to culture of Oedipal resolution, into a self-parody of logic and communication. Julia's suspense offers hope that, no matter how protracted her encounters with the uncanny are, she will put the clues together and remove what stands in the way of their kiss (that is, intimacy).

The intercut story line about the consequences of the rape of Eden Capwell Castillo bears no causal or logical relation to Julia's story (though at a later point Julia's life will be affected by the rapist).[10] They do have a metaphorical connectedness, however, for Eden's story complements Julia's in building suspense around the masculine secrets concealed in the blind space. Eden, in her narrative, deals with the feminine experience of the uncanny through the effect on her life of a masked and unidentifiable rapist. She finds that violation does not inhere only in the elusive rapist, but pervades the community. Significantly, the problem is that analogues of rape exist in a wide variety of "ordinary" male positions. Eden must figure out how to distinguish between the disorders caused by priority on power in the ordinary problematic male and the homicidal will-to-power of the rapist.

In the teaser of #1053, the response of Cruz, Eden's husband, to the rapist's phone call is to try to take control. He repeatedly asks Eden what the anonymous caller said to her. Eden fails to respond to his question, formulating her own instead: she wants to know when the rapist's persecution of her will end. In failing to respond to Cruz's simple question, Eden seems to be possessed by an uncanny disorientation, but also to find Cruz's point of view irrelevant. In the juxtaposed segment of Philip Hamilton at his telephone, the appearance of the uncanny is furthered by his silence. Eden's world is permeated by invasive male gestures.

In act 1, when Ted Capwell (Mason and Eden's youngest brother) arrives at Hamilton's house on business, that uneasy sense of threat pervades their ordinary masculine transaction. Hamilton asks too many "casual" questions about Eden's response to the rape. As Ted and Hamilton speak, Cain Garver bursts into Hamilton's house, roaring threats at him. Garver, like Hamilton, is a Vietnam veteran, and he too carries a violent burden of memories from the war. He and Hamilton hate each other, a carryover from their rivalry for the same Vietnamese woman during the war. This mutual hatred only brings the war back home, adding a distinctly violent tone to the ordinary patterns of male behavior, as Cain not only bellows but advances to make a physical attack on Hamilton. Cain's friendship with Cruz makes him a more complicated character than Hamilton. Hamilton has been defined as a quasi-sinister outsider, but Cain—the very name makes him ambiguous as a comrade—is also sinister. Both the periphery and the interior of Eden's inner circle seem charged with uncanny possibilities.

In an unsettling way, the rape is identified with ordinary daily events rather than with their disruption, thus casting strange reflections on familiar men. Cruz, the most familiar man, is most peculiarly reflected in the lingering glare of the attack when he acts to protect Eden. First, the

methodical Cruz wants both to put a police tap on the phone and to get
Eden an unlisted number—conflicting procedures that render his actions uxorious, even mildly bizarre. As Eden reminds Cruz, if a phone
tap is to be effective, the phone number must be available.

Next, Cruz plans to insure Eden's safety by sending her where the
rapist cannot find her. Though logical, this plan only intensifies Eden's
sense of isolation, brought on in the first place by the rapist. She
therefore refuses to go.

EDEN

Damn it, no! How much do I have to lose before everybody's
satisfied that they did what they could for poor defenseless Eden! I
will not give up my home and my marriage because I might be
punished if I don't!

CRUZ

"Punished"? Eden—

EDEN

Yes, punished—for not doing what I'm told. think about it! If
something were to happen to me tomorrow or the next day, it
would wind up being my fault because I didn't go away, didn't seal
myself up underground like I was told. Don't you see what you're all
doing to me? Why should I have to do anything different? Why
should the responsibility be mine? I'm pregnant. I'm going to have a
baby. I refuse to run off like some unwed mother in a stupid
nineteen-fifties movie. I want my husband with me. . . . Why should
I have to give that up for the man who raped me? You're not
protecting me. You're helping him take more away from me, and I
won't allow it.

(*Santa Barbara*, #1053, act 2, scene 3, pp. 23–24)

Cruz is taken aback by Eden's suggestion that in his loving concern for
her he threatens to deprive her of a fruitful life, but her self-defense
makes his culturally sanctioned desire to protect her seem strangely out
of sync with reality, even to him. Ironically, all men are implicated as
confounding Eden's quest to extricate herself from the labyrinth of the
rapist's influence. Even when Cruz relents and mounts a police guard
rather than sending Eden away, he imperils her, making her more
vulnerable for having been lulled into a sense of false security by the
official protection.

We see her increased vulnerability at the end of #1053, when Eden
leaves the television station where she works. The police presence has

made her feel secure; needing to attend to a last-minute detail, she asks the officer to meet her in the lobby. He agrees and, her work completed, Eden finds herself riding in the elevator with only Major Hamilton for company. Not knowing why Hamilton is at the station at this time of night, she is nervous about being alone with him. Her anxiety is compounded when the elevator suffers a sudden power failure and Eden and Hamilton are stuck together in the dark. Eden's incarceration suggests that all roads in this maze lead to her constraint by frightening men.

In #1053, Eden fights to remain in touch with those she loves, but she ends up in a small dark box that, on a certain level, replicates the feelings of isolation and helplessness of the rape. The episode builds anticipation of Eden's strength even as it builds anxiety about the way the aura of the rapist hovers over ordinary-looking situations. Eden increasingly asserts her right to deal with the maze herself. Despite the suspenseful angst caused by the maze, the journey is a necessary vehicle of growth, not a trap better avoided, as it is in mainstream film. Although she may be trapped temporarily, by traversing the labyrinth the female agent of soap opera will ultimately be enabled to leave the false security of Oedipal subjugation. Traveling the labyrinth is her right. Many a soap opera subject, like Ariadne, begins by sending in a male surrogate, only to discover either that he cannot succeed or that allowing him to act on her behalf only makes her problems more intense.

Multiplots

The suspense structures of Eden's and Julia's narratives imply an identical dialogue: that between the heroine's desire, on the one hand, and repressions rooted in masculine disorders, on the other. The events in each narrative are distinct and singular, yet at the same time they are identical and repetitive. Each heroine faces a hero presented in terms of the historically prevalent definition of masculinity, which privileges control, yet in each case that definition is subverted. In Eden's and Julia's stories, masculinity is distinctly not reassuring; instead it is pervaded by a disorienting threat. Nevertheless, unlike the hero of Hollywood suspense fiction, neither heroine wishes to destroy the threat, for that would mean an undesirable and unnecessary loss. Instead each seeks to negotiate the obstacles to her desire, obstacles placed in her path by male control of social and familial experience. The intercutting of the stories of Eden and Julia amplifies the impact of a discourse gendered differently from that of Hollywood movies.

The multiple-plot structure of soap opera is another aesthetic justification of its non-closed narrative form. It is also a practical necessity for dealing with a daily show that runs over fifteen minutes. Just as important, multiplots compensate for what is lost to the viewer when the consecutive narrative structure is done away with, substituting the gratifications of plenitude for the satisfaction of closure.

The lack of closure in soap opera is an irritant to conventional expectations. Multiple, ongoing plots simply cannot give the usual pleasure of completeness. Instead, a different aesthetic justification is created, decentering conventional satisfactions. The multiplots of soap opera, in short, energize the gaps in the soap opera narrative, delighting the spectator with the infinite variety of situation and the multiple resonances of seemingly unrelated events. Where there is crossover, a single event may take on as many as four different meanings and have four different effects in four different story lines. Thus, the multiplot structure in soap opera has nothing to do with subplots, because there is no necessary hierarchy involved; the major story lines are not subordinated to one dominant story. When one story does seem privileged over the others, it is simply the tastes and preferences of the spectator that make it so. The multiplot structure permits an aesthetic rejection of closure not only by attaching pleasure to maternal abundance in many intersecting stories, but also by detaching desire from the patriarchal deprivations of conclusion.

Here we can see another way in which the aesthetic of closure is gender related. Conventionally, the hero's unrelenting, consecutive narrative protects the spectator against feminine chaos. Even in Hollywood films where no real suspense is involved, the power of the heroine is associated with disruption and anxiety. The domination of the cinema text by one plot is important for her containment—that is, containment of her power to disrupt. As a result, all other story lines must be subordinate to the hero's conquest of her—or, put another way, his mastery will be supported by all actions that are taken.

Soap opera narrative, in contrast, revises this normative pattern, normalizing the gap that Hollywood narrative seeks to close and resisting the power of the consecutive so that it does not apply with its customary, closure-bearing force. In soap opera, the spectator experiences *both* the consecutive and the gap; they are seen as *collaborative* modes of narrative meaning. Each soap opera story has a consecutive pattern; together the stories also have a nonconsecutive relationship. In the case of #1053, the stories of Eden and Julia are each linear; where they are hyphenated to intercut with each other (and other stories), they work in concert to oppose the drive to closure that might be implied in either narrative line by itself. Further, since each narrative separately presents a situation that warns against dangers inherent in the Oedipal text, individually they are in danger of rejection by a patriarchally tutored audience. Jointly, however, they create a context that empowers a resistance to the drive of ordinary linear narrative. Together, the narratives suggest the omnipresent threat of masculine logic and closure, thus reinforcing spectator sympathy with whatever erodes ordinary forward motion.

Melodrama

Multiplot resistance to the linear, Aristotelian conventions of drama makes tragedy impossible in the soap opera form. And although conventional comedy regularly breaks the line of its main plot, soap opera is not a comic genre either. In comedy, diversions from the main story are clearly subplots, not equally important multiplots. Further, comedy's reliance on punch lines, and its rhythms of movement from disorder to order, suggest a reliance on closure that disqualifies daytime serial as a comic form. In any case, few have ever accused soap opera of bearing any relationship to those forms. Melodrama is the dramatic convention normally associated with soap opera—correctly, I maintain, but with an important caveat, which I shall explain below.

Long defined as a lower form of drama, melodrama has in common with soap opera a venerable tradition of bad press. Recently, however, Peter Brooks, in *The Melodramatic Imagination*, has done much to reverse snobbish prejudice against melodrama. By exposing class issues that cloud cultural judgments about melodrama, Brooks places the onus on the critics of the form and makes clear that important aspects of melodrama have long been suppressed from mainstream critical dialogue. And when he takes a page from Jakobson's linguistics and explores the special attributes of melodramatic language, Brooks, who dismisses soap opera in a typical parenthetical aside, opens up some new approaches to the melodramatic aspects of daytime serial of which he is not aware.

Acknowledgment of the illogicality of the association between melodrama—as it is usually understood—and soap opera is rare. Ordinary melodrama, after all, is virtually defined by its closure, whereas soap opera is an endless narrative. In light of the above points, the intuitive sense that soap opera is melodramatic—which it is—requires some analysis. How does melodrama work in an endless narrative?

Brooks is helpful because he focuses less on the role of closure in melodrama and more on its use of language. Brooks begins with a discussion of melodrama as an outgrowth of the revolutionary spirit incubating in France at the end of the eighteenth century, and of the role played by its exaggerated language in the rebellious zeitgeist of the times. Brooks reads melodramatic linguistic excess as a struggle against the repressive symbolic language of the social power structure. Symbolic—logical, verbal—language, he points out, is subverted in all forms of melodrama, as part of its revolutionary impetus to oppose social tyranny and to facilitate reinclusion into the community of the victims of power politics: the abandoned child, the unjustly disinherited son, the daughter of a wrongfully ostracized father. The dramatic rupture of the community is represented in melodrama, at least in part, by linguistic disruption.

This disturbance of ordinary language can be accomplished in two ways. First, melodrama may overload language, perhaps by presenting speeches of such excessive bombast that they "break . . . through everything that constitutes the reality principle," including their own linear logic.[11] Second, melodrama may employ the reverse of linguistic excess; this Brooks calls the "text of muteness." Here, melodrama insists on the power of a vocabulary that speaks in spite of the word, around the word, or instead of the word—the tableau, the gesture, the mute character (including children and animals), and, certainly, music.[12]

It is the linguistic aspect of melodrama, in conjunction with the unorthodox identity of suspense in daytime serial, that is crucial to an aesthetic understanding of soap opera. The technology of partial vision—close-ups, enclosed spaces, horizontal organization, and broad depth-of-field—in soap opera creates a visual labyrinth that in turn provides an uncanny experience of the paternal. At the same time, this visual labyrinth offers an alternative to conventional symbolic language that breaks the hold of verbal grammar and syntax on the making of meaning. Through the camera's labyrinthine weaving between the glances of characters in repetitive patterns of two-shots, close-ups, and rare shot-reverse-shots, the spectator acquires another form of language, one relatively close to what is called the maternal language—language before linear logic and grammar take over the making of meaning. The visual labyrinth creates not only anxious anticipation of the heroine's discovery of the sources of repression, but also a linguistic subtext that offers an alternative to the repressiveness of symbolic language. The melodramatic elements were awkwardly deployed in radio soap opera, but with the evolution of the television daytime serial they have matured into an effective means of articulating the kind of resistance to constraint that characterizes the heroine's story.

Melodrama, in its embrace of the syntax of the maternal, emphasizes the inadequacy of abstract language and the value to be found in the truth of the body. Brooks details how conventional social melodramas often juxtapose the abusive language of the social power structure with the empathetic silent language conveyed by the bodies of the excluded. Alternately, the pent-up feelings of those marginalized characters that cannot be communicated logically may be conveyed through overheated emotionalism in language. In ordinary, closure-bound melodrama, ordinary language is restored to the formerly marginalized characters only when they are reintegrated into society at the happy ending.

In closure-less daytime serial, in contrast, the bombast and muteness are never transformed into "normal" language. Rather, they are permanent, telling features of the soap opera context.

The original production conditions of radio soap opera allowed none of the visual vocabulary of muteness (though music was possible), and so, unfortunately, early soap opera was dominated by the text of bombast—hyperbolic attempts at clarity through the use of immensely detailed language. The tedious speeches resulted from the heroine's struggle against impediments to her agency and desire, but they also constructed a fairly tortuous obstructive labyrinth of their own. Nevertheless, even after the advent of television, as long as the radio-trained soap opera writers held sway, this aspect of the soap opera aesthetic persisted. Doug Marland, for example, speaks of his consternation, as both an actor and a dialogue writer, with the "black pages" of florid dialogue of early television soap opera. When he became a head writer and got his chance to determine the character of soap opera dialogue, he reduced it to the minimalist style now preferred by most daytime serial writers, producers, and actors.[13] The bombastic dialogue of early soap opera was self-defeating, for it discouraged potential members of the soap opera audience who might otherwise have enjoyed its feminine discourse.[14]

After 1978, soap opera discovered and cultivated a rich version of the "text of muteness," belatedly finding the appropriate aspect of melo-drama for the presentation of the female subject. In conventional melo-drama, the needs of narrative closure demanded that the text of muteness be defined as the *failure to speak*. Whatever its charms or attractions, it was essentially *lacking*, and its only hope lay in its being "raised" into the conventional symbolic realm. Melodramatic closure meant a translation of the text of muteness into ordinary language: the ultimate moment of melodrama occurs when the meaning of the mute—the child, the ani-mal, the gesture—is rendered into words. With the end to social abuses, "normal" language can be restored—all is forgiven, and all is well. In soap opera, however, the text of muteness is a legitimate language in itself, which, far from awaiting translation, must continue to exist in order to create the sanction for the meaningful word. Meaning in soap opera, then, results from the fusion of the text of muteness and the verbal. Moreover, here the text of muteness must be distinguished from failure to speak. Failure of speech in daytime serial concerns the reduc-tion of words to *merely* a symbolic form of communication, the charac-teristic of people who seek control and domination, who threaten clo-sure. In soap opera, the ability to speak involves the use of words that derive eloquence both symbolically and in relation to an in-the-body text of muteness.

In #1053, for example, in both story lines, the blind space in which lurks the mystery of abuses perpetrated by men is associated with pseudo-speech—language as obstruction rather than as communication. In Eden's story, the rapist's laconic speech is abusive, invasive, and completely disembodied. As an anonymous voice on the phone, he is the essence of what happens to words that are alienated from materiality. The other male characters in Eden's story, in contrast, are in verbal distress. The emotionally damaged Cain speaks a halting language of rage that culminates in a physical attack. Hamilton, equally emotionally damaged in war, establishes his possible identity as the rapist in the teaser by withholding communication. As far as we are concerned, he expresses nothing; we see him only hanging up the telephone. Cruz, overwhelmed by his inability to understand Eden's situation, breaks off speech repeatedly, following Eden's lead in resorting to the powerful language of the text of muteness, supplementing (failed) abstraction with physical gestures of affection for Eden. Similarly, in Julia's narrative association with Oedipal disturbance is associated with speech deficien-cies. Sonny is a parrot, able to formulate language only as part of someone else's framework of thought—except when Julia brings out the fundamental Mason personality. Gina and Keith speak to each other, either abusively or haltingly, from within an inauthentic parody of reality.

In contrast to all these characters, Julia and Eden both use language in a meaningful and eloquent way. To understand the significance of this eloquence, we must consider the relationship in soap opera between dialogue and the text of gesture and music. Two levels of enunciation are at work in every soap opera scene: on the symbolic level, that which is said; on a more primary level, that which is immanent in gesture and music. In #1053, the fullness of the meaning inherent in gesture and music favors the speech of Eden and Julia and, by contrast, emphasizes the poverty of the purely abstract language of power politics, in Sonny and Gina's scheme and in Cruz's police procedures.

Episode #1053 is typical of all soap opera in its reliance on the omnipresent and untranslatable text of muteness. As the dialogue is spoken, the camera and music weave another text that continually urges the spectator to look beyond the words for another, more powerful level of communication. But then, #1053 is superior in this regard as well, for the talent and intelligence of the actors insure that the mute language of daytime serial is "spoken" with passion, nuance, and great beauty.

In act 1 of #1053, Cruz is on a one-way telephone call (that is, the person on the other end is not heard by the audience) with Lieutenant Boswell, a police colleague, who wants to know about Eden's recent phone call from the rapist. On the level of text, Cruz wants to intensify police security measures to protect Eden; on the level of subtext, however, the visuals portray how closely Cruz and Eden's communication is tied to body. This linkage is achieved by means of what is referred to in the industry as either a "rack focus" or a "focus throw"—the contrast of two visual planes, a visually focused plane with a visually blurred one, for the purpose of making an emotional statement.[15] The focus throws in this scene present Cruz and Eden on two interconnected planes, their heads lined up in a Janus configuration. When the frame distinguishes between them by focusing on one head or the other, disruption of their essential connectedness is suggested (figs. 45–46). However, when the frame brings them both into focus for a sharp two-shot, there is a visual sense of contact. The visual technique of the focus throw is supplemented by rhythmic alternations of head shots (each shot in sharp focus)—as many as eight alternating head shots were used in this scene. The contrast between blurred and sharply defined planes, the resolution of the image with both planes in focus, and the quick alterations of head

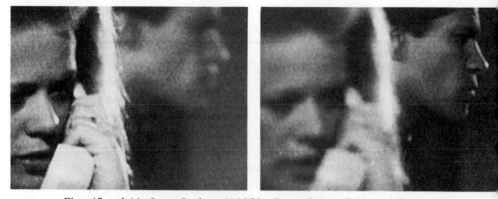

Figs. 45 and 46. *Santa Barbara* (#1053). Focus throws, Eden and Cruz: masculine and feminine planes of consciousness in a Janus configuration.

shots together assume a significance at least equal to the symbolic, verbal language. In this scene, the visual text sets the scene that allows us to interpret, as Eden does, the liabilities of Cruz's logical plan to send Eden away "for her own good."

The Janus-like arrangement of Cruz's and Eden's heads in these focus throws becomes an incarnation of disruption and harmony. The close-ups powerfully evoke the fullness of Cruz and Eden's emotional and visceral bond, in contrast to the blind spaces created by Cruz's rational solution. His abstract wish to send Eden away "for her own good" suggests that logical distance from a situation makes meaning *at the expense of* a terribly important, intimate materiality. Control of the image for the purpose of the linear plot does not occur here. Instead, a part-nership is suggested. In this context, words, no matter how logical, that make meaning at the expense of materiality become suspect. Whereas in the mainstream police film, a woman's complaint at being taken away from those she loves for her protection would render her overemotional, here Eden's silent protest against Cruz's suggestion that she go into hiding, a move that will cut her off from important relationships, pre-vails over his verbal logic of control. In the soap opera, the visual melodrama—its text of muteness—establishes embodied relation (not the logic of the plot) as the linchpin of textual coherence.

The nonverbal sound track amplifies the fullness of the gestural world. As Eden ponders whether she wants to speak with Boswell, the sound of the ocean comes up slowly (the Castillo home is on the beach), transforming and blossoming into electronic music, with high, nonmelodic fluttering notes, under which a low warning note drones, and the sound of crystals resonating off each other. The music continues until Cruz declares his desire for a perfect life for his perfect wife, and then is replaced by a repetitive melodic phrase, played perhaps by piano, guitar, and drum, a doleful, quiet, simple melody with variations, which builds slightly as Eden refuses to be sent away. Like the shot patterns, the music is a counterpoint to the dialogue, diminishing the dependence on words.

For the soap opera spectator, the hyperbolic looking encouraged by the visual texture of camera shots, augmented by music, alters the reading of the cinematic text. Unlike conventional film shot patterns, which mesmerize the spectator with a seamless fantasy world, rendering him or her passive and voyeuristic, the visual patterns of soap opera encourage active watching, an active sense of the disruption between what is seen and felt and what is heard and rationally understood. Thus the melodramatic text of soap opera diminishes the voyeuristic position of the film audience in a way that calls into question the cultural belief in the "typical" overinvolvement of the female spectator—a description normally justified on the basis of Freud's belief that feminine "closeness to the body" prevents the woman from achieving the distance necessary for logical deliberation.[16] Soap opera, that is, challenges the Freudian ideal of objective distance, of voyeuristic detachment, called for by the conventional Hollywood film and requires instead an active spectator, one who engages intuition *and* logic in an empathetic reading of the body.

This partnership between intuition and logic is particularly noticeable during exchanges between intellectually articulate characters, such as Julia and Mason. In #1053, these two consummately verbal characters were played by Nancy Lee Grahn and Lane Davies, actors with extraordinary capacity to shade the most complex diction, as well as to give intelligence to the most emotionally charged of speeches. In their encounter in act 6, they make an especially fine display of the interplay between the dialogue and its rich context of muteness.

While the melodramatic, nonverbal texture of Cruz and Eden's scenes is about connection, the nonverbal texture of Mason and Julia's scenes is about the alienation involved in "ideal" Oedipal distance. The focus here is Julia's struggle to deal with what has happened to Mason because his father tried to raise him "like a man." Mason/Sonny's conditioning has promoted distance all right, but that distance is what destroys the making of meaning.

The scene begins without music. A focus throw sharply defines Mason center screen, with Julia blurred in three-quarters position at the lower right. Despite their discussion of her love so strong that she would sacrifice her life and all her worldly possessions for him, the division of the visual plane creates a space across which words cannot reach. Their richly evocative isolation tells us, beyond Julia's articulation of a desire to desire and Sonny's false declarations about their relationship, how fragmented is this couple's bond. The message contrasts sharply with the mute text embodying the connection, even in verbal dispute, between Cruz and Eden.

The following series of seven alternating head shots of Mason and Julia works as a metonymic presentation of her energy baffled by the uncanny unresponsiveness of Sonny, Mason's blind space. It also represents the inertness of Sonny's utterly unrooted language, a language as insubstantial as the air into which it is expelled in meaningless syllables. The series finishes on Mason, who says that he isn't so bad the way he is. When Julia responds by explosively asking how bad it has to get, a new series of five alternating head shots punctuates Julia's increasingly impassioned twenty-five-second speech about the danger that his excessive drinking poses to the life of both their relationship and their baby daughter. The woven visual text intercuts her energy with his impassivity, which, more than his noncommittal remarks, tells just how bad the damaged Mason/Sonny is, how he constitutes a dead space in the flow of energy needed for interconnectedness.

Music now enters, a repetitive, nonmelodic patterning of a few notes in the high register of a xylophone, beneath which a low growling sound of bass strings sounds in counterpoint. This music continues until the end of the scene, under the following visual pattern. After Julia finishes her speech, asking Mason/Sonny what it will take for him to acknowledge he has a "dependency problem," a series of head shots, beginning and ending with Mason/Sonny, frames them as they exchange glances, Julia's fiery and reaching, his flat, unresponsive, brick wall–like. Mason/Sonny denies the validity of Julia's charges, then disappears from the frame, leaving only her face in the text. He then leaves the scene altogether. After he exits, the camera pushes in on Julia. She turns away and is immediately seen from the reverse direction. The camera follows her in a close head shot as she sinks to the couch in misery.

The expressiveness of Julia's language is contrasted with Sonny's difficulty in verbally formulating a possible position. This contrast culminates in a spectacular shot-reverse-shot pattern of Julia against herself, quite different from the shot-reverse-shot of conventional cinema, which renders the woman the object of the hero. Mason is a void in this scene, and Julia is in visual dialogue with herself. She is essentially alone, having frantically tried to read what is essentially an uncanny text, the hollow body of Mason/Sonny's language. Where logic cannot relate to the text of muteness, it is but hollow, Oedipal mockery. Such language reverses the conventional image of the heroine's relationship to the making of meaning. Utterly abstract discourse is a lie, the evidence of damage in the hero; melodramatic defense of materiality is an aesthetic justification of the heroine making her way through the labyrinth.

Actor Chemistry and Soap Opera Melodrama

The bone and tissue of the current melodramatic language of television soap opera resides in the chemistry of the actors involved. Although actors and actresses and even couples certainly caught public fancy in early television soap opera, chemistry has found its most evolved expression since the 1978 transformation of daytime serial. Significantly, this quality bears no relationship to whether the actors involved personally like each other, or to levels of skill and talent. Chemistry seems to be biological, a wild card that often seems to be the determining factor in the success or failure of a soap opera story.

Actor chemistry, of course, has always played a part in the success of screen fiction. Yet soap opera is curiously resistant to the tried and true casting assumptions of Hollywood cinema, with its rigorous application of cultural stereotypes. Few of the compelling soap opera couples were created by intentional casting decisions. In most cases—Luke and Laura, Shane and Kimberly, Mason and Julia, and Eden and Cruz, to name but a few—the accidental co-appearance on screen of an actor and actress gave someone in a position to make decisions the idea that they might work well together in a long story.

Although Doug Marland thought highly of Tony Geary (Luke) and wished to give him a contract role on *General Hospital*, Geary was originally cast as a day player for a limited and unimportant role.[17] Kimberly was originally set to be coupled with another character named Tony DiMeara on *Days of Our Lives*, but it soon became apparent that the pair had little electricity. Possibly both characters would have vanished from the show had it not been for accidental, and excitement-generating, meetings between Kimberly and Shane Donovan and between Tony DiMeara and Anna, another as yet unpaired character.[18] Julia was brought onto *Santa Barbara* to cause trouble in her sister's marriage and as part of a fairly unsuccessful story involving a lawyer named Jack. When the actress playing Julia, Nancy Grahn, suggested that the character would work best with a highly intelligent man, she was experimentally paired with Mason (Lane Davies). The screen chemistry worked, and story was generated for it.[19] Eden and Cruz initially had no story possibilities with each other either; but producer Jill Farren Phelps noticed something happen on screen when they were in the same scenes and promoted their story line.[20]

A major exception to this trend is the case of Patch and Kayla. Stephen Nichols (Patch), like Geary, was originally cast as a day player for very limited script purposes. Subsequently, when he was singled out as an exciting addition to the cast of contract players, Kayla (Mary Beth Evans) was cast for the return of a character that had left the show, for the specific purpose of playing his love interest.[21] Here, the unusual success of calculated casting may be accounted for by the great resemblance of the chemistry between Luke and Laura and that between Steve and Kayla. Although I can find no evidence that anyone at *Days* consciously considered this similarity in creating the couple, the resemblance between the two couples is, I believe, significant. It suggests, namely, that whereas recognizable chemistry patterns do not transfer intact from conventional cinema to soap opera, there are distinctive soap opera chemistries that do transfer from one daytime serial to another.

Unlike film chemistry, which depends largely on conventional stereotype, soap opera chemistry depends, like all texts of muteness, on subversion. Each instance of spectacular chemistry in post-1978 soap opera has, without fail, depended on an eroticism that destroys rigid gender divisions without conflating the entire gender issue, as postmodern critics suggest television fiction typically does.[22] Soap operas do not deny the concept of gender, but even as they seem to depict Masculinity and Femininity, they also depict a range of possible masculinities and probable femininities.

Luke Spencer and Laura Webber, the first of the chemical wonders of soap opera, radicalized the text of muteness by asserting a masculinity and femininity relatively unconstrained by the Oedipal categories of other screen fictions. Tony Geary, for example, shucked the physical signs of the Oedipal power hierarchy in his incarnation of Luke. Geary's Luke was a skinny, clownlike figure, whose body assumed the pose of the comic double-take, or the stance of flight in situations of danger, and whose intense erotic attachment to the heroine embraced a maternal quality. Genie Francis, as Laura, embodied the golden heroine, in a rather conventional way; yet her melodramatic physical text amply communicated to Luke her desire for a man who removed her from the orbit of the conventionally masculine.

While the success of Luke and Laura inspired no conscious attention to the subversion of rigid gender roles, it did provoke a readiness to accept the gift of unexpected combinations, which in turn has resulted in an increasing departure from stereotypes. Thus, even though the masculine and the feminine continue to be portrayed as essentially different, the eros of soap opera has begun to challenge the historical rigidity of thinking about these differences.

The pairing of Cruz and Eden is one of a group of major successes that followed in the wake of Luke and Laura. Although Cruz and Eden fit the erotic stereotype of the dark man and the fair woman, they scramble traditional masculinity and femininity more thoroughly than did any of their *General Hospital* predecessors. Marcy Walker, as Eden, portrays a unique fusion not only of "male" aggressiveness and "female" receptiveness, but also of female qualities conventionally kept separate. With the white, pink, and gold coloring that is generally reserved for the petite and the childish, Walker is nevertheless a woman of mature and motherly proportions, suggesting an unusual hybrid of the dainty and the nurturing. Departing in a second way from the passivity of the pastel ingenue, Eden has bodily muscle tone and a challenging physical independence. She projects a sexual energy not easily classifiable in terms of the screen's conventional coding of the fair-haired woman. Expressing neither the brazen, mocking character of the predatory platinum Harlow bombshell, nor the anemic virginity of the Eva Marie Saint blonde, Eden is instead both desirous *and* wholesome. Stubborn, sweet, enveloping, and athletic at the same time, Eden combines receptivity and initiative, a range of personhood usually denied the conventional screen heroine.

A. Martinez, as Cruz, embodies a complementary, and similarly unique, masculinity. To Eden's Nordic appeal, Cruz contrasts a Mediterranean or perhaps native American aura. Where the conventional Hispanic screen figure has tended to divide among the bandito of *The Treasure of the Sierra Madre*, the smooth ladies' man portrayed by Fernando Lamas, and the monosyllabic noble savage, Cruz is an original blend of worldly civility and primitive purity. Not conventionally handsome, Cruz is taut, compact, and muscular, suggesting a readiness to strike at a moment's notice—a readiness that in mainstream film often implies sexual cruelty. In erotic moments, however, his body displays unexpected softness, which invites Eden's physical initiative as much as it portends his own sexual advance. His sharply boned facial structure, unorthodoxly expressing aspects of both feral ferocity and puppylike sweetness, also conveys piercing ethical intelligence and concentration, and a depth of responsive feeling. The casting of Eden and Cruz is in itself a "text of muteness" that, beyond the dialogue, conveys a crucial melodramatic message. This couple defies Oedipal definition of what is male and what is female, by embodying an erotic masculine-feminine charge even while subverting Hollywood's images.

Julia and Mason baffle the ordinary categories even more strongly. Nancy Grahn, as Julia, is the shape and size of "the girl" made popular in the movies of Katharine Hepburn and her post–World War II namesake, Audrey Hepburn. Julia is slim and lithe, her face structured by those well-defined cheekbones that mark the photographically beautiful boyish girl–woman. Like the Hepburns, Julia conveys intelligence and spirit through that face. Yet Julia is tawny rather than porcelain, emanating an earthy majesty rather than conventional European glamour, suggesting not the mercurial flightiness of the Hepburn variety of boyish heroine, but rather a kind of rooted steadfastness. Where the Hepburns as sylphs each maintained a physical containment that made them, in their own distinctive ways, difficult to attain as objects, Julia is a passionate sprite who is active whether she contains or is contained. Variously sinuous, earnest, playful, and intellectually piercing, Grahn's Julia fills the screen with the stereotype-shattering form of a highly intelligent, transcendent elf infused with the ancient materiality of the Earth Mother. She may indeed be a personification of mother wit.

Lane Davies, who played Mason from the show's inception in 1984 until July 1989, complemented Grahn's Julia with a devastating assault on the stereotype of the mainstream, upper-class sophisticate. This figure demonstrates how difficult it is for Hollywood to imagine the masculinity of an introspective man given more to the complexities of thought than to the simple either/or of the fist. When David Niven played this kind of man, for instance, he was typically portrayed as somewhat superior but also suspiciously effeminate, and he almost always yielded to the agency of the more conventional "hunk." Similarly, James Mason as this type, though almost always superior, was either sinister—the Cassius who thinks too much to be a true-blue man—or ineffectual. The popularity of Cary Grant, who always got the girl, and of the powerful yet womanly Marlene Dietrich and Mae West testifies to the satisfactions of Hollywood's Freudian slips, when, by some glitch, the rigid gender categories are somehow confounded in conventional films. In Hollywood, the departures are rarely institutionalized. In soap, the opposite is the case, though rarely does the effort meet with as much success as in Lane Davies's Mason. Davies suggests the same combination of feminine introspection and masculine charm as did Cary Grant, but he also calls more attention to the disturbing fissure in the Oedipal ego.

Davies's Mason is, like Grant's typical screen persona, a conventionally handsome man who is both the subject and object of desire. He emanates the languid air of the Victorian dandy, the lion's "masculine" command; but he also projects "feminine" imperiousness, the expectation that others will, as a matter of course, expend the energy necessary for his survival. Davies's particularly deep and mellifluous voice substitutes vocal range and articulation for the physical prowess of the conventional hero, replacing muscle with the power of abstraction. Cary Grant was a radical deviation for Hollywood's choice of leading man. Although he was devastatingly masculine and so could suggest male force and cruelty, he could also convey the slightly daffy disorientation of the feminized absent-minded professor. Davies's Mason, because he grew out of soap opera, not cinema, had more scope for development of all this complexity of character. In addition to the above, he was permitted to express a world-weary, self-parodying tone of self-loathing, reflecting the conventional hatred of the hero for what is feminine in himself in a setting in which that self-hatred is not approved. This split is expressed physically in Mason's scenes with Julia. The Cary Grant character often waited for his heroines to embrace *him*, but there was a kind of cold withholding in his tolerance of the woman's sexual aggression that allowed him to maintain the upper hand. Davies's Mason plays complexly with the Cary Grant sangfroid, which the character aspires to but cannot maintain. Much as he would like to, Mason does not stop at cavalierly permitting Julia's emotional and sexual initiative; rather, he is energized by her drive. Mason's combination of disdain and need allows the audience to see both the physical cruelty and the pathos inherent in the pose of the Grant character—that desperate Oedipal assertion that in matters of passion, the woman is out of control and he, as one superior to her, is not.

When Terry Lester took on the role of Mason briefly between 1989 and 1990, he brought his own interpretation to the part. Lester moved

Mason toward a point of periodic freedom from the torment and ner-
vousness he experienced over his intense feeling for Julia. At the same
time, Lester was able to convey the continuing evolution of Mason's
combination of urbane defensiveness and vulnerability. Physically fair
where Davies was dark, Lester radiated a golden, intellectual grace
rooted in an arch certainty of superiority, reminding one of the panache
of the serio-comic public persona that the young William Buckley at his
most ingratiating could turn on. Struggling with the paternal cloud that
ever obscured his light, Lester's Mason presented himself to the world-
at-large as a lordly and unbending "fair-haired boy," though the audience was privileged to see in him a private man growing ever more able
to cope with secret humiliations. Lester altered the original concept of
Mason's desire to remain aloof in love and eschew emotional displays.
Although Lester's Mason—like Davies's—certainly would have felt
safer at a controlling distance from women, Lester permitted Mason a
somewhat surer delight in Julia's energy. Now the audience saw a man
grown freer, because of his struggles with love, from the need to appear
untouchable at all times. Lester's Mason subverted stereotype by combining the ego of a Renaissance duke with a growing capacity to enjoy
his need for Julia's exuberance, even her ability to throw him off balance—now and then.

Female agency in soap opera means opening up stock conventions
about the heroine—and about the hero, who is portrayed as a man with
the typical male penchant for abstraction, or violence, or control, but
who at the same time exhibits his own receptivity to and inner turmoil
about the conventional logic of masculinity. Eden and Cruz, and Mason
and Julia, are superior examples of the ways many soap opera couples
confound Hollywood traditions by bombarding the spectator with images of sexuality that acknowledge as compelling much that the Hollywood fantasy has discarded in terror: the female subject, and the male
who is found desirable by HER.

In soap opera, all of Hollywood's warnings turn out to be written on
the wind. In conventional cinema, when the hero is "in a lonely place,"
he is vulnerable to the way "the woman" dissolves meaning and leads
him into a fatal series of plot convolutions. In soap opera, the melodramatic text of muteness is evidence of the way soap opera's endlessness
subverts the femophobic Hollywood plot. A Mason starts out weak and
convoluted but gains the opportunity for a powerful masculinity because a Julia desires him. A Cruz begins with the perfect control that

might move mountains but also kill love and is helped to a more flexible, satisfying mastery by understanding the desire of an Eden.

Conclusion

Aesthetically, soap opera reconstitutes the conventions of mainstream cinema, but in a new context, that of narrative without closure. Consisting of endless installments, soap opera imagines closure as a threat and in response involuntarily constructs an aesthetic that resists repression. Thus the possibility of imagining HER desire is allowed. Whereas Hollywood cinema employs the aesthetic of suspense to create its own kind of pleasure in denying HER and HER desires, soap opera's pleasures release HER by means of a suspense that affirms spectator anxiety about the repressions of a male-dominated society. Soap opera's multiple plots also structurally remove the onus from maternal desire by constructing interrupted linearity as a formal element, not as HER incursion into the logical progress of events.

Soap opera's particular type of melodrama goes further than conventional melodrama. Central to conventional melodrama is a temporary suspension of our belief in the beneficence of the power hierarchy through the diminished powers of the verbal and the emergent power of gesture. Under these temporary conditions, the abuses of patriarchal power are made real by audience sympathy for a mute victim. However, the narrative purpose is to create a place and an ordinary voice for the injured party in a more just, but still patriarchal, system. Soap opera, in contrast, provides a permanent hiatus from the tyranny of the language of logic and reason—and patriarchy; there, the language of gesture and the culpability of the father are a permanent feature.

To what extent does soap opera's aesthetic make it a genuinely feminine text? Like Hollywood screen fiction, soap opera assumes both universal feminine essence and universal masculine essence. Yet instead of narratively binding these essences into the typical gender-coded hierarchy of dominance and subordination, soap opera moves the masculine and feminine back and forth in unclosed narratives of mutuality. Critics who reject the idea of an essential gender division have emphasized that any discourse that neatly polarizes femininity and masculinity risks sliding into hierarchy and exclusion. Certainly, from time to time, such slippage occurs in soap opera, but only as a blunder on the part of those unskilled at operating within the terms of the form. It is worth noting, moreover, that this kind of slippage is almost always accompanied by a sterile period, one often quite painful to the regular audience of the show. Usually, however, such a period will be followed by an upswing in which new circumstances undo whatever slippage has occurred.

The momentum of soap opera aesthetics serves as a corrective to slippage, and often as a preventative. Soap opera's use of suspense is so effective at depleting the narrative pleasure Hollywood takes in neutralizing a dreadful mother that it tends to encourage whoever is writing, producing, and acting to thwart Hollywood narrative practice. Its multi-plots and melodramatic texture dissolve the Hollywood movie norm of linearity, which mandates that the inclusive maternal linguistic must be suppressed as an incestuous threat to coherence. The aesthetic of soap opera works best when it is in the hands of the real stars of the genre, but even the tasteless and dull cannot stay in daytime serial unless they accommodate to the new angles of vision opened by the remarkable formal discourse of the daily soap opera.

CHAPTER FIVE

Persephone's "Wild Zone": Difference, Interiority, and Linear Historicity in Soap Opera

The stories we have examined thus far in this study, those of Mary Noble, Helen Trent, Viki Lord, Laura Webber, Kimberly and Kayla Brady, and Julia Wainwright, have been discussed ahistorically. I chose to explore the gender issues in these stories in isolation from cultural, racial, religious, and class considerations because the most pervasive fantasies in soap opera touch so lightly on social issues. Helen Trent and Mary Noble imply no more than a shadowy critique of the way class impacts on feminine identity. The same may be said of *One Life to Live*'s Viki and her pointedly upper-class, powerful father. *General Hospital*'s Laura and *Santa Barbara*'s Julia, both narratively placed with men of classes different from their own, pursue their desires with only tangential reference to economics. On *Days of Our Lives*, Kayla and Kimberly, desiring men respectively beneath and above their own socio-economic group origins, have almost nothing to say about what their confrontation with masculine voyeurism and masculine rage for control means for the working-class Irish girls that they are. These story lines are representative of American soap opera in making only passing reference to socioeconomic considerations. However, the fantasy narrative of the soap opera heroine is not the whole daytime story. Sometimes HER narrative *does* open the way to historical concerns about how time and place shape our selfhood.

In the popular imagination, soap opera and history have a paradoxical relationship. For the most part, daytime serial reminds us grindingly of Anytown, U.S.A., but it nevertheless *feels* like fantasy. Yet although daytime serial does infrequently indulge in obvious flights of whimsy about Ice Princesses and the like, its omnipresent, ineffably fantastic aura is a matter of perspective rather than plot. Its substitution of anxiety about the hidden paternal threat for conventional anxiety about feminine disruption, its conditional validation of abstract language so long as it is not purely self-referential but instead is cognizant of the body, its break with the tradition of the single protagonist—all these elements "distort" the historical character of the male power structure. From the perspective of the hierarchical "real world," a discourse that portrays family, police, government, and business in a manner that resists domination and mastery seems ahistorical, fantastic.

It is that fantasy transformation of ordinary life that creates the opportunity for soap opera's nontraditional ways of looking at history. The same elements that cause soap opera to be gendered differently from Hollywood movies also cause its relationship to history to differ from Hollywood's. Hollywood, with its tendency to produce linear narrative, favors a conventional, monolithic historical narrative, one that many current students of society contend has distorted our understanding of cultural identities. Several commentators point specifically to gender issues in our unbalanced understanding of past and present. They state that traditional history is not only monolithic; it is restricted to a masculine focus as well. If restoration of balance in historical texts means in part the inclusion of a feminine point of view, then soap opera, with its feminine text and its multiple plots, is the mass media narrative that can best dramatize that revised form of narrative.

The historian Hayden White suggests that we have impaired our understanding of our past by imposing excessive linearity on history. Emphasis on the paternal axis of combination in "telling history," he says, omits huge areas of our cultural heritage by reducing the historical text largely to discussions of who won what from whom. In his view, this kind of narrative must be supplemented by discussion of multiple (his word is *synchronic*) perspectives on events of the past.[1]

In *The Chalice and the Blade*, Riane Eisler is even more emphatic than White about the gender questions posed by our monolithic historical narrative. She argues that much of the story of the human race has been repressed because of its domination by one, linear perspective favoring a repressive Oedipal form of culture, that of the "dominator society." She seeks, therefore, to reestablish the vitality of an additional perspective to the familiar linear, historical mode. Eisler discusses archeological evidence of ancient cultures that preceded the historically pervasive dominator society, evidence that suggests a pervasive matriarchal order. To Eisler, "matriarchy" does not mean a dominator society with women in charge, as the term is ordinarily understood, but rather a society that embodies a cooperative mode of social order. Such cultures she calls "partnership" societies. She argues that we must establish new connections with the repressed partnership perspective, because only then can we hope for a truly just society. In Eisler's view, the banishment of the feminine partnership mode from history is the prototype for subsequent repressions: namely, racism and bigotry.[2]

Edwin Ardener also concentrates on gender issues in the monolithic perspective on history, suggesting that a full discussion of history requires co-present masculine and feminine interpretations of the world. Ardener theorizes that a large area of reality is shared by masculine and feminine perspectives but dominated by the masculine point of view. He also identifies ways of organizing information that are peripheral to tradition and convention, perhaps the source of new ideas; these they designate as cultural wild zones, one feminine and one masculine. Ardener assumes that the new ideas that come from the masculine wild zone are assimilated with relative ease into the dominant cultural traditions because there masculine discourse prevails. Whatever emanates from the feminine wild zone, however, is likely to be repressed, or at least to operate unacknowledged by mainstream history. It remains wild, invisible, unheard—because of the monolithic character of dominant masculine discourse. The isolation of the feminine wild zone from the body of historical narrative, they contend, renders the official canon of history incomplete.[3]

Soap opera discourse, with its obligatory proliferation of plots, will, as a matter of course, treat history synchronically if history is introduced into its text. In contrast to Hollywood (or television news, for that matter), which presents the past and present from the perspective of the power establishment, soap opera is a kind of wild zone. In soap opera, the impact linear history has on the characters is similar to the impact of a Victor Lord, a Frank Smith, a Victor Kiriakis, or a C. C. Capwell: like the patriarchal adversaries who seek to control and dominate, linear, conventional history operates within the multiperspective text of soap opera as a mode of repression and control, an invasive attack on the cooperative network of relationships in the soap opera community. Because soap opera is a feminine narrative that privileges synchronicity and partnership, it has the capacity to resist the marginalizations inherent in linear history by presenting social categories from the perspective of individuals on whom those categories impinge.

If the creative community of soap opera chooses, it can use its unusual, disrupted narrative to spin a topical story of resistance to the invasive power struggles instigated by abstractions about culture, race, and religion.[4] Topical stories have not been the rule on American network soap opera. However, where they do appear they suggest the underused potential of the form to bring a fresh historical perspective to mass media entertainment.

Historical Difference: Culture and Religion

The mass media rarely treat cultural difference as an element of subject identity, although they do trade heavily on cultural stereotypes to denote the more dangerous elements of the feminine. Thus, as in the kind of film of which *Ivanhoe* is a prototype, the beautiful "Jewess," the dark, mysterious Latina, or the Celtic/Catholic/oriental spitfire exists as a foil for establishing the masculinity of a movie protagonist, although his proper object is assumed to be the mainstream woman. Sometimes the culturally differentiated character is a man who acts as the hero's sidekick, as in the adventure film of which the television show "The Lone Ranger" is a prototype. This person—like a woman—is significant in the narrative only as part of the "regular" hero's story. In 1986, on *Days of Our Lives*, a narrative about the romance between a Christian and a Jew broke this pattern in two important ways. First, it constructed subject positions for both Christians and Jews. Second, it presented the continuum of events in *Days* as an alternative to the continuum of events in familiar linear history, an alternative that blurred the sharp, exclusive divisions between the historical categories of Jew and Christian.

This narrative concerned Robin Jacobs (Derya Ruggles), a doctor and an Orthodox Jewish woman, and Michael Horton (Michael Weiss), also a doctor, but a Protestant and a member of the socially prominent Horton family, one of the serial's core families. Where the Brady women only hint at the issue of Irish ethnicity, Robin claimed a clear place in the narrative for both the feminine difference and the historical difference of the Jew. She was joined on the show by her father, Eli Jacobs (S. Marc

Jordan), her uncle, Robert Le Clair (Robert Clary), and, inevitably it would seem, the Holocaust.

Official historical movie discourse sees Jewish difference and Christian centrality as part of a global linear discourse. In that "text," the Jew belongs to the history of the Christian, significant only in relation to Christian definitions and hierarchy. In this fact, movies mirror historical narrative, as we see from the way the historical time line is divided into the periods before and after Christ. Similarly, the Bible is not divided simply into Jewish and Christian testaments; rather, there is a new testament, which the old one exists to be supplanted by. Since World War II, the historical discourse of mass media screen fiction has expressed these identities more benignly than Western culture has in many hundreds of years—through the anti-Nazi narrative, in which the Nazi is a disguised recognition of what was once the pervasive repression of (Jewish) Otherness. The defeat of the Nazi, *by the Allied forces*, not the Jews themselves, is its closure. In telling of the Allied rescue of the Jews, this narrative maintains Oedipal assurances that a power hierarchy remains intact by simultaneously privileging Allied repression over Nazi repression and making the Allied victory a continuation of subject-object politics between Christian and Jew. Thus, Hollywood simultaneously attacks anti-Semitism and maintains the Other (Jew) in the same object position that the heroine has in the action film.

On *Days of Our Lives*, the text of Robin and her family was quite different from this Hollywood model. First, the *Days* story marginalized the official narrative. Although the obligatory Nazi war criminal appeared, it was only briefly, and although the *Days* Nazi was defeated in a fight by Michael, and not by Robin or any other Jewish character, Michael's victory is the closure only of the Nazi, not of the Jewish-Christian difference. Robin and Michael's narrative, in fact, insists on a pervasive difficulty inherent in the historical politics of religious differences. Thus, while it applauds the defeat of the Nazis, the *Days* text continues to problematize the attitudes toward Otherness in linear history. The historical definition of Jewish and Christian categories invades the "normally" synchronic soap opera world.

While the Nazi story was nothing more than a blip in the Horton-Jacobs narrative, the emotional history of Michael Horton was an enduring issue. The suffering caused by his denied need for intimacy—a denial familiar as part of the "normal" male self—is identified in this story with the separation Michael feels as a Christian from the woman he loves. But Robin is not an exotic Jewish object in Michael's story of loneliness. No

Rebecca to Michael's Ivanhoe, Robin has her own loneliness and her own perspective in which her Jewishness is identified both as a cherished part of her identity and as what separates her from her desire. Robin and Michael as subjects are impeded by the power relationship between their separate traditions, which boxes them into such choices as which holidays will be celebrated. The mundaneness of the problems—which many actual Jewish-Christian couples negotiate handily—on this show had the effect of underscoring the invasiveness of linear history and its traditions.

The narrative carefully acknowledges the integrity of the two traditions, and at the same time dramatizes the negative aspects of their exclusiveness, creating two perspectives on the same romance: the linear perspective, which defines the two traditions in terms of hierarchy and dominance; and the nonlinear perspective, which privileges the timeless horizontal need for connection. The narrative does not rewrite the history of mutual exclusion of the two traditions, but it does decenter the role of the clash. If this were an ordinary narrative, Michael would appear as a subject defined by his relationship to the paternal power structure that grants him his masculinity, while Robin would be an object he could take only in defiance of that hierarchy (and at peril to his masculinity) and of the hierarchy to which Robin's father belongs. Yet because on *Days* Michael and Robin exist primarily as emotional *subjects* independent of the way their traditions define them, his masculinity and her femininity are defined by their needs and desires, which take on an importance as great as those claimed by the traditions that would deny Robin and Michael fulfillment. We see this clearly when Robin, trying to be a "good Jewish girl," marries an attractive, intelligent Jewish man in a lovingly presented traditional wedding ceremony. However, the interplay between Michael and Robin before, during, and after the wedding suggests that, lovely as it is, this ritual is in direct conflict with the more important passions of the hero and heroine. Indeed, the wedding, never consummated, is soon annulled owing to lack of desire between the culturally matched couple. In the soap opera story, subject positions grow out of preexisting roots in masculinity and femininity that create the kinds of problems that are open to dialogue and mediation. From the soap opera perspective, it is linear history that imposes the either/or constraints of religious traditions on the *Days* characters. What is normal in conventional history is questionable in soap opera. More, it is an abuse.[5]

Despite the fact that the Robin-Michael story was not brought to life by really fascinating actors, it did open up, in an atypical way, issues that the mass media prefer to leave alone. The introduction of Jewish issues into *Days* also created one truly compelling moment relative to the identity of a Jewish man in a Christian society, in the brief, intersecting story line of Robin's Uncle Robert (pronounced Ro-bair). A French character, played by an obviously French actor, Robert had appeared for years on the show as a light-hearted, comic-romantic cabaret entertainer and manager, and he was brought back to the show for Robin's story. Part of his function was to let Michael save him heroically from the Nazi villain. But Robert also has to grapple with the sudden reappearance of his past in the *Days* continuum.

During the Robin and Michael narrative, a new aspect of Robert's character was introduced. Robert, it turns out, was a Jewish child in France and had been imprisoned in a concentration camp.[6] One day in Salem, Robert recognizes a doctor visiting the local hospital: he is one of the infamous camp doctors, now in hiding. To insure the capture of the war criminal, Robert must reveal his past—including his Jewishness, his Otherness, a fact heretofore concealed from the Salem community. The sudden and belated eruption of this new aspect of his identity, one that brands him as simultaneously different and familiar, blurs the boundaries that, in extradiegetic historical discourse and mainstream historical film, are maintained with vigor. More compelling than either the intrusive fight scene, where Michael beats the Nazi up, or the tepid love story between Robin and Michael was the assault on the denial of cultural difference, through a moment that exemplifies the power of the essentialist text to resist social context.

Diana Fuss has written, "The essentialist holds that the natural is *repressed* by the social, the constructionist maintains that the natural is *produced* by the social."[7] Although this formulation poses a perhaps too neat distinction between essentialism and constructionism, Fuss does illuminate a possible contrast between the two positions when she implies that constructionists hold no monopoly on resistance to social repression. The prevailing constructionist belief that nothing in humans is innate provides a rationale for revolution: there is no social category or structure that must be tolerated; all social "realities" are open to revision. Yet essentialist faith in a preexisting, innate reality may also offer a form of resistance to social constructs—one more contemplative. The essentialist offers a larger reality that, by contrast, may impugn the validity of any aspect of society. The evocation of such a larger reality took place on *Days* when Robert's recognition of the doctor led him to reveal his

Jewish identity to Doug Williams (Bill Hayes), another character of long standing in the *Days* community. This extraordinary scene added a piercing new perspective on people who for years had been known only in relation to Doug's nightclub, where Doug doubled as singer and owner and Robert worked as entertainer and manager.

The long friendship between Doug Williams, a handsome, mellow crooner, and Robert, a wiry, frenetic dynamo of theatrical energy, was known to the *Days* audience as a kind of comic/romantic buddy pairing much like the Bing Crosby–Bob Hope and Dean Martin–Jerry Lewis partnerships of Hollywood. Part of the charm of these movies is their obliviousness to historical power structures, an oversight that preserves the Hollywood myth of a homogeneous mainstream. All the problems of such character pairs are presented as wacky misadventures with power conventions to which they will eventually be reconciled. For the "funny buddy," the sidekick Robert, suddenly to talk about his experiences in a concentration camp, so long a secret, is to reveal everything that kind of *show* business is meant to deny. Robert's emergence as a Jew reveals that our protective devices against the unbearable violence inherent in linear history includes the falsification of identity to avoid disturbing the illusion of a safe, monolithic community. This moment was all Robert's, a rare, nonlinear treatment of the Nazi atrocity.

Robert demonstrates how the official linear historical narrative ordinarily masks the narrative of the Jew's loss and recovery to the community as both Other and kind. The Robin-and-Michael story, and the story of Robin's Uncle Robert, were parts of a brief interlude in the *Days*' narrative, as historical narratives have thus far tended to be on soap opera. But for that brief time, the multiple perspectives inherent in the daytime serial structure created for the *Days* audience a number of co-presences, a synchronic narration of Christianity and Judaism in a time continuum that revealed exclusions from the threadbare linear narrative of history.

Historical Difference: Race

The official narrative of black-white race relations is another part of the conventional discourse of linear history. The Hollywood prescription for dealing with black characters has allowed the American film capital to preserve the hierarchy between the races—even while enacting dramas of Civil War liberation. It maintains the Oedipal dominator mode of history by clearly portraying the black slave as the object of a whole army of subjects, in the persons of the Northern, white liberators. This stereotype has been extended, through black and white male buddy movies, to movie narratives of the civil rights movement. In contrast, when *Days* presented a story that referred to both the Civil War and the civil rights movement, the issue of race was brought to the fore in a way that resisted the conventional dichotomy between a Caucasian subject and an African-American object. Significantly, this emergence of a subject position for a black character, Marcus Hunter (Richard Biggs), was connected with the show's presentation of the Civil War through a female voice, as expressed in an old diary written by a woman—almost a comment on the narrative's role in a synchronic view of history.

Unlike Robin's Uncle Robert, Marcus entered into the *Days* community as a clear Other, for with a few interesting exceptions, even black characters who appear regularly on a soap opera remain part of the narratives of the white core characters.[8] Marcus initially was brought on to figure as Steve Johnson's "best friend." Briefly, however, in a bold and effective story created by Anne Howard Bailey, Marcus gained his own plot line.

The story begins with a number of seemingly random "accidents" endangering Marcus's life, which in turn provoke an insistent, unexplained aural memory of little girls singing. At first it seems that Marcus's story will be a typical subordinate element in a romantic story about Steve and Kayla. In their story, they relive—in imagination—the lives of a southern woman and her northern lover, recounted in the woman's Civil War diary. But soon Steve and Kayla's play fantasy gives way before Marcus's stark reality. When Marcus realizes that some unknown assailant is trying to kill him, the conventional linear plot brings the police and the ISA in to help him. Under their direction, Steve Johnson and Shane Donovan go undercover to investigate. But all the militaristic solutions are contextualized in a way that only questions their validity. Steve's efforts, for example, are seen in relation to the Civil War diary. In that account, Emily, the long-dead author of the diary, sympathizes with the plight of her slaves but is graphic about how altering their social status *through violence* only hurts everyone. As Steve and Kayla read in Emily's diary about how the Civil War tore people from those they love, we see families being similarly torn apart by the racial attack on Marcus. Kayla and Steve are separated. Shane's efforts are likewise seen in relation to his forced separation from his wife,

Kimberly, so that he can go undercover to fight what is supposed to be the good fight. Moreover, the action plot that in fact calls for all this sacrifice is marginalized to such an extent that the sacrifice of intimacy seems not just unfortunate, but also senseless. In the *Days* narrative, the police-type solution is called into question by a co-present perspective on Marcus's inner journey.

By shifting toward interiority, Marcus's narrative privileges history-as-recovery over history-as-repression; in reclaiming his history internally, Marcus avoids falling into the conventional femininized object position of the usual Hollywood black-oriented narrative. Nor need he qualify for the subject role in his narrative by imitating the Oedipal subject and repressing his own Other, the mode of choice for a Hollywood character who wishes to qualify as a subject. Instead he assumes his position as the subject of an alternative form of narrative.

Marcus's personal experience of recurrent, significantly incomplete memories and dreams takes him back to his childhood. At first, the flashbacks are only auditory, the sound of sweet, feminine children's voices singing a hymn. The images proliferate with time, however, and Marcus remembers himself as a child, running with a dog and hearing the singing of the little girls, but the memories are accompanied by intense sensations of horror and fear. The sweet voices lead him on a pilgrimage to a small South Carolina town. There, Marcus regains his memory of how his parents were killed by a group of white racists who are now trying to find Marcus, the witness to their bombing of a black church and consequent murder of the children. The sweet children's voices turn out to be those of the three little girls killed by a bomb as they practiced their hymns in the church. He also rediscovers Lizzie Putnam (Adrian Ricard), a black woman who spirited him away to an orphanage so he would be safe from the criminals who sought his end. Marcus thus finds his lost roots—not through official intelligence agencies, but through the reversal of linear time that allows his memory to forge the present by breaching the repressions of linear (white) history and finding his continuing relationship to *his* past.

In this story Marcus was a true subject, and police control of racism was either peripheral or problematic. Both Steve and Shane help Marcus only up to a point, not just because in essential ways Marcus's memory held the key to his own recovery, but also because the series' treatment of racism as a socially pervasive invasion of the body politic threatened their identities as well.

Patriarchal historical discourse interprets the feminine as disruption and the linear as continuity. Marcus Hunter's tragedy, however, is defined as patriarchally enforced linear narrative that in some ways is most disturbing because of its utter repression of femininity. It is also unsettling in its suggestion that the murderers of the little girls have found a place where they can disguise their criminality in the patriarchal institutions of church and state—for we eventually discover that the murderers are already in the narrative, but known to us as a minister, the fundamental evangelist Saul Taylor (James Hampton), and a former U.S. intelligence officer, Col. Alfred Jerricho (Steven Eastin), now a rich and powerful drug dealer as well as the head of the ISA. From these positions of power they continue to violate Marcus while pretending to protect him. Shane and Steve, working to help Marcus under the direction of the very men who are trying to kill him, thus become victims of the same power structure that is responsible for the suppression of Marcus's past.

The first stage of emotional repression begins when Reverend Taylor and Colonel Jerricho murder the little girls, Marcus's family, and Marcus's childhood, in reality and in memory. Now, Marcus is still afflicted by Colonel Jerricho, who, in the tradition of *General Hospital*'s Frank Smith, is both legitimate and corrupt. Not only is he the invisible source of the threats on Marcus's life, but in his visible position as a corrupt officer of the ISA he also commands Gail Carson (Patrice Channel-Carter), a young black woman who works as an ISA agent. Just as Jerricho destroys the relationship between Shane and Kimberly while ostensibly deploying Shane in a righteous battle, so his control over Gail forces her to "protect" Marcus through the strategies of power politics, which ultimately destroy the possibility of intimacy for her and Marcus. What is more, it turns out that Gail is related to Lizzie Putnam and so would have been a natural link between Marcus and his roots. However, forbidden by her employers to tell Marcus what the organization knows about his childhood, Gail, who loves Marcus, is forced against her will to become another obstacle for him to overcome.

With the devaluing of the role of the corrupt ISA, a minor revolution takes place. Told from Marcus's point of view, the story removed him from the narrative control of the representative white heroes, who, from the Civil War on, have fought the antiracist battle on behalf of their black "brothers," and in so doing effectively reduced them to the feminine status of object (as in *Mississippi Burning*). Here the significance of the white heroes to Marcus's struggle is markedly diminished. Take Shane Donovan as a case in point. Although Shane's story would certainly take precedence over Marcus's in any official narrative, in soap opera the multiplot structure permits a perspective from which Shane's supposed death is mentioned as a peripheral incident in Marcus's story.

Shane is missing, and although he is not dead as everyone believes, he is out of the action, having accomplished nothing, when Marcus undergoes the intense experience of recovering the memory of his parents, a process that is the inverse of the ISA's characteristic repressions. Shane's position as a subordinate factor in Marcus's odyssey is quite clear in *Days of Our Lives* episode #6067, where Marcus confronts Lizzie Putnam and her silence about Marcus's reality:

MARCUS

. . . You know there's nothing to be afraid of. No one's going to hurt you now. Those two men are dead.

LIZZIE

Oh, child, some things are so evil they don't die with the human soul. That's where the real hurt comes from.

MARCUS

I know all about real hurt, Mrs. Putnam.

LIZZIE

I knew you'd come back. You had that look in your eye. Wanting to know things better left alone.

MARCUS

Don't you see, it's those things that haunt me. I know pieces but I have to know the rest.

LIZZIE

Best you just forget.

MARCUS

Forget three little girls in a church. Forget seeing them die. Forget knowing they were murdered by two men and a hatred so strong I locked the memory away for twenty-six years.

LIZZIE

It should have stayed locked away.

MARCUS

But it didn't. And it's cost me too much getting here. I lost a friend. Almost lost my own life. I lost the woman I loved.

(*Days of Our Lives*, #6067, act 3, pp. 53–54)

In this exchange, Shane disappears as an issue. Not even mentioned by name, he is only a "lost friend." The opposite, of course, is the case in the Shane-Kimberly story, where his disappearance is very much an issue. Each character is central from his own perspective and marginal from that of the other. Nevertheless, an overall sense of community is created in which Marcus and Shane, Kimberly and Gail, Steve and Kayla, are all united against the racism that afflicts them through the double nature of the ISA. In short, racism is in all their narratives as a historical construct that grows out of the abuses inherent in hierarchy. Anne Howard Bailey's story for Marcus is one of two major narratives of black identity on soap opera (before *Generations*), the other having been told by Gordon Russell on *One Life to Live* in the late sixties, early seventies.

Topical stories on soap opera are very vulnerable to criticism. Negative fan mail while the story is being played out can stimulate decision makers to make immediate changes in an effort to prevent poor ratings. Although no one involved with *Days* said anything to me to confirm that Marcus's story was influenced by audience response, that apparently was the case. Vicious racist mail did arrive concerning Marcus's role in the series, and subsequently the long story projection for Marcus was abandoned.[9] The attraction to Marcus felt by Faith Taylor, the innocent daughter of the murderous Reverend Saul Taylor, was originally projected to move an interracial romance story into the void left once the romance between Marcus and Gail failed. Instead, a scene was written in which Marcus tenderly rejected Faith. Then Marcus was returned, as quickly as possible, to the "back burner," resuming his old role simply as Steve's best friend. Here, the same kind of racism that was so well decentered in the story appears to have assumed great power over the production conditions of the soap opera.

The more than unfortunate politics of this situation should not obscure two important points. First, the airing of Marcus's story, as far as it went, permitted a glimpse of what soap opera fantasy can do in the way of resisting racism, by identifying it with the worst excesses of the Oedipal power broker. Second, the fact is that the hate mail could not completely destroy Marcus's story. Its momentum carried the spectator to a confrontation with the tragic situations of Gail and Lizzie; a recovery of Marcus's parents, lost to him because of racism; and a scene in which Marcus publicly accused the faithless minister of his crimes. Marcus's confrontation of his parents' murderer must be acknowledged as quite different from the acts of black characters in conventional screen fiction, where they are usually denied their subject status by a single-perspective plot structure.[10]

Historical Difference: Homosexuality

On occasion—writers, network, and audience permit-ting—soap opera can suggest a complete recovery of cultural Other as subject. This occurred on *As the World Turns* in the late eighties. In most ways a conservative show, *World Turns* exhibits relatively few of the changes sparked by the 1978–80 influence of *General Hospital*. One of its narratives, however, caused a quietly radical renarration of the con-ventional historical response to homosexuality, through the introduc-tion of Hank Eliot (Brian Starcher), a gay character, into the multiplot framework of the series. As head writer Douglas Marland has said, Hank's story—as a probing of the response of the other members of the community to him, rather than as an account of incident—could not have succeeded in any other dramatic form.[11] Indeed, soap opera's narrative may be the only mass media example of a fiction in which a character is permitted subjecthood despite his existence almost purely as part of the stories of other core characters.

Although he had no narrative of his own, Hank was given a subject perspective in order to play out a rejection of conventional homophobia. The rejection was dramatized through the acceptance of Hank by the vast majority of characters, with adverse response to his difference re-stricted to figures identifiable in some way as Oedipal fathers. Primary among those was James Stenbeck (Anthony Herrera), the necessary soap opera antagonist, the power broker. In his limited stay on *World Turns*, Hank was the show's androgynous knight, the one person who could challenge Stenbeck successfully. It was his job, one usually assigned to the soap opera heroine, to split the cruel, repressive father-son bond between Stenbeck and his son, Paul. Thus, although Hank was male, he was in the powerful position of the soap opera heroine. His liberation of Stenbeck's son did not, however, include the sexual intimacy with Paul that would have been the case had the task been performed by a soap opera heroine.

In *The Chalice and the Blade*, Riane Eisler speaks of the historical importance of the *Oresteia* trilogy by Aeschylus.[12] When Athena hands down a judgment justifying Orestes' murder of his mother, matricide is in effect deemed acceptable and even necessary under certain circumstances to insure the stability of society. The *Oresteia*, says Eisler, is an imaginative depiction of the moment when the feminine was eliminated as a form of historical co-presence and when her subordination to the masculine introduced the Oedipal myth as the norm of historical narrative. In just such a way, the intervention of Hank Eliot in the relationship between Paul and his father reflects a moment—though not as culturally powerful—of imaginative resistance to the Oedipal mode of historical narrative through a startling inversion on the *Oresteia* gambit. Eliot's story, that is, makes a case for the unorthodox concept of the necessary patricide.

Hank Eliot was a crucial figure in the story of James Stenbeck's death. Stenbeck's demise, at the hands of his own son, is part of a narrative that emphasizes the elder Stenbeck's hatred of his former wife and the boy's mother, Barbara Ryan (Colleen Zenk), a loving parent but a woman of dubious reputation—she lies and she cheats. Stenbeck justifies his plan to take Paul from his mother by citing her less-than-acceptable performance in the nonmaternal realm of her life, a premise that *World Turns*, in vindicating his murder, rejects. Hollywood, in contrast, historically blesses such control over the son as the father's right, even when the mother is a model of propriety. On *World Turns* the patriarchal prerogative is posed as utterly destructive; not only is his claim to control invalid, the series suggests, but it is also so excessive that Paul's murder of his own father is legally and ethically correct. Even more fascinating is that the moment the narrative chooses to reveal his father's excesses to Paul is the moment when Stenbeck attacks Hank.

Paul, of college age during the Hank Eliot arc of the narrative, acts out the conventional family romance as defined by classical developmental theories. Paul wants the bond with his father but is conflicted because the elder Stenbeck has made it clear to Paul that he must choose between father and mother. There is a difference, however, between the social attitude toward Paul's dilemma that prevails in our culture and that which is presented on *World Turns*. Our culture tells the developing boy wonderful stories about the father and frightening stories about the mother, sometimes disguised by a show of idealization; on *World Turns*, in contrast, everyone tells Paul horrifying anecdotes about his father's ruthlessness, and while many characters dislike Barbara, only James attacks Paul's regard for his mother.

Paul's unconventional manhood struggle with his father's demands hinges on his relationship with Hank. Paul, initially unaware that Hank was gay, had looked up to his friend as a male role model; then, when he learns of Hank's difference, Paul indulges in a rather conventional homophobia—a reaction that is gently criticized by all the characters on the show whom the audience has come to respect. Narrative events also strongly undermine Paul's first response upon learning that Hank is gay, when in the course of the story we see that Paul's own heterosexual manhood depends on his freedom *from excessive intimacy with his father* and his rethinking of his homophobia.

In an extreme form of resistance to predominant mass media Oedipal narrativity, the threat to Paul's heterosexual manhood lies neither in Hank's difference, nor in Paul's connection with his mother, but in James himself. The danger is dramatized when James makes what appears to be his final attempt to make Paul his, in New York, where Hank and Barbara, on a business trip, are accompanied by Paul. Lured to a heliport, Paul is about to be talked into leaving with James even at the cost of permanently severing the connection with his mother, when Hank, the only person in a position to thwart James's plan, arrives on the scene. Enraged by the interference, James shoots Hank. Paul is strongly affected by Stenbeck's brutality, the first he has ever really witnessed firsthand, and refuses to go away with his father. Seeing Stenbeck try to kill Hank to get his own way causes in Paul the shock of recognition that severs Stenbeck's hold over his son. It is also the beginning of Paul's accepting of Hank, and a bold statement that sexual difference does not require repression from the narrative. This position on sexual difference is underlined by the story's refusal to allow the rescue to be made by Barbara Ryan's policeman lover, who arrives only after Hank has changed Paul's mind about Stenbeck.

Through Paul, Hank, and Stenbeck, *As the World Turns* created an alternate historical discourse, one that challenges the patriarchal narrative of power. Here, Stenbeck's control of the world by violence threatens not only Hank's sexual difference and the flawed Barbara Ryan's *Mutterrecht*—rights as a mother—but also Paul's heterosexual manhood—for it is separation from James that frees Paul for his first sexual experience, with Emily, Stenbeck's former mistress. Although this choice of a partner would seem to justify Oedipal warnings, subsequent events indicate that Paul's close relationship with a woman who once belonged to his father was part of a necessary maturation process.

Paul's rejection of his father, made possible by Hank, remained a dynamic narrative element on the show, leading at last to the almost unprecedented exoneration of Paul as a patricide. Several arcs after the scene with Hank at the heliport, Paul kills his father to defend Emily from Stenbeck's rage on learning of their affair. Paul now seems to have fulfilled the Oedipal prediction of what happens when there is too much intimacy with the maternal. However, defended by a black woman lawyer, Paul is vindicated, primarily on the basis of Hank's testimony about James's violence at the heliport. In soap opera, everyone marginalized by the standard cinematic text potentially has a hand in overturning the rule of the paternal power broker so central to the Hollywood gender hierarchy.

Paul's complete exoneration before the law-of-the-father tribunal and, to this date, the absence of any other form of punishment seem fantastic in their optimistic treatment of the integration into the community of homosexual difference. In fact, however, soap opera gave that unorthodox perspective a platform in front of a mass audience and was validated by positive viewer response both to Hank Eliot's friendship with Paul and to the exoneration of Paul as a patricide.[13] Clearly, the soap opera form has created a forum for discussing, in increasingly provocative ways, the plight of those whom patriarchy has defined as historical Other.

Hank ceased to be a core member of the *World Turns* community soon after the incident in New York. Yet he left on his feet instead of dying there at the heliport in the arms of those he served—thereby being recuperated for patriarchy—as those characters who rise above ordinary definitions of their difference often do in conventional screen fiction: the faithful black-Jewish-Mexican-Indian sidekick, the good-bad girl, Madame Butterfly, and so forth.

Soap opera's narrative distance from conventional social definitions creates unorthodox subject positions in the Horton-Jacobs story, in the story of Marcus Hunter, and in the story of Hank Eliot. These three stories, moreover, do not exhaust the instances of topicalism on daytime serial. I know of two other approaches to gay identity on daytime serial, one on *Days of Our Lives* in the seventies, in which Julie Williams discovered she was looked on with desire by another woman, and one on *All My Children* in the eighties, in which Devon moved into an apartment shared by a woman she subsequently discovered was gay. In addition, *Ryan's Hope*, *Generations*, and *All My Children* provide extensive examples of conscious attempts to treat cultural, racial, and class issues. There are surely others. Cultural diversity has been a part of daytime serial since the very infancy of soap opera, when Irna Phillips used the ethnically inflected voices of a Mrs. Kransky and a Mrs. Cunningham in the radio version of *Guiding Light*.

Soap opera can decenter conventional perspectives on cultural, racial, and sexual Others. If topical narrative is done well and is perceived as a valuable and valued part of the form, it will stay on the air. Moreover, reference to specific members of marginalized groups—Jews, blacks, and gays—is not the only way soap opera's lack of closure resists the thrust toward domination and exclusion in conventional historical narrative. Soap opera also makes possible bursts of increased fantasy, which energize the gender issue to such a degree that what is ordinarily understood as time—the linear, historical continuum—is reduced to a partial view, nothing more (or less) than one cosmic model.

Interiority: A Different History

The story of Marcus Hunter on *One Life to Live* suggests through intermittent flashback imagery and aural recall that interiority can serve to recover what has been lost in the course of linear history. Two soap opera narratives that take that insight even further were dramatized on *One Life to Live* and *Santa Barbara*.

In 1987, a story line on *One Life to Live* gave Viki (see chapter 2) a global relationship to time that enabled her to redeem linear history by temporarily freeing herself of its constraints. In the *One Life to Live* of the late eighties, Joe Reilly is dead, and Viki (now played by Erika Slezak) is remarried, to Clint Buchanan (Clint Ritchie). The Viki/Niki split has been healed; Viki, an integrated personality, "has it all," as a professional woman, a wife, and the mother of three children, two by Joe and a new baby with Clint, Jessica. Viki thus functions as a conventional historical reflection: the eighties woman, supposedly "post-feminist," who suggests by her life-style that liberation has been achieved. Women are supposedly no longer forced to choose between sexuality and competence. But in Viki's new narrative arc, all that she has achieved appears to be threatened by linear history. Her past is not dead; neither is Clint's. Old problems resurface for both of them, endangering Viki and her family.

Viki is once more afflicted by terrible headaches, heretofore a signal of the imminent eruption of her alter ego, Niki. At the same time, Viki is visited by Tom, Joe Reilly's brother. Played by Lee Patterson, the original Joe, he is, of course, Joe's double. This combination of circumstances causes Viki to lose track of temporality and to experience a psychic return to the days of her love for Joe, which were also the days of Niki and the tyranny of Viki's father. Joe's "reappearance" is an uncanny assault on Viki, reactivating in her problems associated with the "awful father." This event is complemented by a simultaneous eruption of her husband Clint's experience of the conventional uncanny, which promotes dread of an imminent attack by the "terrible mother." Out of Clint's buried past comes Maria (Barbara Luna), a Hollywood-style dangerous woman with whom Clint had a child. As Tom gets close to Viki, in partial recapitulation of the old love between Viki and Joe, a parallel recapitulation takes place as Maria becomes increasingly determined to reestablish her relationship with Clint and supplant Viki. The two narratives interconnect when Maria discovers the history of Viki's alter ego and fabricates evidence to suggest that Niki is returning. Indeed, to all appearances Niki is more of a threat than ever, since, thanks to Maria's engineering, "Niki" has become desperate and vicious enough to kidnap Jessica.

If characters live only in linear time, as most of us generally assume we must, then only violent repression can "solve" the problems caused by the resurgence of Tom and Maria—or, in a movie, exorcism of the ghosts of times past. Here, however, a metahistorical discourse intervenes, permitting Viki to leave linear time and space to confront the difficulties posed in her narrative. Tania Modleski has written of the need to abandon the notion of women as mute bodies outside history; women must have textual representation as speaking bodies with historical significance.[14] In response to the incursions of Tom and Maria into her life, Viki presents the spectator with a particular version of that option: the physical and situational tensions of the uncanny narratives send Viki into a coma. Although to the anxious men who surround her the coma is a frightening interruption, the gap introduced by Viki's absorption into her body is, for the soap opera spectator, the site of reconciliation and the only hope for negotiating the threats posed by ordinary historical biography.

For about two weeks, Viki's narrative withdrew from the external linear world and reconvened in Viki's interior space, fantastically visualized as a dazzling, white starship. Resembling any number of space vehicles that have graced the screen, Viki's starship is futuristic in design and highly stylized. Its view, through large control room windows, is of a black universe bejeweled with a myriad of pinpoint dots of light moving centrifugally without cessation. All the personnel on the starship are dressed in white, but not in the stripped-down, boyish bodysuits of the conventional sci-fi wardrobe. Instead, men and women alike are robed in snowy, feminized, flowing Grecian garments, washed into brilliant whiteness by the unnaturally bright lighting of the set.

Viki's interior space, then, is presented in opposition to the conventional assumption that the darkness and danger of female interiority has required that men build culture and history to protect themselves. The brilliance and beauty of the starship, an unambiguous space of feminine interiority, is delineated as a wonderful alternate historical space in two unequivocal ways. First, the starship is peopled with the deceased characters of major importance from Viki's previous story arcs, played by the same actors. Second, in the spirit of co-presence so typical of soap opera, there exists in this space one anomalous character, representing the conventional, linear historical perspective: Vergil (John Fiedler). The only character in this space that has never before appeared in Viki's life, Vergil, both by name and by appearance, clearly alludes to patriarchal time: he dresses in white, like everyone else, but in the rigidly role-defining three-button suit, not the voluminous garments of the other men and women. Vergil is Viki's sad-faced, nervous guide, who takes her to her starship and watches her struggle with the conflicting forces in her life.

Vergil, as the emissary from linear history, is defined not only by his clothes and his role (recalling the guide who led Dante toward the patriarchal paradise), but also by the part he played in the linear history of Viki's Main Line family. (At one point on the starship, Victor Lord fulminates against Vergil because his mistake prevented the Lord family from arriving in America on the Mayflower, a faux pas that Viki's tyrannical father says he will never forgive.) Vergil, of course, is also male, and hence he has a certain amount of power as a representative of that order; nevertheless, he is also a bungler. In short, he embodies the limitations of the ordinary understanding of history—and he is completely peripheral to Viki's encounters with her mother, her father, Joe, and her most frightening adversaries, who still have the power to harm her, though they are dead. Nor can Vergil stay the hand of the dangerous Maria, who clearly intends to kill Viki while she is helpless and vulnerable. Only Viki's successful self-regeneration while she is out of linear time can affect the dangers she and Clint face within that time.

Viki faces two ordeals in her interior starship, the first with Mitch

Lawrence (Roscoe Borne), a departed villain from *One Life*, and the second with Niki (also played by Erika Slezak), her alter ego. Mitch is memorable as a ruthless embodiment of the spirit of social Darwinism: if ever there was a man who believed in manhood as mastery and conquest, it is Mitch. Alien to everything Viki is, Mitch can never be anything but an anomaly in her internal space. He appears in Viki's all-white starship as the only figure in black, with chains around his neck and hands. He exists in Viki's interior space as a seemingly devastating form of her internalization of the patriarchal prohibition of feminine subjecthood— as he all but tells her when he announces himself to Viki as "the dark side of your mirror," "the keeper of your secrets," "the symbol of everything you fear," "the warehouse of your weakness," "the ultimate test of what your soul can stand." Although Viki is at first terrified of Mitch, she eventually finds that he has no real power, except what she gives him. His image fades and dissolves as Viki proclaims that she has passed her test and will resume life through the power of love, which will, she triumphantly proclaims, always prevail.

As a historical position, this story line is more than optimistic; it is a "euphoric text."[15] Since the masculinity that Mitch represents is the rule in Oedipal history, the fading of his image into thin air seems to buy a feminine historical co-presence at the price of denial. *One Life to Live* in fact has a tradition of resisting closure through application of unwarranted optimism about the power of the feminine vis-à-vis the Oedipal. Its use of this pattern makes the show, in some ways, a throwback to the early radio serials discussed in chapter 2. However, the exaggerated empowerment of the feminine in *One Life* has its charms. One of them is the pleasure in watching the mean, masterful Mitch fade when Viki exerts herself, and the other is the delightful surprise that he is not even her ultimate trial, as both Viki and Mitch himself mistakenly believe.

Viki's encounter with Mitch suggests that what makes a woman's life problematic is not the tyranny of men, but the more potent internalization of the role men have defined for her: her identification with the glamorized but demeaned object. Masculine aggression is only as strong as a woman allows it to be. Viki's major adversary is neither Mitch nor Maria, the Medusan revenant who threatens Clint and is actually trying to kill Viki; it is the angry, dispossessed fragment in herself, Niki Smith. When Niki first reveals her presence on the starship, she seems to be one obstacle that Viki will never surmount. But there is a dramatic turn as Viki and Niki speak to each other: both agree on Niki's place as a part of Viki that has become fragmented and needs to be reintegrated. In Viki's interiority, the problem of the man-created woman is resolved, and she and Niki bid an affectionate farewell to each other.

Viki then receives permission to return to linear time from a male authority on the starship, an event that would seem to reabsorb her back into a patriarchal historical order; the role of the "permission," however, is ambiguous. Like Persephone, Viki seems to have done the job on her own, with the male authority serving only as a witness. Viki's ambiguous relationship to male agency is emphasized in her last farewell, to Joe, before she leaves for the hospital to return to her body trapped in linear time. Vergil is initially banished from Viki's final scene of reconciliation—an erotically charged farewell dance with Joe to Nat "King" Cole's "Stardust Memories"—despite his plea that this is the part he "wanted to see the most." As Viki and Joe dance, however, Vergil rematerializes and stares intently at them, reflecting a most intense form of, yes, pity and fear (figs. 47–50). Viki's special relationship to her past is cathartic for this representative from linear time.

This arc of Viki's story effectively casts doubt on the popularly accepted theory of the unified ego. Here, the continuous co-presence of the selves she has been at different times in her life is beneficial, not a sign of disturbance. This is a revised version of Viki's old story of division. When the division is enforced by her father, it is debilitating. Yet when Viki moves by her own desire among her many selves, she liberates herself from the power of the Oedipal dyad (the old domination by her father). This freedom of movement outside of time also, paradoxically, allows her a more flexible existence in linear time. She is her own woman. Her connection to, yet freedom from, her father and Joe represents the fulfillment of a desire that is totally alien to Vergil. Viki's ability to achieve a feminine identity by moving in and out of a world made by men is emphasized by her scenes with her dead mother, the only one of her starship encounters that she promises to renew "at some unspecified date."

Indeed, the issue of the relationship between linear history and a feminine perspective receives further definition when Viki returns to ordinary life. Ostensibly she comes back in order to keep Maria from turning off the respirator and killing her. Yet when Viki does break into "real" time, she finds that Maria has already stopped herself. At the last moment, Maria, Hollywood's supposedly uncanny, unstoppable threat from the past, goes against the grain of her own stereotype by coming to the realization that it is crazy to kill for love. Knowing more than Maria, however, the spectator understands that Viki's pilgrimage to her starship has in fact influenced Maria's decision.

Figs. 47, 48, 49, and 50. *One Life to Live*. Vergil (John Fiedler) watches Viki and Joe (Lee Patterson) dance on Viki's starship: the masculine representative of history experiences pity and fear.

Through the eloquence of her body, Viki forms a nexus between the linear and the nonlinear, the temporal and the atemporal. As such, she reverses the usual historical priorities. The fading of Mitch suggests the illusory nature of Oedipal recourse to power and repression, and the efficacy of mediating multiple perspectives. Viki's regressive mistaking of Tom for Joe is ended not by repression, but by synthesizing the eroticism she shared with Joe into her present. Without denying her relationship with Clint, she can now also affirm Joe and make a clear distinction between Joe and his brother, Tom. After that, Tom no longer holds her captive to a fantasy, nor does he pose any threat to her marriage. When Viki arrives at her new synthesis, Maria arrives at a new perspective too. In this context, Maria's initial appearance of implacability dissipates in such pointed juxtaposition to Viki's act of mediation between history and her interior time and space that a connection, whether conscious or unconscious, seems inevitable.

The evocation of history, subject, and time in this narrative was daring, particularly in their evocation through flashback and its aesthetic companion, montage. The starship events were not in flashback, of course, for although they involved characters from previous stories, they were not presented from old tapes. Indeed, transformed by setting, situation, and extraordinary costume, the recollected characters were all fantastic transformations of once-familiar images. Flashback and montage were used only on the last day of the starship fantasy, as a reprise of the events that had taken place on that privileged ship during Viki's return to consciousness. This narrative technique brilliantly marked Viki's transition back into linear history. In sophisticated use of flashback, as Gilles Deleuze has pointed out, we witness the birth of memory: "Memory could never evoke and report the past if it had not already been constituted at the moment when past was still present. . . . It is in the present that we make a memory, in order to make use of it in the future when the present will be past."[16] On the starship, the flashback montage reveals the point at which the presentness of that experience is being transformed into memory. Viki's return to linearity thus positions her own form of history in active coexistence with that of the larger patriarchal order.

The bold resolution of Viki's and Clint's relationships with their past lives through Viki's vision is a landmark use of history in soap opera narrative. The euphoria in the *One Life to Live* text affords solace and consolation. It imagines for its heroine a lost chivalric hero (Joe), whose delight in her power is recovered. It imagines the reformation of Hollywood's uncanny woman by integrating Maria peacefully into the present instead of repressing her back into the past. It imagines the mediation of history's nightmare by the feminine dream. This euphoria makes *One Life to Live* remarkable for its imaginative boldness, but it also mars the triumph of its heroine's agency by portraying it with improbable ease. Because of *One Life*'s simplistic solutions to the tangled problems created by gender conflicts, the writers were forced to resort to bombastic melodrama in some of Viki's crucial speeches, thus undercutting the show's effectiveness by moments of inadvertent self-parody. For a less starry-eyed, more incisive soap opera exploration of time, identity, and the linear history of the fathers of culture, we must look to *Santa Barbara*.

Santa Barbara, in its formative period, was brought to life by a community of writers, actors, directors, and producers who hoped to challenge the limits of soap opera structure. The show provides consolations less intoxicating than *One Life to Live*, but ultimately more reassuring, because more leavened by comedy; but it still incorporates anger, doubt, intractability, and complexity into the resolution of problems. *Santa Barbara* has on numerous occasions explored the human condition by taking its characters out of the linear space/time frame, notably in retellings of Dickens's *A Christmas Carol* (starring Mason as the *Santa Barbara* version of Scrooge), of Capra's *It's a Wonderful Life* (starring Cruz in the Jimmy Stewart role), and of the New Testament Christmas story (implying that Eden's baby is a kind of holy child). The series has also sent Mason to a heaven decorated with the NBC peacock and chaired by a network executive—spoken of as God in the script, and played by an actual NBC executive. *Santa Barbara*'s most original and challenging transformation of time and space, however, occurred in episode #1234, written by Patrick Mulcahey, which aired on June 20, 1989. In that episode, Greg Hughes (Paul Johansson), the illegitimate young son of C. C. Capwell (Jed Allen), deals with the new knowledge of the identity of his father, re-creating himself in order to accept that bond without cutting himself off from his mother. *Santa Barbara* #1234 offered the possibility of a hard-won "heritage of the mothers," a process by which identity is achieved in an Oedipal minefield by a traditional male subject through an integration, rather than a repression, of the feminine wild zone.[17]

Greg has grown up believing that his father died when he, Greg, was an infant. Now Greg's mother, Megan Richardson (Meg Bennett), facing death from a blood disease, regrets her lie, one that covered her shame at conceiving Greg during a brief affair with C. C. Capwell, a man she hardly knew. She wishes to restore Greg's father to him before she dies. Greg, however, can only view his father and his father's family as aliens; he clings to his mother, and rages against acknowledging the reality of C. C.'s paternity.

Greg's situation provides a wonderful example of soap opera's refusal to dignify domination, whether it be by father or by mother, since this story offers the spectator a boy whose mother has in fact spared him from an overbearing, tyrannous father. The task here is somehow to acknowledge the hard facts of reality without losing self. Greg's resistance leads him into a fantasy outside the parameters of paternal space and time; in the end, though, it also brings him back, at peace with the reality of his father's power but without having lost the heritage of his mother.

In the preceding show, *Santa Barbara* #1233, Greg has sought

Fig. 51. *Santa Barbara* (#1234). The Capwell Zone, Masone (Lane Davies) and Julieight (Nancy Grahn): familiar yet strange.

release from his anger at being presented with C. C. Capwell as his father by taking a surfboard out into an unsafe sea; at the end of the show he is dragged back to shore unconscious. That segment shows Greg within linear time, metaphorically acting out his feeling of being stuck between his father's house and the dangers of the (maternal) ocean. Episode #1234, which unfolds in Greg's interior time and space, allows Greg and the audience to see that it is only within the monolithic logic of linear history that his sole alternative to entering the historical time of the father is death in the chaos of the mother. Indeed, the alternate perspective in Greg's interior space presents Greg's decision as the anatomy of the choice that everyone makes in some way. While Greg is "unconscious," or in the body, he is granted a reprieve from the seeming tyranny of linear time in a temporary, fantastic hiatus. Greg's story presents a male subject with an atypical historical significance. The male place in history has conventionally been guaranteed by male bonding. Here, in contrast, Greg finds his historical meaning by moving beyond the implications of the language and logic of the father. In fantasy he finds that which complements the domain of the father, and this produces a sense of wholeness and choice.

At the beginning of the fantasy, Greg seems to wake up under a star-covered sky, confronted by automaton likenesses of Mason (Lane Davies) and Julia (Nancy Grahn) wearing metallic jumpsuits and speaking in mechanical voices. Visually, the world Greg confronts is both familiar and strange. Mason and Julia are present, but in a new form, with fantastic physical features, strange expressions, and futuristic garb (fig. 51). Greg is set in a context where walls disappear and doors present themselves at unnatural angles (fig. 52). These defamiliarizations recon-

Fig. 52. *Santa Barbara* (#1234).
The Capwell Zone, Masone,
Julieight, and Gregorthree (Paul
Johannsson): a dreamscape opens
new perceptual possibilities.

struct the scene as a timeless place where, as they tell him, Greg "is what
he didn't know he was, and will see what he didn't know he sees." Mason
and Julia, as *Santa Barbara*'s two focuses of resistance to the order of the
father, are Greg's guides through this vision. The force of their journey
with him is that the co-presence of another perspective ("what we
become in sleep and silence") makes wholeness possible within the
constraints of linear history. They are there to speak of the synthesis of
logic and disruption that creates for us a fully human life. They tell him
of a question he must answer—"Do you consent?"—while admitting
that they know of no words that will clarify what he must consent to. As
the vision unfolds, we find that Greg is in a place where he will learn to
consent to the power of the father by understanding his mother—and all
women—as human beings with separate needs from his.

Everything in Greg's strange dream world is and is not a reflection of
Greg's ordinary life. The familiar yet strange-looking Mason calls himself Masone (Mase-one), and Julia is introduced as Julieight (Julie-
eight). They tell Greg he is Gregorthree. The Capwell family, Greg's
mother, Megan, and his girlfriend, Emily, at first appear to him in
metallic jumpsuits with reptilian tails, surrounding him like the living
dead to enclose him in their family circle. Unlike the site of nonlinear
historical perspective that was Viki's starship, the "Capwell Zone" is not
a "clean well-lighted place." Instead, it is a jumble of juxtapositions—
some deformed versions of the ordinary reality Greg knows, some true
fantasy limbos. Here, interiority will shed light, but it is no bright,
reassuring enclave.

As Greg's voyage progresses, the alien appearance of those whose
claims to intimacy at first terrify him eventually takes on an increasingly

human aspect. Different vignettes make Greg understand these claims in a new, bearable way, because he ceases to perceive intimacy in terms of a maternal that is all-enveloping, indistinguishable from the baby's ego. At the same time, a fragmentary symbolic narration of Mason's life in real time warns Greg against the other extreme: absolute division from the maternal.

Mason's disastrous life is relentlessly told in linear historical discourse that, in Greg's vision, is defined in terms of Mason's destabilizing rejection of feminine subjecthood. Julieight and Masone show Greg a scene between Mason and Julia (in their ordinary appearance) in which Mason rejects closeness with Julia, calling it an albatross around his neck. Julia struggles with her sense that this is what "boys" are like, and wonders what it will take to make Mason comfortable with belonging with the people who love him. But Julieight, Julia's nonlinear historical cognate, knows that this is not the only way for a boy to develop. Masone disappears, and it is Julieight alone who performs the task Dorothy Dinnerstein, in *The Mermaid and the Minotaur*, proposes as the historical project of feminine consciousness: to acknowledge the limitations of conventional gender arrangements by understanding the isolation and degeneracy involved in Oedipal rejection of the claims of intimacy.[18] Julieight shows Greg a linear projection of Mason, twenty years in the future, if his present attitude persists. In this projection, Mason returns home after a disappearance, a pariah accused of socially irresponsible business practices, partly able to verbalize his repressed yearning for Julia and his children but unable to find his way back to them. Then Julieight leaves Greg to watch alone, finding it too painful to witness Mason, an old, homeless drunk with no memory of love, uncomprehendingly rejecting photos of his grandchildren proffered to him by his brother. In the same way that Viki's Vergil represents patriarchal trauma at viewing the feminine historical perspective, so for Julieight the trauma of linear inevitability is unbearable—even though she herself points out to Greg that, because it is a linear projection, the vision of Mason's future is not inevitable. To Greg's question of whether Mason is doomed to this future, she replies, in iambic meter, "Each motion changes every moment. / You saw a future plotted straight, direct. / Such calculations are seldom correct." Greg, in other words, must learn to maintain a critical distance from linear narrative, thus placing limits on his necessary submission to the linear logic of the father.

"The Capwell Zone" is a brief narrative-within-a-narrative about a

Fig. 53. *Santa Barbara* (#1234). The Capwell Zone: Julieight's third eye.

privileged sort of awareness and perception. Relationships and structures of reality that are repressed by linearity are visible in the Zone. The organ of recovery is symbolized as the third eye that both Masone and Julieight can open in the middle of their foreheads—"like putting on reading glasses," Masone tells Greg (fig. 53). Another of Mulcahey's charming inventions to evoke the co-presence of the maternal and the paternal is Julieight's use of the number-names, which imbues numbers with emotional as well as abstract meaning and thus establishes a paradoxical harmony between individuation and empathy. The number-names chart the course of development, and change as the individual changes. Significantly, the numbers do not change in a linear fashion: for a man (whose names are formed with odd numbers), advancing toward the number one—signaling individuation—may be the desired direction at early stages of development, but later on higher numbers are desirable; that is, individuation should serve as the foundation of empathy, not as a goal in itself. As she guides Greg in his development, Julieight reveals that she seeks to inspire in Masone greater empathy and has applied, without Masone's knowledge, for a revision of his status to Maseven. Other men of that status, she informs Greg, include Irving Berlin and Bishop Tutu: not conquerors, but creators and nurturers, are the historical role models. The women's even numbers inscribe a separate structure for the feminine difference, one that implies individuation and empathy—in women a given condition requiring no evolution. There is a limit to what can be done in a one-hour episode, of course, and the significance of the feminine numbers is not established in the script. However, Juli*eight*'s status seems to include an a priori combination of

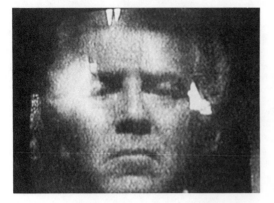

Fig. 54. *Santa Barbara* (#1234). The Capwell Zone: dealing with paternal hegemony, the head of C. C. Capwell (Jed Allan) superimposed over a questioning Greg.

separation and filiation. If in linear history masculine priorities of power and individuation establish the norm of human development, here human development is evaluated through its ability to use power in combination with the feminine traits of empathy and intimacy.

As in Viki's starship, Greg's Capwell Zone is an altered perspective that cooperates with, but does not supplant, the linear perspective of history. When Greg, at the end of the vision, cries out that there is only one answer, we are not told what that answer is, but abruptly the grim, superimposed face of the patriarch, C. C. Capwell, fills the screen (fig. 54). The world of the father must be accepted.

Not at all euphoric, this historical perspective is voiced through Julieight, who knows of the possible catastrophe that linear discourse can invoke, but who also knows that that catastrophe is not inevitable—if the larger, nonlinear perspective is co-present. Faith in the reality of discontinuity and disruption makes bearable the necessary patriarchal illusion of linear calculations, which, no matter how predestined they seem, "are seldom correct." Julieight's knowledge constitutes a consolation for the necessary acceptance of the father. The threat to intimacy, difference, and filiation by the historical discourse of patriarchal power structures is not understated, but it is not invincible either. Possibilities are and are not foreclosed by it.

Not popular enough—if the ratings are an accurate measure—to gain network carte blanche for its highly original use of the soap opera form, this show was vulnerable to decisions calculated to enlarge the viewership. In the end, however, all that happened was that *Santa Barbara*'s spirit was effectively killed. Still, for a number of years, this show served as the imaginative vanguard of the form.

Conclusion

Soap opera is written by bad writers and by good writers. It is performed by intelligent, compelling actors and by trite, insipid actors. It is produced and directed by people of great vision who are sensitive to the medium and by desperate hacks whose sole purpose is to get an image on the screen every day. These are the accidents of all dramatic forms. Basic to the identity of soap opera, however, is its existence as a narrative without end. Soap opera's resistance to closure implies a resistance to mainstream veneration of physical prowess, social skills, and power-driven institutions that result in control and domination. Regardless of whether it is broadcast on radio or television, regardless of whether the daily episode is fifteen minutes, a half-hour, or an hour, daytime serial requires a transformation—or at least a reinterpretation—of the erotics of domination. Beyond this, soap opera is a narrative that reclaims all forms of Otherness. The keys to this recovery are the multiplot structure of soap opera, the long duration of an individual series, and the conscious intentions of the writers in using the multiplots. The narrative fact that soap opera does not privilege any one hero or heroine's perspective opens opportunities for all perspectives—of man or woman, adult or child, black, Jew, or homosexual, rich or poor. A character can be positioned marginally at one point in the narrative and be moved to the center of subject perception years later, or he or she can be moved out of linear time entirely, and thus allowed to see how he or she is dominated by historical realities—the fantasy glance, creating a freedom from, but cooperation with, ordinary cultural hierarchy.

In the *New York Times*, Ken Burns, director of the television miniseries "The Civil War," is quoted as seeing a Homeric, epic potential in television. By this he means that the postponement of closure in the miniseries allows time to give historical significance to those normally excluded from historical accounts—the "spear carriers," as he calls them.[19] How much truer this potential is in the "macroseries" form known as soap opera has been suggested by the examples in this chapter.

British television, too, has demonstrated a sustained and intentional approach to historicity in the soap opera *Eastenders*, named for a section of London that stands for social marginality. In fact, the entire reason for the series' existence is to deal with a pluralistic community representing different races, ethnicities, classes, religions, and sexual orientations. The difference between *Eastenders* and American soap opera is that the creators of the English show know the discourse of the medium in which they work, and have made it a respected creative vehicle. The American media, where soap opera was born, have yet to end their self-destructive insistence on demeaning this flexible and potent narrative form. Such small-mindedness has caused us to be culturally obtuse, unable to differentiate between the better and the worse in the soap opera community. Blanket contempt for soap opera has deprived a large number of very talented artists of the recognition they deserve; it has perpetuated an attitude toward the form calculated to demoralize those who make it work and empower the callow and the cynical—in short, to become a self-fulfilling prophecy.

Rich in qualitative power, the boldly conceived *Santa Barbara* has on occasion after occasion celebrated what the form, at its best, can do, and it has reflected on its own differentness—an alterity I have identified as feminine narrative in the tradition of the ancient Persephone story. On *Santa Barbara* #1234, Masone tells Greg, "You have sustained the shock every human child must endure, the shock of finding you have never been who you were told you were." If this is the discovery that both Persephone and Oedipus make, the puzzle of identity is soon named in non-Oedipal terms when to this Julieight adds the great hope and consolation of the soap opera form: "My father had a child that had my name, but it was not me. Do not be deceived by the Cleavers, the Waltons, the Huxtables, Jim, Margaret, Princess, Kitten, and Bud. Only infants are born; men and women are decided, and in between you belong to no one."

Julieight mocks the historical discourse of the fathers in other forms of screen fiction, a discourse that she finds silly and reductive. Here the visionary form of Julia, even in her ordinary guise one of the brightest creations television has to offer, speaks for the discourse that is soap opera, for soap opera's recovery of a possible subjecthood for marginalized humanity—for woman, cultural Other, and the repressed part of the conventionally conditioned masculine subject. She places us all both in and beyond the paternal name.

Epilogue: What Is Normal?

In the preceding pages, I have discussed soap opera as a legitimate discourse: one that has its own truth, its own beauty, and its own inner logic of self-preservation. I have explored this discourse as a way of making meaning though a feminine syntax. As the Hollywood film tends toward a masculine narrative because its syntax is dictated by the aesthetics of closure, soap opera tends toward a feminine story because its syntax is dictated by the resistance to closure.

From this it follows that soap opera is valuable as a site from which we may gain perspective on the true and the beautiful as gendered constructs. Truth in the Hollywood film is the truth of linearity, the truth of mastery and control. Truth is domination: Rhett Butler carrying Scarlet O'Hara up the stairs. Truth is singular: the chaotic feminine multiple perspectives of the Hall of Mirrors in *The Lady from Shanghai* resolving to the pristine monocular vision of the hero. Truth is Oedipal: Superman's either/or choice in *Superman II* between emotional fulfillment with Lois Lane on the one hand and the continued strength and viability of the United States of America on the other. These narratives reflect what is normally accepted as truth. In contrast with that of soap opera, however, Hollywood's truth is a reductive form of normality.

In soap opera, truth is the multiple-perspective reality of the unclosed line, of mutuality and intimacy. In soap opera there are *truths*. If Shane understands Kimberly as an object of desire, Kimberly needs to deal with her assumptions about male appropriation of her body (*Days of Our Lives*). In soap opera, masculinity is as problematic as femininity. If Julia cannot adopt her mother's model of behavior, she must also struggle with the eerie blind spots in male patterns of identity (*Santa Barbara*). In soap opera, the choices offered within the constraints of linear history are insufficient: Viki must make her star voyage of discovery and reconciliation (*One Life to Live*).

Beauty in conventional screen fiction also establishes an exclusive norm. Hollywood reduces beauty to mastery. Beauty in Hollywood is Alfred Hitchcock's elegant crane shots giving the spectator ocular possession of a situation. It is the aesthetics of violence in the western, the war story, the detective story. It is the erotic possession of the glamorous woman by the camera eye, which acts as a surrogate for the controlling hero.

Beauty in soap opera is the beauty of dialogue, mutuality, and connection. It is the aesthetics of intimacy in the family story, the couple story, the story of a community network. It is director Michael Gliona's elegant invention of the rhythmic, simultaneous appearance of the hero and heroine on the two sides of an empty frame (*Santa Barbara*). It is the evolution of the focus throw or rack focus (the use of focus to delineate the relationship between two planes of the frame) as a means of emotional storytelling.[1] It is the pointillist technique of multiple cross-cut close-up shots of two characters in a conversation to create the visual texture of their emotional interchange.

As a form with its own truth and beauty, soap opera widens the concept of normality and opens up new and important options. For that alone, it should be accorded respect. It should be valued for its difference from closure-bound screen fictions, and therefore evaluated differently. Academicians who refer to it as a mock-Aristotelian form, and network executives who impose on the creative community of soap opera a conventional understanding of visual and dramatic storytelling all miss the point of the soap opera form. Critical assessments that promote better soap operas and better understanding of them must begin with an attempt to understand the implications for storytelling of a screen narrative without absolute closure.

There was no useful commentary on the soap opera form until Tania Modleski noted that resistance to closure was the central fact of daytime structure.[2] It was on that basis that she—and those who read her, myself included—began to make any real sense of what the daytime serial audience was watching and what the daytime serial community was producing. In the industry itself, only those executive producers with a sensitivity to the nonlinear nature of their narratives produce television that takes full advantage of the possibilities of the medium. Since there is, at present, no public discourse in mass culture about nonlinear narrative, each successful producer has created his or her own terminology for discussing soap opera; each in his or her own fashion has found a practical way to deal with the truths (and beauty) of a narrative form with a deemphasized linear axis of combination.

Gloria Monty energized *General Hospital* with her plan to "pick up the pace" of the show. Industry myth has it that she threatened to put her cast and crew all on skates if that was what it took to make the show snappier. No one can call this a theoretical statement on a narrative without closure. In practice, however, Monty's approach meant a greater number of shorter scenes in the daily episode. Without any attention to the theoretical ramifications of her actions, Monty had pulled soap opera away from the linearity of the long scene. She thought she was making the genre more "cinematic," but the use of quick cuts reminiscent of those used in film editing produced instead an aesthetic effect specific to the endless narrative and the normalization of the gap—the basic features of the soap opera form.

Al Rabin's successful leadership on *Days of Our Lives* grows out of a superficially different sense of what is important to soap opera, but one that has in common with Monty's an understanding that taps into the special strengths of the endless form. For Rabin, the crux of the soap opera genre is the emotional bonding it creates between character and spectator. The characters may lie to each other, he says, but never will they lie to the viewer.[3] It is the norm on *Days* that everything—story line, camera work, costumes, sets—is subordinated to the viewer's emotional rapport with the character. Different on the surface from Monty's emphasis on pace, Rabin's priority on emotional truth shares Monty's intuition about the need for a nonlinear approach for a distinctive, and compelling, use of the form.

More different still to the casual eye is the *Santa Barbara* approach. From the beginning, this show was driven by the desire to take soap opera "as far as it can go," in the words of Jill Farren Phelps, executive producer from 1985 until 1990.[4] Bridget and Jerry Dobson's goal in creating the show in the first place was to tell the truth about the rivalry between father and son. Toward that end, the Dobsons created the tortuous love-hate relationship between Mason Capwell and his father, C. C., to correct what they saw as general soap opera sentimentality about the family relationship.[5]

The Dobsons, like all soap opera originators, have had uneven access to control over their creation. Nevertheless, they gave the show a solid and consistent core in which the role of the father's power is openly interrogated. This questioning has kept the show closer to the non-Oedipal, nonclosed narrative of daytime serial than other soap operas. Even *One Life to Live*, *General Hospital*, and *Days of Our Lives*, all of which have found superior ways of tapping into the discourse of soap opera, indulge to a certain extent in conventional pieties about fathers. On the margins of *Days of Our Lives*, for example, are the narratively inert good old daddies, primarily Tom Horton (McDonald Carey) and Shawn Brady (Frank Parker), men who maintain masculine stereotypes. Brought to life only on the rare occasions when they enter the heroine's quest or become temporarily problematic, they are otherwise much like furniture. *Santa Barbara*'s continued commitment to tough resistance against conventional images of father-son bonding, in contrast, has kept Oedipal sentimentality impressively low.

The Dobsons' insistence on the problematic father committed them to a male point of view: Mason's. However, the formal propensities of soap opera built the original Dobson impulse into a narrative that, at its best, burst through the limitations of that original conception. As the show developed, the problem of C. C. Capwell showed itself to be most exciting in fostering the development of the female characters, notably Julia, Eden, and Gina—women who must pursue their desires in opposition to a hierarchy dominated by C. C. The evolution of the Capwell context into a wonderful place for soap opera narrative to unfold can be credited to the vision of Jill Farren Phelps, who gave the Capwells a brilliant, humorous spin during her tenure as executive producer. Phelps was receptive to the inclusion in the daily episode of disruptive humor and direct address to the camera. Similarly, under her influence *Santa Barbara* further defined its style by interrupting its ongoing narratives with shows that, though related, were complete in themselves, as, for example, the "Capwell Zone" episode discussed in chapter 5.[6] In that show, Greg's fantasy was not in the minds of the main protagonists, a quirky choice that only complemented the disruption of linearity and monocular focus that is a natural part of the soap opera form.

Neither the Dobsons, nor Jill Farren Phelps, nor the writers who form the collective unconscious of *Santa Barbara* articulate their goals for the show in terms even vaguely related to the psychology I have discussed in this book. Yet they have a doubly nonlinear orientation that has put this show, as they have conceived it, on the cutting edge of soap opera. *Santa Barbara*'s excitement, that is, derives from a two-pronged approach to narrative that energizes the structure of the daytime serial discourse: it foregrounds the pain of the Oedipal wars, and it further disrupts its own already-hyphenated stories by laughing at conventional pieties.

People who do good work with soap opera know it to be a medium with characteristics all its own. At times, they are proud of themselves; more often they are harried and frantic. All too frequently the use they make of their creative energy seems to grind them down more than it buoys them up, even in periods that I have identified as imaginatively productive. Most soap opera professionals would chalk up the wear and tear to the enormous difficulties of putting on a one-hour television show every day of the week, but I wonder if lack of discussion about the value of the form is not more burdensome. The more I talk with the people who make soap operas and the more I write, the more I have been forced to reflect on the "default factor" in what happens in soap opera. It seems impossible to imagine soap opera without the influence of random elements, those wonderful developments that burst into life under the pressure of daily production. And yet, it seems equally impossible to imagine a thriving future for soap opera unless there is more conscious experimentation and discovery about the form than at present. Although the interchangeability of the daytime serials is a virtual commonplace, there are in fact stunning differences among the shows, many more than I have been able to deal with in this study. Lack of a discourse with which to articulate the distinctions cannot be productive for either creativity or spectatorship. Similarly, not all soap operas are equally admirable, nor are all admirable soap operas consistently imaginative or effective in their uses of the form. It is unfortunate that, aside from the acknowledgment of what commands a large audience, there are almost no effective criteria for judging excellence in soap opera.

A small number of highly rated daytime serials, most notably *The Young and the Restless* and *The Bold and the Beautiful*, embody a sadomasochistic resistance to the gender of the soap opera narrative that urgently merits attention. In *The Young and the Restless*, the odd combination of mawkishness and ruthlessness in its central father, John Abbott, making him an odd conflation of the "marmee" of *Little Women* and Genghis Khan, empowers feminine values while disenfranchising the female characters on the show. The operation of John Abbott and other such creations, wherever they occur in soap opera, cry out for exploration. For both practical and theoretical purposes, it is insufficient to note simply that the show is popular.

My study is not encyclopedic enough in its detailing of soap opera particulars to generate full clarity about artistic standards of quality relevant to its unusual narrative style. This study is, by design, another in a series of attempts—begun by Tania Modleski and Robert Clyde Allen—to recontextualize the discussion of soap opera. At the moment, an encyclopedic work that would help to make the poetics of soap opera a vivid part of public discourse is not possible. Present assumptions about the value of soap opera (or lack thereof) inhibits access to materials for serious critics of the soap opera form. No one who reads this book, for example, can easily refer back to most of the episodes I discuss above. No library houses a respectable number of aural and videotapes of soap operas. Old movies and early television shows by the score are available for purchase by the consumer in videotape format; among television soap operas, however, only *Dark Shadows* is easy to find. The Museum of Broadcasting, my best source outside my own collection, has no more than a dozen radio tapes and a dozen videotapes in its collection. Some soap opera scripts have been published, but by no means are enough available for a really exhaustive analysis of the form. My sources have been largely my personal collection of tapes, those of friends and helpful industry professionals, and the materials collected in the Irna Phillips Papers at the State Historical Society of Wisconsin at Madison.

The only real counterforce to the oppressiveness of the commercial television emphasis on ratings and income from sponsors is knowledge. The quality of a form is most easily imagined by its practitioners and its audience through knowledge of and respect for the history of the form: what it has been and how it has grown. The notion of quality that has brought distinguished programming to cable television and PBS stations will not be provided by the many soap opera fanzines that have sprung up. These are an inferior means of filling the steadily rising need of the soap opera fan to know more about what he or she loves; they are too intimately tied to the discourse of commercial television, which defines a "better" show as one with a ratings share that will increase station revenue. This definition has tyrannized the daytime serial to such an extent that most people in and out of the industry confuse network political pressures with soap opera's identity as a form.

The ambiguous situation of soap opera is not to be dismissed. We must ponder the strength of desire in creators and spectators that has caused a narrative with a feminine structure to survive in a male-dominated society. We must question the "normal" discourse that has obscured the legitimacy of that desire and denied it social recognition. That denial is neither as big as a barn nor as deep as a well, but it has served efficiently to foreclose intellectual curiosity about soap opera. Normal discussion of the daytime serial genre has been largely relegated to the province of gossip. Normal acknowledgment of daytime achievement has been largely reduced to the banalities of the popularity contest. Is there a kind of civilized villainy at work in normal attitudes to soap opera? I contend that there is. In this area, as in so many, the white picket fence of ordinary received opinion conceals the dark, unexamined panic about gender difference.

Notes

Prologue

1. William Outhwaite, "Hans-Georg Gadamer," in *The Return of the Grand Theory in the Human Sciences*, ed. Quentin Skinner (Cambridge: Cambridge University Press, 1985), 30.

2. See, for example, Tania Modleski's *Loving With a Vengence: Mass-produced Fantasies for Women* (New York: Methuen, 1984) and *The Women Who Knew Too Much: Hitchcock and Feminist Theory* (New York: Methuen, 1988); and Mary Ann Doane's *The Desire to Desire* (Bloomington: Indiana University Press, 1987).

3. For an example of such reactionary theorizing, see Camille Paglia, *Sexual Personae: Art and Decadence from Nefertiti to Emily Dickinson* (New Haven: Yale University Press, 1990).

4. Susan Bordo, "Feminism, Postmodernism, and Gender-Scepticism," in *Feminism/Postmodernism*, ed. Linda Nicholson (New York: Routledge, 1990), 139.

5. Diana Fuss, *Essentially Speaking: Feminism, Nature, and Difference* (New York: Routledge, 1989).

6. Mark Philp, "Michel Foucault," in Skinner (ed.), *Return of the Grand Theory*, 69.

7. See, for example, Nancy Chodorow, *The Reproduction of Mothering: Psychoanalysis and the Sociology of Gender* (Berkeley and Los Angeles: University of California Press, 1979); Carol Gilligan, *In a Different Voice* (Cambridge, Mass.: Harvard University Press, 1982); Mary Field Belenky et al., *Women's Ways of Knowing: The Development of Self, Voice, and Mind* (New York: Basic Books, 1986); and Mary Daly, *Beyond God the Father: Toward a Philosophy of Women's Liberation* (Boston: Beacon Press, 1985).

8. Jackie Byars, *All That Hollywood Allows: Re-reading Gender in 1950s Melodrama* (Chapel Hill: University of North Carolina Press, 1991), 4.

9. Terry Lester, Interview, June 28, 1990.

10. Nancy Grahn, Interview, July 26, 1990.

11. Interviews with Anne Schoettle, November 18, 1989; and Charles Shaughnessy, July 26, 1990.

12. Irna Phillips Papers, State Historical Society of Wisconsin, Madison.

Chapter 1

1. Robert Clyde Allen, *Speaking of Soap Operas* (Chapel Hill: University of North Carolina Press, 1985), 108, 110–11.

2. Ibid., 114.

3. A sample text of *The Guiding Light* demonstrates rather poor skill with dialogue but makes my point that Phillips's real work as a soap opera writer had nothing to do with selling soap. This excerpt from a late-thirties script (reprinted in Robert LaGuardia's *Soap World* [n.p.: Priam Books, 1983], 211–12) demonstrates a sharp division between pressure on the audience to buy a product and the appeal of the dramatic situation:

ORGAN MUSIC

ANNOUNCER

The Guiding Light
MORE ORGAN MUSIC

ANNOUNCER

Well, friends, here's wonderful news for you—

WOMAN

Just a minute. If you say one more word about all those people who won all that money in your contest I'll just . . .

ANNOUNCER

Now don't worry . . . here's good news for you. Starting today, another big P & G Soap contest gets underway. . . . Now remember, just add twenty-five words or less to the statement "I like P & G because . . ." . . . Entries judged for sincerity, originality, and aptness of thought. Judges' decision final.
MORE ORGAN MUSIC

ANNOUNCER

And now . . . *The Guiding Light* . . . (announcer softens voice) There are times in our lives when we seem to have lost all sense of direction, all sense of identity, when we as individuals seem suspended in mid air . . . when living seems hopeless, without objective. It was an apathetic, listless young woman who returned to her apartment in San Francisco this morning. . . . Martin Kane, sensitive to the mood of the young woman, suggested that they go to a quiet restaurant. . . . Seated across the table from the girl whom he hopes someday to marry, he suddenly loses patience with her apparent disinterest in him, and says—

MARTIN

Snap out of it, Mona.

MONA

Is there anything to snap out of, Martin?

MARTIN

It seems to me there is . . . look here, you're not being very fair.

MONA

You don't think so?

MARTIN

No, I don't.

While the single announcer provides a link between sponsor and dramatic text, the alteration in tone and discourse signals a clear distinction between the two.

4. "Who Is Kitty Foyle?" Irna Phillips Papers, State Historical Society of Wisconsin, Madison, Box 4. Ellipses in original.

5. LaGuardia, *Soap World*, 34.

6. Agnes Nixon, Interview, September 22, 1989.

7. Anti-essentialist critics will almost certainly object to this assessment, arguing that, in maintaining universal gender distinctions, soap opera opens the way to hierarchy, exclusion, and stereotyping. It is to everyone's advantage, however, to consider as objectively as possible the extent to which recovery remains possible within soap opera through structural alteration of the traditional narrative dynamics of the essentially masculine and the essentially feminine. As we will see, soap opera's essentialist text renders conventional male identity problematic for both the male and the female spectator.

8. Douglas Marland, Interview, May 10, 1989.

9. Allen, *Speaking of Soap Operas*, 21.

10. Ibid., 22.

11. Molly Haskell, *From Reverence to Rape: The Treatment of Women in the Movies* (New York: Holt, Rinehart & Winston, 1973), 154–55.

12. See, for example, Gilligan, *In a Different Voice* (Cambridge, Mass.: Harvard University Press, 1982); Jean Baker Miller, *Toward a New Psychology of Women*, 2d ed. (Boston: Beacon Press, 1986); and Belenky et al., *Women's Ways of Knowing: The Development of Self, Voice, and Mind* (New York: Basic Books, 1986).

13. See, for example, Elizabeth Spelman, *Inessential Woman: Problems of Exclusion in Feminist Thought* (Boston: Beacon Press, 1988).

14. Tania Modleski, "The Search For Tomorrow in Today's Soap Operas," *Film Quarterly* 33, no. 1 (1979): 12–21.

15 My discussion of psychoanalytic film criticism is not intended as exhaustive. Moreover, a number of psychoanalytic film critics would take issue with my references to masculinity and feminity, given their belief that gender is entirely constructed. For example, Teresa de Lauretis (*Technologies of Gender: Essays on*

Theory, Film, and Fiction [Bloomington: Indiana University Press, 1987]) and similar critics use film to dispute the assumption that there is a feminine nature.

16. Initially a disciple of Freud, Lacan is best known for his exploration of the relationship between language, desire, and the subject. His work is hence crucial to the debate about the possibility of a female subject. See his *Ecrits: A Selection*, trans. Alan Sheridan (New York: Norton, 1977). For a description of the mirror stage, see J. Laplanche and J.-B. Pontalis, *The Language of Psychoanalysis* (New York: Norton, 1973), 250–52.

17. Christian Metz, "Identification, Mirror," in *The Imaginary Signifier: Psychoanalysis and the Cinema*, trans. Celia Britton, Annwyl Williams, Ben Brewster, and Alfred Guzzetti (Bloomington: Indiana University Press, 1977), 42–58.

18. Laura Mulvey, "Visual Pleasure and Narrative Cinema," *Screen* 16, no. 3 (1975): 6–18.

19. Laura Mulvey, "Afterthoughts on 'Visual Pleasure and Narrative Cinema,' Inspired by *Duel in the Sun*," *Framework*, no. 10 (Spring 1979): 3–10.

20. De Lauretis, *Technologies of Gender*, 127, quoting Silvia Bovenschen, "Is There a Feminine Aesthetic?" trans. Beth Weckmuller, *New German Critique*, no. 10 (Winter 1977): 111–37.

21. Doane, *The Desire to Desire* (Bloomington: Indiana University Press, 1987), 78.

22. Modleski, *The Women Who Knew Too Much: Hitchcock and Feminist Theory* (New York: Methuen, 1988), 67.

23. See the introduction to Ellen G. Friedman and Miriam Fuchs, eds., *Breaking the Sequence: Women's Experimental Fiction* (Princeton: Princeton University Press, 1989).

24. For a thorough discussion, see Roman Jakobson and Morris Halle, *The Fundamentals of Language* (The Hague: Mouton, 1971).

25. Julia Kristeva, "From One Identity to Another," in *Desire in Language: A Semiotic Approach to Literature and Art* (New York: Columbia University Press, 1980), 136.

26. See, for example, Chodorow, *The Reproduction of Mothering: Psychoanalysis and the Sociology of Gender* (Berkeley and Los Angeles: University of California Press, 1979); Gilligan, *In a Different Voice*; Miller, *Toward a New Psychology of Women*. See also Irene P. Stiver, "Beyond the Oedipus Complex: Mothers and Daughters," *Work in Progress* 26 (Wellesley, Mass.: Stone Center of Developmental Services and Studies, Wellesley College, 1986); Judith V. Jordan, "Clarity in Connection: Empathic Knowing, Desire, and Sexuality," in *Work in Progress* 29 (1987); Janet Surrey, "Self-in-Relation: A Theory of Women's Development," in *Work in Progress* 13 (1985); and Alexandra Kaplan, "Dichotomous Thought and Relational Processes in Psychotherapy," *Stone Center Colloquium Series*, Wellesley, Mass., March 1987.

27. In *Power: The Inner Experience* (New York: Irvington, 1975) David McClelland mentions the Persephone myth as exemplifying the feminine attitude toward power, while Carol Gilligan remarks on the myth's recognition of the importance of connection in the life of human beings. Luce Irigaray, however, sees in it only modified feminine subjectivity. Irigaray, who credits a version

of the story in which Persephone loses her voice, emphasizes that on her return from Hades Persephone has been further stripped of self-determination by having had her name changed from Kore to Persephone. (Irigaray's reading of the myth is cited in Elaine Hoffman Baruch and Lucienne J. Serrano, *Women Analyze Women: In France, England, and the United States* [New York: NYU Press, 1988], 157, 186–87.)

Some readers may wonder whether the myth of Persephone qualifies as anything more than a fanciful allusion, whether it can bear the weight of my claim regarding its centrality to the issue of human development. Nonetheless, my claim is borne out in the story's principal source, the Homeric *Hymn to Demeter* (*The Homeric Hymns*, trans. Thelma Sargent [New York: Norton, 1975], 2–15). In the hymn, Persephone is abducted by Hades, the lord of the underworld, while she is picking narcissus in a field at some distance from her companions. When Demeter learns that her daughter's disappearance was in fact arranged by Zeus to provide his brother with a ravishing bride, she leaves Olympus in rage and despair. After various adventures on earth she returns to Olympus, unreconciled to the loss of her daughter, and threatens to render the earth barren unless the girl is returned to her. Zeus gives in to her demand, but as Persephone is about to leave, Hades secretly asks her to eat a pomegranate. This act locks her into eternal marriage with Hades, with the result that Persephone cannot be fully restored to her mother.

Now that the stage has been set by Demeter, who has fortified her demand for the return of her daughter with a powerful threat, and by Persephone, who has complicated the situation immeasurably by eating the pomegranate, Zeus offers a compromise. Backing down from his initial, typically patriarchal, either/ or stance, he now suggests that Persephone live with Hades for one-third of the year and with her mother for the other two-thirds. The Homeric hymn makes it clear that the women have taught Zeus something about relationships and that he is only saving face by being the one to articulate the inclusiveness that Persephone and Demeter have already built into the situation. This is one of our few narratives in which women successfully reconstitute the prevailing either/or thinking of men.

No feminist will be surprised to learn that the rest of history has conspired to transform Zeus into the hero of this heroine's tale. Ovid's re-creation of the tale in his *Metamorphoses* suppresses the role of Demeter—and it is this version of the story that was passed along to modern society in *Bulfinch's Mythology*, thereby eclipsing the earlier, Homeric version. How much is at stake in this re-narration was brought home to me during a screenwriting class I was teaching at the Tisch School of the Arts. I was shocked at the vehement insistence of a group of young men that Zeus did indeed solve this dilemma. They actually banded together to shout me down when I tried to explore with them the original version of the myth in relationship to a script-in-progress.

Nevertheless, the Homeric hymn, through its description of Persephone's consumption of the sweet, delicious pomegranate, constitutes Persephone as a female agent. That is, her act of eating the fruit suggests itself as the image of *her* desire (see Gilligan, *In a Different Voice*, 23). Since the pomegranate was a symbol of marriage, the image also serves to suggest that Persephone's desire constructed her marriage, at least in part. One might also wonder why Persephone happened to wander away from the other girls, thus allowing Hades the opportunity to abduct her. If we interpret this, as I believe we can, as another indication of her desire, we have a great deal of textual evidence that her bond with Hades—if not the violence with which he attempts to define it—is partially her creation and hence as important as Demeter's demands in creating the conditions for the compromise, which Zeus merely affirms. True, in the "Hymn to Demeter" we never hear Persephone speak with her husband or discuss her feelings about him; nor does Persephone reveal to her mother anything other than a wish not to be entirely separated from her. The choice is never made in Persephone's own voice.

Neither, however, does Oedipus choose his destiny. And this did not prevent Freud from seeing in that myth a depiction of the ruin and dishonor that ensue when a son fails to exclude and distance his mother. In contrast, the story of Persephone emphasizes *in*clusion. Once we grant the heroine a right to desire and to act on her desire, she is transformed into the agent of that inclusion. Through a silent action Persephone insures her continued connection with her husband, even as she vocally affirms her connection with her mother. She is thus a fully realized female figure, who exemplifies the feminine developmental choice.

28. See especially Jean Baudrillard, "The System of Objects" and "The Masses: The Implosion of the Social in the Media," in *Selected Writings*, ed. Mark Poster (Stanford: Stanford University Press, 1988), 10–28 and 207–19; and E. Ann Kaplan, *Rocking Around the Clock: Music Television, Postmodernism, and Consumer Culture* (New York: Methuen, 1987).

29. Douglas Marland, Interview, May 10, 1989.

30. E. Ann Kaplan, "Whose Imaginary?" in *Female Spectators: Looking At Film and Television*, ed. Deirdre Pribram (New York: Routledge, 1988), 154.

Chapter 2

1. See Miller, *Toward a New Psychology of Women*, 60–74.

2. A skeptical view of realism has long been a feature of feminist film criticism. The prevalent stance, however, has been that "realism" is a bourgeois convention which prevents the presentation of a female subject by replicating in fictional form the patriarchal ideology that places woman as object. Christine Gledhill sums up this position in "Recent Developments in Feminist Film Criticism," *Quarterly Review of Film Studies* 3, no. 4 (1978): 457–93). Gledhill herself relies on Louis Althusser for her critique of realism: "the attempt to represent the social formation can produce only the natural world of the dominant ideology" (469); that is, any familiar image tends to be interpreted by the viewer through the conventional ideological grid. Only the strange image holds out the opportunity for a new mode of thinking. I think Althusser's formulation is generally true; I emphasize that soap opera fantasy is especially useful for the

production of a female subject in that it positions Oedipal resolution as a fantasy obstacle to female development.

3. Miller, *Toward a New Psychology of Women*, 61.

4. Ibid., 116.

5. Mulvey, "Visual Pleasure and Narrative Cinema," 12.

6. The terms are those of Peter Elbow; see Belenky et al., *Women's Ways of Knowing*, 104, 113. Also see Elbow's *Writing Without Teachers* (London: Oxford University Press, 1973), 173.

7. Doane, *Desire to Desire*, 97, 107.

8. Modleski, *Women Who Knew Too Much*, 73–85.

9. Jeff was written out of the show (he died in a car crash), ostensibly because Mark Rydell, the actor portraying the character, wanted to move on to new opportunities (LaGuardia, *Soap World*, 112). Nonetheless, the death of a character is not the only recourse when a cast member leaves the show; decisions relative to cast changes are usually dictated by the directions of the characters. Simply put, the Penny-Jeff partnership did not suggest a sufficiently interesting future direction to the writers of that time, or Jeff would have been recast.

10. Several actresses have played Viki (and her alter ego, Niki; see below) over the course of the show, but Gillian Spencer and Erika Slezak have had the most responsibility for the development of the character.

11. Despite superficial resemblances between Tracy Lord and Viki Lord, both of the Main Line, Agnes Nixon did not find in *The Philadelphia Story* her inspiration for *One Life to Live*. Nixon was, however, conscious of certain feminist notions in creating Viki. Having worked in the soap opera form since 1946, when she became an associate and friend of Irna Phillips, she was very familiar with the usual soap opera heroine. She therefore understood that her use of the double personality was unique to the genre. Revealing the Jungian shadow of a female personality through such a fiction was Nixon's intended feminist contribution to the genre. She also purposefully made Victor Lord responsible for the pent-up energy of Viki's shadow, Niki. She asserts that his tyranny, together with Viki's lack of a mother, left Viki with repressed emotions and an unlived portion of her personality.

Nixon is candid about how Viki's story grew from her own life. Although she had a very strong mother and so was spared the domination of a tyrannical father, she found herself wondering what would have happened had it been the other way around. What are the cultural roots of this story? She does not appear to have made intentional allusion to any of the texts that resonate in Viki's story; she read *The Three Faces of Eve* only after having conceived the new story, and although she had seen *The Philadelphia Story*, she says she made no specific use of it for the show (Interview, September 22, 1989). Viki seems to have been a flashpoint at which the possibilities of the medium combined with the author's personal fantasies to yield a truly new direction for soap opera.

12. Laplanche and Pontalis, *Language of Psychoanalysis*, 314.

13. In 1989, the writers of *One Life to Live* created a new story for Viki that involved rewriting the genesis of the Viki/Niki split. Significantly, despite some changed details, the new narrative continued to assign the blame to the patriarchal destruction of the mother-daughter bond. In this version, Viki dis-

covers that she has a daughter who was born to her when she was in college. Following a trail of clues, she learns that her father had had the child, a daughter, taken away from her abruptly and forcibly, because her motherhood did not fit her father's idea of how she should be living her life. In this version, Viki was so overwhelmed by the humiliating and enraging impotence she experienced over what her father had the power to do to her that she repressed all consciousness of her baby and her first lover. Niki was then created as her rebellious alter ego, a place to safely store her painful memory. This revised narrative bears some resemblance to *Track 29*, directed by Nicholas Roeg and written by Dennis Potter, a film released in 1987, around the time of the recreation on *One Life to Live* of the Viki/Niki genesis. In this film, too, the deterioration of the heroine's identity is placed at the door of patriarchal destruction of the mother-child connection. Although this film achieves altered perception of feminine identity by subverting the major narrative conventions, it is about the favored relationship in film, mother-son. By contrast, *One Life* takes on a discussion of the mother-daughter connection in the patriarchal context.

14. On the medical discourse, see Doane, *Desire to Desire*, 38–69.

15. Ibid., 49.

16. Belenky et al., *Women's Ways of Knowing*, 52–75.

17. Modleski, *Women Who Knew Too Much*; see especially the essay "Femininity by Design: *Vertigo*," 87–101.

18. Ibid., 99.

19. Ibid.

Chapter 3

1. Bovenschen, "Is There a Feminine Aesthetic?" 119; quoted by de Lauretis, *Technologies of Gender*, 127.

2. Sheri Anderson, one of the writers who created the Luke and Laura story, emphatically resists the description of their first love scene as a rape. Laura's use of the term, Anderson says, is for Laura's husband's benefit and comes from her inability to find language to tell him about her relationship to Luke in any other way. Anderson was unhappily surprised to find that the press also had no other language with which to describe a scene involving emotions so obviously unrelated to the hatred and violence of the rape act (Interview, December 8, 1989).

3. The ups and downs of the character of Scotty Baldwin demonstrate well what works for soap opera. Scotty originally succeeded quite well as Laura's first love interest before she and Luke ran away. Interestingly, however, Laura and Scotty were a popular couple only *before* he got on good terms with his father; once they married and Scotty began imitating his dad by wearing suits and going to law school, all the vigor of the relationship was depleted. Scotty as betrayed "good man" held so little interest that the character was temporarily terminated on the show. Yet ultimately he made a triumphant return and achieved renewed

viability; the changes that brought about this reacceptance are instructive. The actor remained the same (Kin Shriner), but he was no longer a "good" person; rather, he had become a bitter, cynical man, full of rage and violence as a result of his experience with Laura. As a man with a problematic masculine identity, he has been extremely popular and useful in generating new stories.

4. Laura Mulvey ("Visual Pleasure and Narrative Cinema," 11–13) has discussed at length the way the erotic image, identified with the female—and which, she points out, is an alien presence in mainstream narrative cinema— works to "freeze the flow of action in moments of erotic contemplation."

5. The glamorized female on television soap opera probably began with Lisa on *As the World Turns* in the fifties. In 1970, *All My Children* intensified the presentation of the female fetish with Erika Kane, a highly specular figure, the first of a galaxy of transitional black-haired temptresses that became a standard feature of the daytime serial in the seventies. Other such figures include Dorian on *One Life to Live*, Raven on *The Edge of Night*, and Rachel on *Another World*. Each was a manipulating, much-married woman who dressed herself as a glamorized fetish. Modleski, commenting on these figures in an article written just as the changes on *General Hospital* were taking place, spoke of these women as complicated representatives of "the bad mother," outlets for female anger at the helplessness of "the good mother" ("Search for Tomorrow in Today's Soap Operas"). Yet in hindsight, we can see that they are really less impressive than Niki, on *One Life to Live*, in serving as partially formed subjects. They were useful in narrative as long as soap opera was stuck with a Mary Noble–type heroine, for the fight between these two types of women created a dialogue between feminine anger and the denial of that anger. But unlike Viki and Niki, the temptress and Mary Noble maintained the appearance of that good girl/bad girl dichotomy. These women were viable, in other words, only as long as the developing heroine was permitted relatively little access to her anger. After Viki's appearance on *One Life* soap opera heroines changed, and the temptresses either disappeared or "matured" into fascinating, egocentric, but spunky women. They are still featured in narrative as adventuresses, but they no longer are the bane of the heroine's existence. Instead they have their own identity problems, which cause them to walk a fine line between an imperialistic desire to stake out territory and a readiness to work with the community when their more freewheeling approach to problem solving is called for.

6. Belenky et al., *Women's Ways of Knowing*, 109.

7. Sheri Anderson, Interview, December 1, 1989.

8. Modleski, *Women Who Knew Too Much*, 60.

9. Interviews with Sheri Anderson, December 1, 8, 1989; Leah Laiman, October 29, 1989; Anne Schoettle, November 18, 1989; Charles Shaughnessy, July 26, 1990.

10. The Brady sons, Kimberly's brothers Roman and Bo, are as interesting as Shane as vehicles for exploring male and female identity, but discussion of them here would be digressive, since the focal point here is the hero as he affects his lover, not his sister. Although Kimberly does resist her brothers' pronounced tendency to violence, each has been important to the series as a problematic masculine figure in relationship to whom a heroine has worked out her defini-

tion of herself, almost always in conjunction with Kiriakis or the father/criminal who preceded him, Stefano DiMeara.

11. "Friends and Lovers," the song written for the show as theme music for Shane and Kimberly, musically contextualizes this passionate couple as lovers struggling against the domination-submission model of male-female relationship. The words in the refrain tell the story:

So I'll be your friend
And I'll be your lover
For we know in our hearts we agree
We don't have to be one or the other.

12. Doane, *Desire to Desire*, 38–69. See also the discussion of the medical discourse in chapter 2, with respect to Laura's narrative on *General Hospital*.

13. At one of his low points, Steve kidnapped Kayla's sister-in-law, Hope, tied her up, and placed her under a shelf on which he told her a bottle of acid was balanced which would spill on her face if she tried to escape. To Hope's fearful response, Patch had nothing more compassionate to say than that he enjoyed watching her bosom heave up and down in terror. He represents a crude variation on Victor Kiriakis's extreme Oedipal rage to control and subjugate. The actor, Steve Nichols, has said that he viewed this "Patch" period in Steve's narrative as being motivated by Steve's abandonment by his family. Nichols interprets the character as a man who was never taught anything, who had to make the rules up as he went along to survive (Interview, July 26, 1990). Nichols's sympathy for the character indicates an appreciation of the unfortunate influence of the Oedipal narrative on men. Either because of his work playing Steve, or because of an inborn resistance to Hollywood's version of the "mother-son problem," Nichols accepts the narrative's implication that there is a problem for a boy when he is denied access to the mother by the aggressive model of manhood he is theoretically supposed to bond with.

14. Linda Williams, "When the Woman Looks," in *Re-Vision: Essays in Feminist Film Criticism*, ed. Mary Ann Doane, Patricia Mellencamp, and Linda Williams, American Film Institute Monograph Series, vol. 3 (Frederick, Md.: University Publications of America, 1984), 83–99.

15. Bruno Bettelheim, *The Uses of Enchantment: The Meaning and the Importance of Fairy Tales* (New York: Vintage Books, 1977), 143–50.

16. Doane, *Desire to Desire*, 16.

17. Interviews with Patrick Mulcahey, June 29, 1989; and Courtney Simon, January 12, 1989; February 5, 1990.

18. The result of this deconstruction is not so different from the deconstruction undertaken in the short story "A Most Parisian Episode" by Alphonse Allais, referred to by Umberto Eco in "Lecteur in Fabula," *The Role of the Reader: Explorations in the Semiotics of Texts* (Bloomington: Indiana University Press, 1979), 200–260. Eco discusses logically and mathematically the way Allais deconstructs closure-bound narrative by demonstrating that inevitably such a narrative undermines its own logic and meaning. See 200–204 for the original French text of Allais's story ("Un drame bien parisien"); appendix 2 for an English translation; and 204–19 and appendix 1 for explication. Julia's story suggests a similar conclusion. However, Allais's story is an intellectual joke that

chides ordinary narrative for *insufficient* control, power, and logic, whereas Julia's story makes fun of ordinary narrative for being *too* logical, for its ludicrous attempt to assert mastery over the elusive, fluid world of desire.

19. Mulvey, "Visual Pleasure and Narrative Cinema."

20. Modleski, *Women Who Knew Too Much*, 73–85.

21. Interviews with Patrick Mulcahey, June 28, 1989; Courtney Simon, January 12, 1989; and Bridget and Jerry Dobson, October 26, 1989.

22. Modleski, *Women Who Knew Too Much*, 77.

23. In a chapter titled "Mans/laughter" (ibid.), Modleski cites Freud's description of the role of a woman in an obscene joke as an object between two male subjects. She then goes on to demonstrate how the heroine of Hitchcock's *Blackmail*, who begins the film a free woman (laughing *with* a man or at a remark her lover does not hear), is gradually made into that object (ending the movie between two men who smile at a joke on her), as the patriarchal order creates an obscenity of her situation (19). Julia's narrative might on that basis earn the subtitle of "womans/laughter." Here Sonny, the dysfunctional male ego produced by the male power structure, is caught between two female subjects—Julia and Gina—and reduced to an obscene joke.

24. Ibid., 95.

25. For those readers who cannot call back the lyric simply from the title, or have never heard the song, I reprint the words:

CRAZY

Crazy . . .
Crazy for feelin' so lonely.
I'm crazy . . .
Crazy for feelin' so blue.
I knew you'd love me as long as you wanted,
And then, someday, you'd leave me
For somebody new.

Worry . . .
Why do I let myself worry?
Wond'rin' . . .
What in the world did I do?

Crazy . . .
For thinking that my love could hold you.
I'm crazy for tryin'
Crazy for cryin'
And I'm crazy for lovin' you.

Chapter 4

1. Sigmund Freud, "The 'Uncanny,'" in *On Creativity and the Unconscious: Papers on the Psychology of Art, Literature, Love, Religion*, ed. Benjamin Nelson (New York: Harper Torchbooks, 1958).

2. Pascal Bonitzer, "Partial Vision: Film and the Labyrinth," trans. Fabrice Ziolkowski, *Wide Angle* 4, no. 4 (1981): 56–64.

3. Daly, *Beyond God the Father*, 23.

4. Christine Gledhill, "Pleasurable Negotiations," in Pribram (ed.), *Female Spectators*, 77–88.

5. Patrick Mulcahey, Interview, June 29, 1989.

6. Interviews with Leah Laiman, October 29, 1989; and Anne Schoettle, November 18, 1989.

7. Agnes Nixon, Interview, September 22, 1990.

8. Robert Graves, "Theseus in Crete," in *The Greek Myths*, vol. 1 (Baltimore: Penguin Books, 1955), 336–49; H.D.F. Kitto, *The Greeks* (Edinburgh: Penguin Books, 1957), 17; and "Theseus and the Minotaur," in *Myth or Legend?* ed. G. E. Daniel (New York: Capricorn Books, 1968), 49–59.

9. All subsequent quotes from this episode are taken from the script, #1053. Unfortunately, because of the paucity of material on soap operas in library collections, this script is not available to interested scholars. I used a copy from my personal collection.

10. Later on, in the larger context of the long story, the juxtaposition of Julia's and Eden's narratives will directly link the Oedipal dominance pattern of the rapist with Mason's inability to deal with Julia as a desiring subject. About two months after show #1053, in real time, and somewhat after Julia has left Mason/Sonny at the altar in narrative time, Julia is abducted, drugged, and held hostage (but not sexually attacked) by the rapist who had previously attacked Eden. After her rescue, and still feeling isolated from Mason, Julia copes with the trauma of the abduction by seeking sexual intimacy with Michael, a man who has been a good friend to her. This situation leads to an inversion of the image that broke up Julia's wedding plans. Once Mason becomes aware of Julia's ordeal, desire for her well-being wins him control of his personality. He rushes to Julia's house, where, seeing her with Michael, he assumes the same position in which Julia found herself when she saw Sonny with Gina. His sight bracketed by a window of her home, Mason glimpses Julia as a woman with desires separate from him and, in Oedipally correct fashion, gives Sonny control again. Here the reminder of the framed screen once again constitutes the female subject not as lack, but as plenitude, though it is a fullness that disorients Mason.

11. Peter Brooks, *The Melodramatic Imagination* (New Haven: Yale University Press, 1976), 41.

12. Ibid., 48.

13. Douglas Marland, Interview, April 19, 1989.

14. Douglas Marland's comments notwithstanding, the television soap operas that still make use of the text of bombast are the shows produced by Proctor & Gamble: *Another World, As the World Turns,* and *Guiding Light.* Marland, as head writer of *As the World Turns,* has discouraged such dialogue; but in comparison with the non–P & G shows, *World Turns* still relies on extensive verbalization of emotional and relational situations. In one extraordinary display of verbiage, a *Guiding Light* heroine confronts the man who sexually molested her as a child and recites a monologue of over five (interminable) pages detailing the emotions she felt when, at the age of twelve, she was violated by him

(*Guiding Light*, #10731). In the same show, a different character read the entire story of Peter Rabbit, in a six-page monologue, during which time another character, observing him, discovered a secret of his past.

15. Interview with Steve Wyman, Director, *Days of Our Lives*, July 27, 1990.

16. On the Freudian reading of the involvement of the female spectator, see Doane, *Desire to Desire*, esp. 67–69, 176–83; by calling attention to what has the force of a truism, she opens these assumptions up for examination. For another critique of the Freudian idea of spectator distance, see Modleski, *Women Who Knew Too Much*, 8.

17. Douglas Marland, Interview, May 10, 1989.

18. Sheri Anderson, Interview, December 8, 1989.

19. Interviews with Courtney Simon, January 12, 1989; and Nancy Grahn, July 26, 1990.

20. Interviews with Patrick Mulcahey, February 13, 1990; and Jill Farren Phelps, July 27, 1990.

21. Interviews with Sheri Anderson, December 8, 1989; Al Rabin, July 25, 1990; and Stephen Nichols, July 26, 1990.

22. The destruction of stereotype in soap opera characters has completely eluded William Galperin, who, in "Sliding Off the Stereotype: Gender Difference in the Future of Television" (in *Postmodernism and Its Discontents: Theories, Practises*, ed. E. Ann Kaplan [London: Verso, 1988]), suggests that characters in soap opera are intensely stereotypical. Galperin uses as a theoretical base for his examination of character cliché Roland Barthes's important distinction between *écrivance*, "the emplacement of discourse where the body is missing," and *écriture*, where the body is "effectively released from culture" (147). Galperin asserts that the *écrivance* (stereotype) of *The Young and the Restless* is so intense that it slips into *écriture* (a disruptive text) and thus undermines itself through excess. The application of this distinction clearly resonates against Brooks's text of melodramatic bombast. However, in applying that theory to soap opera Galperin errs in two important ways. First, he makes no distinction between the narrative forms of daytime serial, on the one hand, and prime-time melodrama, on the other. Thus, he fails to integrate into his commentary the issue of the vastly different relationships to closure between a serial that is on air every day and one with regulation hiatus periods between thirteen-week seasonal contracts, not to mention no new shows during the summer season. Second, his inattentiveness to the closure issue causes him to search in the wrong place for the release from culture that he intuits in daytime serial. Third, Galperin's use of *The Young and the Restless*, the most atypical of all the network soap operas, as his only example from daytime serial is a further demonstration of the incompleteness of his analysis.

All other soap operas have arrived at a rather straightforward, if involuntary, feminine discourse in responding to the requirements of daily programming. *The Young and the Restless*, in contrast, has a kind of sadomasochistic relationship to the needs of its narrative. Apparently unaware of the effect of narrative on character, Galperin uses the figure of John Abbott to prove his point, claiming that John Abbott is the cliché of the patriarch, but so exaggerated as to undermine even itself as a cliché. In fact, John Abbott is part patriarch, part matriarch, the only male agent on soap opera today who functions narratively to usurp the role of the soap opera heroine. Unlike representative power-broker patriarchs like Victor Lord, James Stenbeck (see chapter 5), Victor Kiriakis, C. C. Capwell, and Frank Smith, Abbott spends a good deal of time presenting a set of a feminized, pre-Oedipal priorities. Masquerading as both mother and father to his daughters, he mouths platitudes that privilege family over power relations. At the same time, however, Abbott mocks what are ordinarily called feminine values by giving them no more than lip service. Abbott's priority on family is all verbal; in fact he provides for neither filiation nor intimacy. When plot complications so require, he justifies his three-piece Oedipal suit by forming a troublesome dyad with his son, Jack. He is at the same time a mechanism for resisting closure, and for imposing it. In acting as a hermaphroditic subject who obviates the need for a mother by symbolically incorporating her within him, John Abbott is a one-man anxiety-provoking image of what causes the uncanny sensation about the fearful aspects of patriarchy. Abbott's unending involvement in frustration and betrayal may be one reason for the continuous popularity of the show, attesting to a widespread desire to explore the problematic aspects of a figure who so graphically embodies a patriarchal fantasy that the best woman is a man.

Chapter 5

1. Hayden White, "New Historicism: A Comment," in *The New Historicism*, ed. H. Abram Veeser (New York: Routledge, 1989), 300. The enduring feature of "serious" Hollywood historical discourse is its determined Oedipal resistance to feminine co-presence. This resistance is particularly striking in films that tell stories about historical epochs when women were conspicuously present, as, for example, during World War II. Among others, Linda Williams ("Feminist Film Theory: *Mildred Pierce* and the Second World War," in Pribram [ed.], *Female Spectators*, 12–30) has explored the complex manipulations of historical context that World War II films employ to maintain the conventional Oedipal stance while portraying on screen the historical agency of the feminine that the war necessitated. Williams has shrewdly noted that the "new women" of those films divided between two types, each of which is denied historical agency for a different reason. In one category, the woman subject is clearly marked as a temporary substitute for her man; her ephemeral agency marks not her desire but his, which she serves by making sacrifices to reserve his place until he returns (*Since You Went Away*). The second type of woman—Joan Crawford as Mildred Pierce, for example—experiences the "exhilarations of matriarchal power" only because reference to the war is suppressed in the film, and along with it any possible historical role for the feminine. As Williams points out, in *Mildred Pierce* the time frame of the action is vaguely established. The mise-en-scène evokes wartime without making specific diegetic reference to World War II, either in and of itself or as the reason for the absence of Mildred's husband. Unlike *Since You Went Away*, *Mildred Pierce* does not explain away the feminine desire of

Mildred's agency. Instead it postulates an "Oedipus takes a holiday" hole in time in which the dangerous Mildred runs wild. By recounting her adventures through an intricate series of flashbacks, the film proffers Oedipal assurances that this anomaly is safely bracketed, protecting the present from her threat. Closure brings the reappearance of linear time and her husband and the end to Mildred's ahistorical rampage. By implication, all women's war achievements are relegated to extrahistorical limbo.

2. Riane Eisler, *The Chalice and the Blade: Our History, Our Future* (San Francisco: Harper & Row, 1987). Eisler sets out her theory about partnership and dominator cultures in her introduction. The following chapters sift the historical evidence.

3. On Ardener's theory, see Elaine Showalter, "Feminist Criticism in the Wilderness," *Critical Inquiry* 8 (Winter 1981): 179–205; and Edwin Ardener, "The 'Problem' Revisited," in *Perceiving Women*, ed. Shirly Ardener (New York: Wiley, 1975). Although Showalter uses Ardener's idea to pursue an argument that rejects silence as an important part of the way women make meaning, the same diagram has been demonstrated to be an effective heuristic in pursuing the opposite argument, as I do. Part of the consequences for the feminine identity of Lizzie and Gail in Marcus's story is the silence that racism forces upon them. Linda Williams ("A Jury of Their Peers: Marlene Gorris's *A Question of Silence*," in Kaplan [ed.], *Postmodernism and Its Discontents*, 107–16) finds a similar construction of silence in the film *A Question of Silence*. Williams uses Ardener's concept of the unknown feminine wild zone to explain the inability of any of the authorities in the film to interpret the actions of three women. Her critique also illuminates the film as a powerful dramatization of the place of femininity in conventional historical constructions. The film's narrative is about the chance meeting of three strangers, all women, in a dress boutique, who band together to kill the male boutique owner when he tries to prevent one of them from shoplifting. Subsequently their defense lawyer, a woman, comes to understand the feminine character of the deed, from a perspective that neither the law nor language can articulate.

Favoring the linguistic perspective of the pre-Oedipal maternal way of making meaning, the film interprets silence as polysemic. Silence is both what shrouds the historically repressed contents of the feminine wild zone and a linguistic principle. History is silent about women, and women's historical judgments cannot be rendered in the words that by nature repress them: the film, Williams writes, "offers a silence that questions all language, a laughter that subverts authority, a judgement that never gets pronounced" (113). Williams's interpretation of Gorris suggests masculine silence about the feminine as a kind of lack, and feminine silence as a kind of plenitude that disrupts masculine structures. Such silence is rendered criminal only within the patriarchal historical vise. As Williams sees it, Gorris tells us that articulate structures of society are completely dominated by the Oedipal content of the masculine wild zone; the feminine wild zone, conversely, can only be guessed at in those random moments in which a gap appears in the dominant discourse. Further, the film suggests that the rage of the muted and contained feminine becomes the likely subtext of feminine silence under the repressive circumstances of patriarchal history.

4. All people in the creative community of soap opera know that the topical story that brings historical discourse into play involves both a conscious choice and a risk. Soap opera writers are wary of topical stories as being disliked by the networks, which clear story lines before they are scripted and aired. And writers are also sensitive to the aesthetic risks of "the issue" for the special needs of soap opera narrative. As Patrick Mulcahey says, "A drama dominated by issue is possible for two hours, but not two hundred hours" (Interview, February 13, 1990). To use the topical story, a soap opera storyteller must make sure that the character is not reduced to his or her issue. What Hayden White refers to as the decentering of the axis of combination in historical narrative, the soap opera creative community calls embedding topical issues in the emotional concerns of the characters. Soap opera writers know that to make issue stories work they must make sure that belief systems are not on the front burner. Therefore, when soap opera focuses on a character who is culturally Other, great care is taken to give him or her an exposition that makes sensibility more important than the character's definition in terms of conventional social hierarchy.

Embedding the issue in the character rather than the character in the issue is more than a method of storytelling; it is also a way of humanizing for the audience people who have been wrongheadedly rejected under the influence of unfortunate belief systems (Interviews with Douglas Marland, February 5, 1990; and Agnes Nixon, February 8, 1990). Many of these topical stories are very dear to the hearts of the writers who create them. Agnes Nixon, for example, has a passionate desire to tell stories that force viewers to recognize the complexity of social problems and rethink them in human and not narrowly rationalistic terms. She has told stories of mothers losing sons in the Vietnam War, of the victims of child abuse and drugs. Her story about teen-aged prostitution on *All My Children* was one of her more explosive narratives, for it involved a black pimp and a white prostitute who were shown in bed together. Nixon says that once her research showed that this configuration was prevalent, she had no fears about offending viewers by putting the images on screen. Her most urgent concern in creating the story was to insure that the misery she showed was not glamorized in terms of the power the pimp held (Interview, February 8, 1990). Similarly, Douglas Marland sees in the topical story the stuff of powerful, original, emotional narrative, provided the presentation is not didactic in tone but part of the emotional perspectives of the core characters. His commitment to the humanizing of audience perspectives about groups considered different is evident in his introduction of the story of Hank Eliot, a gay man, into *As the World Turns* (Interview, February 5, 1990; on Eliot, see below).

Most discussion about the dramatization of historical realities in soap opera, however, reveals only the inadequacy of conventional discourse. Many soap opera creators "do historical issues but can't talk about it." Al Rabin, executive producer of *Days of Our Lives*, has been responsible for topical stories as compelling as those promoted by Marland and Nixon but *says* that type of story is not appropriate on soap opera, as if the fantasy on *Days* had no bearing on historical reality. His attitude is echoed by the best and brightest who work with that show (Interviews with Al Rabin, July 25, 1990; Steve Wyman, July 27, 1990; and Charles Shaughnessy, July 26, 1990). All agree it would be nice if soap opera could deal with "reality," but all believe that "reality" is incompatible with the entertainment value of soap opera. One exception to this *Days* point of view is voiced by Steve Nichols, who created the role of Steve "Patch" Johnson (Interview, July 26, 1990). He speaks passionately in favor of verisimilitude; in fact, his desire for "more reality" than he could find on *Days* prompted his decision to leave the show. I would suggest that the major culprit in this apparent lack of agreement is the inadequate language available for discussing soap opera, which basically restricts members of the soap opera community to terms that are hostile to the truth conveyed by the fantasy re-vision of life which is daytime narrative's greatest strength.

5. Leah Laiman, the writer on whose initiative the Jacobs-Horton story was pursued, extracted a promise that Robin and Michael would never be allowed to marry, out of respect to her own Jewish tradition (Interview, October 29, 1989). Accordingly, Robin left Michael, and the show, after taking the position that their religious differences made marriage impossible. Several years later Robin returned (played by the original actress, Derya Ruggles), with a child she had had by Michael—of whom he knew nothing—and with a different attitude about marriage. Michael, however, now committed to another woman, rejected Robin, and she left the show once more. But when the actor who played Michael (Michael J. Weiss) wanted to leave the show, the story took another turn: Michael's decision to go to Israel to join Robin and their child was scripted into the narrative. Even though the audience was not told that Robin and Michael would marry, the implication was that Michael wished to put his obligations to Robin and their child first in his life. Some may see the progress of this narrative as an example of what happens to promises in daytime television production. Another way of looking at the way Robin and Michael meandered into a commitment to each other is to understand that the chaotic confluence of circumstances of soap opera production tends to erode the imposition of abstract priorities alien to its characteristic, disruptive nature.

6. Robert Clary, the actor who played Robert Le Clair, in fact is a French Jew who spent part of his childhood in a concentration camp and most of his professional life in this country hiding both his Jewish identity and the traumatic events of his past. Thus, the revelation on the show of the character's denial of his Jewish identity reflected the actual historical position of the actor. At around the time the Robin-and-Michael story line brought Clary back to the show after an absence of some years, the actor had just initiated public discussion of his background in order better to understand the Holocaust and his own life. When Le Clair was written out of the show, the character was said to be embarking on a similar educational campaign. This identity between character and actor adds an autobiographical issue, not unknown in the relationship between actor and story on daytime serial, to the question of historical reflection in daytime serial.

7. Diana Fuss, *Essentially Speaking: Feminism, Nature, and Difference* (New York: Routledge, 1989), 3.

8. The major breakthrough for core black characters was created for *Generations*, the only soap opera ever to have such a family in its Bible. Put on the air in 1989, *Generations* was terminated because of poor ratings in 1991. In the late sixties–early seventies, too, we can identify in this category the narrative told by

then head writer Gordon Russell on *One Life to Live*. On *One Life* during that time period, an important narrative line concerned a character named Carla Benari/Clara Grey (Ellen Holly). Played by a light-skinned black actress, the character first appears as Carla Benari, a singer who is accepted as an exotic-looking Caucasian by the white community. Here, as in Robert Le Clair's story on *Days*, the spectator is subject to a blurring of the distinction between Other and subject when it is disclosed that the character is both: involved in a romantic triangle with two doctors, one black and one white, Carla finally reveals her suppressed identity as a black woman passing for a white. Carla Benari is really Clara Grey, the daughter of Sadie Grey (Lillian Hayman), a black cleaning woman on the show. In the series, a long sequence during which Carla denies her connection to her mother was juxtaposed with a parallel sequence involving the interracial romantic triangle. Through Carla's story, the *One Life* narrative treated racial difference in a bold and interesting way, associating the disruption of connection between lovers and between mother and daughter with a racism built into linear patriarchal history.

In a wrenching, unusual scene, Holly and Hayman, both talented actresses, unleash the mutual frustrations of Carla and Sadie that led to Carla's rejection of Sadie and her racial heritage. Remarkable on many counts, the scene is narratively distinguished by the sense of the specifically racial consequences for maternal desire and the mother-daughter bond in a racist society. Sadie's sense of humiliation at being referred to as "the maid" in public by her own daughter is matched by Carla's feelings about a certain pattern of incidents from her childhood, forgotten by the mother but burned forever into her own memory, in which the dark-skinned mother herself taught the light-skinned daughter to respect the politics of difference. Whenever the two of them walked through a black neighborhood, Carla reminds her mother, Sadie would hold Carla's hand, but as they came into the presence of whites the physical intimacy would cease. Carla does more than jog Sadie's memory in this scene. She makes her see the consequences of her internalization of racist hatred. Carla knew without being told that Sadie was pretending to be caring, in a hired capacity, for a white child so that Carla could experience higher social esteem than her mother ever would. Like the distress caused by racism for Gail and Lizzie in Marcus's narrative on *Days*, here too the peculiar feminine loneliness and silence generated by racism is evoked.

The power of the scene between Carla and Sadie matches and even surpasses the most daring Hollywood movies that recount similar dilemmas of light-skinned Black women: *Pinky*, directed by Elia Kazan; and *Imitation of Life*, directed by Douglas Sirk. These directors, working in a medium structured to suppress the possible female subject, were less free than *One Life* to explore the impact on feminine agency of racism.

9. Interviews with Richard Biggs and Charles Shaughnessy, July 26, 1990.

10. I do not wish to underplay the effectiveness of racist hate mail in doing damage both to the show and to Richard Biggs, who plays Marcus. Unfortunately, when hate mail—including a petition signed by fifty people abusively protesting Marcus's interracial involvement with Faith—arrives at a television station, it does not go unnoticed. Because soap opera actors depend on erotic

involvement with a heroine to make them viable heroes, it seems certain that the termination of Marcus's potentially exciting romance with Faith had a detrimental effect on Biggs's career (Richard Biggs, Interview, July 16, 1990). It should also be noted that the termination of the story line was injurious to Mindy Clarke, the young actress who played Faith, Saul Taylor's daughter, as well. Both Clarke and Biggs were sidetracked to other story lines so insipid that they dissipated of their own colorlessness. Clarke was written off the show.

11. Douglas Marland, Interview, May 10, 1989.

12. Eisler, *Chalice and the Blade*, 78–85.

13. Douglas Marland, Interview, February 7, 1990.

14. Tania Modleski, "Some Functions of Feminist Criticism; or, The Scandal of the Mute Body," in *Femininism Without Women* (New York: Routledge, 1991), 52.

15. In the preface to *The Heroine's Text* (New York: Columbia University Press, 1986), Nancy K. Miller establishes the definitions of euphoric and dysphoric text; she then, in the following chapters, applies these categories to a range of heroines.

16. Gilles Deleuze, *Cinema 2: The Time-Image*, trans. Hugh Tomlinson and Robert Galeta (Minneapolis: University of Minnesota Press, 1989), 52.

17. The great period of *Santa Barbara* is defined by the work of long-standing writers Patrick Mulcahey and Courtney Simon, executive producer Jill Farren Phelps, director Michael Gliona, and the members of its superb cast: Jed Allan (C. C. Capwell), Lane Davies (Mason Capwell 1984–89), Justin Deas (Keith Timmons), Nancy Grahn (Julia Wainwright), Terry Lester (Mason Capwell 1989–90), Judith McConnell (Sophia Capwell), A. Martinez (Cruz Castillo), Robin Mattson (Gina Blake Capwell Capwell Timmons Capwell Timmons), and Marcy Walker (Eden Capwell Castillo). Although Sheri Anderson, Ann Howard Bailey, Leah Laiman, Douglas Marland, Agnes Nixon, and Anne Schoettle have all skillfully and courageously told stories of cultural difference on their own soap operas, unlike the *Santa Barbara* team they have had no designs on structural originality. Although I claim that other shows have in fact disrupted conventional historical discourse, their creators, I believe, would contend that they had done nothing but tell the story in the most interesting and effective way they could. The creative people working on *Santa Barbara* will certainly not agree with all my points. Indeed, the show's creators, Bridget and Jerry Dobson, regard the period I have identified as *Santa Barbara*'s most productive time as too antic (Interview, Bridget and Jerry Dobson, October 26, 1989). However, everyone connected with the show has been forthcoming about how they tried, in their own ways, to do something different with the form.

With the exception of Nancy Grahn and Patrick Mulcahey, who took great pride in Greg's episode-long dream, the cast, writers, and production and direction staff on *Santa Barbara* believe that the "Capwell Zone" show was an idea better in theory than execution. Yet only a vehicle such as *Santa Barbara* could have given Mulcahey the freedom to write what I hope they will all someday recognize to be one of the best shows ever to air on day- or nighttime American television. Together they have had the vision of a show that disrupts the conventions of narrative for the purposes of entertainment, honesty, and the sharpening of perception about emotional complexities. For all their use of direct smile, sneer, and smirk at the camera, for all their self-parody, for all their day-trips to fantasy parallel universes, they felt deeply about and treated their characters and spectators with respect (Interviews with Courtney Simon, January 12, February 2, 1989; Patrick Mulcahey, June 28, 1989, February 13, 1990; Terry Lester, June 27, July 26, 1990; Charlotte Savitz, July 27, 1990; Jill Farren Phelps, July 27, October 2, 1990; Michael Gliona, July 27, 1990; Nancy Grahn, July 26, 1990; and Lane Davies, August 21, 1990).

18. Dinnerstein, *The Mermaid and the Minotaur.*

19. Ken Burns, "Reliving the War Between Brothers," *New York Times*, Arts and Leisure sec., September 16, 1990, 1, 43.

Epilogue

1. Michael Gliona, *Santa Barbara.*
2. Modleski, "Search for Tomorrow in Today's Soap Operas."
3. Al Rabin, Interview, July 26, 1990.
4. Jill Farren Phelps, Interview, July 27, 1990.
5. Bridget and Jerry Dobson, Interview, October 26, 1989.
6. Jill Farren Phelps, Interview, October 2, 1990.

References

Interviews

Anderson, Sheri. December 1, 8, 1989.
Biggs, Richard. July 26, 1990.
Davies, Lane. August 21, 1990.
Dobson, Bridget and Jerry. October 26, 1989.
Ford, Nancy. March 3, 1989.
Gliona, Michael. July 27, 1990.
Grahn, Nancy. July 26, August 10, 1990.
Laiman, Leah. October 29, 1989.
Lester, Terry. June 27, July 26, 1990.
Marland, Douglas. April 19, May 10, 1989; February 5, 1990.
Mulcahey, Patrick. June 29, 1989; February 13, 1990.
Nichols, Stephen. July 25, 1990.
Nixon, Agnes. September 22, 1989; February 8, 1990.
Perlman, Barbara K. January 20, 1989.
Phelps, Jill Farren. July 27, October 2, 1990.
Rabin, Al. July 25, 1990.
Savitz, Charlotte. July 27, 1990.
Schoettle, Anne. November 18, 1989; February 16, 1990.
Shaughnessy, Charles. July 26, 1990.
Simon, Courtney. January 12, 1989; February 5, 1990.
Taggert, Millee. July 11, 1989.
Wyman, Stephen. July 27, 1990.

Archival Documents

Irna Phillips Papers. Film and Manuscripts Archive. State Historical Society of Wisconsin, Madison.

Radio and Television Episodes Available at the Museum of Broadcasting

As The World Turns (CBS-TV). March 25, 1958; January 3, 1961 (video).
The Guiding Light (CBS-TV). July 10, 1952; January 17, 1956; January 3, 1961; January 2, 1962; October 2, 1963 (video).
Mary Noble, Backstage Wife (radio). N.d. (audio).
Our Gal Sunday (radio). September 21, 1939 (audio).
Romance of Helen Trent (radio). September 21, 1939 (audio).
Young Doctor Malone (NBC-TV). October 2, 1962 (video).

Works Cited

Allen, Robert Clyde. *Speaking of Soap Operas*. Chapel Hill: University of North Carolina Press, 1985.
Ang, Ien. *Watching Dallas: Soap Opera and the Melodramatic Imagination*. Translated by Della Couling. London: Methuen, 1982.
Ardener, Edwin. "The 'Problem' Revisited." In *Perceiving Women*, edited by Shirley Ardener. New York: Wiley.
Barthes, Roland. *The Pleasure of the Text*. Translated by Richard Miller. New York: Hill & Wang, 1975.
Baruch, Elaine Hoffman, and Lucienne J. Serrano. *Women Analyze Women: In France, England, and the United States*. New York: NYU Press, 1988.
Bataille, Georges. *Eroticism: Death and Sexuality*. Translated by M. Dalwood. San Francisco: City Lights Books, 1965.
Baudrillard, Jean. *Selected Writings*. Edited by Mark Poster. Stanford: Stanford University Press, 1988.
Baudry, Jean Louis. "The Apparatus." *Camera Obscura*, no. 1 (Fall 1976): 105–26.
———. "Ideological Effects of the Basic Cinemagraphic Apparatus." *Film Quarterly* 28, no. 2 (1974/75): 39–47.
Belenky, Mary Field, et al. *Women's Ways of Knowing: The Development of Self, Voice, and Mind*. New York: Basic Books, 1986.
Bettelheim, Bruno. *The Uses of Enchantment: The Meaning and the Importance of Fairy Tales*. New York: Vintage Books, 1977.

Bonitzer, Pascal. "Partial Vision: Film and the Labyrinth." Translated by Fabrice Ziolkowski. *Wide Angle* 4, no. 4 (1981): 56–64.

Bordo, Susan. "Feminism, Postmodernism, and Gender-Scepticism." In *Feminism/Postmodernism*, edited by Linda Nicholson. New York: Routledge, 1990.

Bovenschen, Silvia. "Is There a Feminine Aesthetic?" Translated by Beth Weckmuller. *New German Critique*, no. 10 (Winter 1977): 111–37.

Brooks, Peter. *The Melodramatic Imagination*. New Haven: Yale University Press, 1976.

Buerkel-Rothfuss, Nancy L., and Sandra Mayes. "Soap Opera Viewing: The Cultivation Effect." *Journal of Communication* 31 (Summer 1981): 108–15.

Bulfinch's Mythology: The Age of Fable, the Age of Chivalry, the Legends of Charlemagne. New York: Thomas Y. Crowell, 1970.

Burns, Ken. "Reliving the War Between Brothers." *New York Times*, Arts and Leisure section, September 16, 1990, 1, 43.

Byars, Jackie. *All That Hollywood Allows: Re-reading Gender in 1950s Melodrama*. Chapel Hill: University of North Carolina Press, 1991.

Cassata, Mary, and Thomas Skill, eds. *Life on Daytime Television: Tuning in American Serial Drama*. Norwood, N.J.: Ablex, 1983.

Caughie, John, ed. *Theories of Authorship*. London: Routledge & Kegan Paul, 1981.

Chatman, Seymour. *Story and Discourse: Narrative Structure in Fiction and Film*. Ithaca: Cornell University Press, 1978.

Chodorow, Nancy. *The Reproduction of Mothering: Psychoanalysis and the Sociology of Gender*. Berkeley and Los Angeles: University of California Press, 1979.

Cixous, Hélène. "Castration or Decapitation?" Translated by Annette Kuhn. *Signs* 7, no. 1 (Autumn 1981): 41–55.

Cook, Pam. "Melodrama and the Woman's Picture." In *The Gainsborough Melodrama*, edited by Sue Aspinall and Sue Harper. London: British Film Institute, 1983.

Daly, Mary. *Beyond God the Father: Toward a Philosophy of Women's Liberation*. Boston: Beacon Press, 1985.

Daniel, G. E., et al., eds. *Myth or Legend?* New York: Capricorn Books, 1968.

de Lauretis, Teresa. *Technologies of Gender: Essays on Theory, Film, and Fiction*. Bloomington: Indiana University Press, 1987.

Deleuze, Gilles. *Anti-Oedipus: Capitalism and Schizophrenia*. Translated by Robert Hurley, Mark Seem, and Helen R. Lane. Minneapolis: University of Minnesota Press, 1983.

———. *Cinema 2: The Time-Image*. Translated by Hugh Tomlinson and Robert Galeta. Minneapolis: University of Minnesota Press, 1989.

———. *Masochism: An Interpretation of Coldness and Cruelty*. Translated by Jean McNeil. New York: George Braziller, 1971.

Derrida, Jacques. *Of Grammatology*. Translated by Gayatri Spivak. Baltimore: Johns Hopkins University Press, 1974.

———. *Positions*. Translated by Alan Bass. Chicago: Chicago University Press, 1981.

Dinnerstein, Dorothy. *The Mermaid and the Minotaur: Sexual Arrangements and Human Malaise*. New York: Harper & Row, 1977.

Doane, Mary Ann. *The Desire to Desire*. Bloomington: Indiana University Press, 1987.

Doane, Mary Ann, Patricia Mellencamp, and Linda Williams, eds. *Re-Vision: Essays in Feminist Film Criticism*. American Film Institute Monograph Series, vol. 3. Frederick, Md.: University Publications of America, 1984.

Eberwein, Robert. "Reflections on the Breast." *Wide Angle* 4, no. 3 (1981): 48–53.

Eco, Umberto. *The Role of the Reader: Explorations in the Semiotics of Texts*. Bloomington: Indiana University Press, 1979.

Eisler, Riane. *The Chalice and the Blade: Our History, Our Future*. San Francisco: Harper & Row, 1987.

Elbow, Peter. *Writing Without Teachers*. London: Oxford University Press, 1973.

Elsaesser, Thomas. "Tales of Sound and Fury: Observations on the Family Melodrama." *Monogram*, no. 4 (1972): 2–15.

Foster, Hal, ed. *The Anti-Aesthetic*. Washington: Bay Press, 1983.

Freud, Sigmund. *Beyond the Pleasure Principle*. Translated by James Strachey. New York: Norton, 1961.

———. "'A Child is Being Beaten': A Contribution to the Study of the Origin of Sexual Perversions." In *The Standard Edition of the Complete Psychological Works of Sigmund Freud*, vol. 17. Translated by James Strachey. New York: Norton, 1961.

———. "Female Sexuality." In *The Standard Edition of the Complete Psychological Works of Sigmund Freud*, vol. 21. Translated by James Strachey. New York: Norton, 1961.

———. *The Interpretation of Dreams*. In *The Standard Edition of the Complete Psychological Works of Sigmund Freud*, vols. 4–5. London: Hogarth Press, 1953.

———. *Three Essays on the History of Sexuality*. Translated by James Strachey. New York: Basic Books, 1962.

———. "The 'Uncanny.'" In *On Creativity and the Unconscious: Papers on the Psychology of Art, Literature, Love, Religion*. Edited by Benjamin Nelson. New York: Harper Torchbooks, 1958.

Freytag, Gustave. *Freytag's Technique of the Drama*. Chicago: Griggs, 1893.

Friedman, Ellen G., and Miriam Fuchs, eds. *Breaking the Sequence: Women's Experimental Fiction*. Princeton: Princeton University Press, 1989.

Fuss, Diana. *Essentially Speaking: Feminism, Nature, and Difference*. New York: Routledge, 1989.

Galperin, William. "Sliding Off the Stereotype: Gender Difference in the Future of Television." In *Postmodernism and Its Discontents: Theories, Practises*, edited by E. Ann Kaplan. London: Verso, 1988.

Gentile, Mary C. *Film Feminisms: Theory and Practice*. Westport, Conn.: Greenwood Press, 1985.

Gilligan, Carol. *In a Different Voice*. Cambridge, Mass.: Harvard University Press, 1982.

Gledhill, Christine. "Pleasurable Negotiations." In *Female Spectators: Looking At Film and Television*, edited by Deirdre Pribram. New York: Routledge, 1988.

———. "Recent Developments in Feminist Film Criticism." *Quarterly Review of Film Studies* 3, no. 4 (1978): 457–93.

Graves, Robert. *The Greek Myths*. Vol. 1. Baltimore: Penguin Books, 1955.

Hansen, Miriam. "Pleasure, Ambivalence, Identification: Valentino and Female Spectatorship." *Cinema Journal* 25, no. 4 (Summer, 1986): 6–32.

Haskell, Molly. *From Reverence to Rape: The Treatment of Women in the Movies*. New York: Holt, Rinehart & Winston, 1973.

Hollenstein, Elmar. *Roman Jakobson's Approach to Language*. Translated by Catherine Schelbert and Tarcisius Schelbert. Bloomington: Indiana University Press, 1976.

The Homeric Hymns. Translated by Thelma Sargent. New York: Norton, 1975.

Irigary, Luce. *The Speculum of the Other Woman*. Translated by Gillian C. Gill. Ithaca: Cornell University Press, 1985.

Jakobson, Roman, and Morris Halle. *The Fundamentals of Language*. The Hague: Mouton, 1971.

Jameson, Fredric. "Pleasure: A Political Issue." In *Formations of Pleasure*. London: Routledge and Kegan Paul, 1983.

———. *The Political Unconscious: Narrative as a Socially Symbolic Act*. Ithaca: Cornell University Press, 1981.

Jordan, Judith V. "Clarity in Connection: Empathic Knowing, Desire, and Sexuality." In *Work in Progress* 29. Wellesley, Mass.: Stone Center for Developmental Services and Studies, Wellesley College, 1987.

Kaplan, Alexandra. "Dichotomous Thought and Relational Processes in Psychotherapy." *Stone Center Colloqium Series*, Wellesley, Mass., March, 1987.

Kaplan, E. Ann, ed. *Postmodernism and Its Discontents: Theories, Practises*. London: Verso, 1988.

———. *Psychoanalysis and Cinema*. New York: Routledge, 1990.

———. *Rocking Around the Clock: Music Television, Postmodernism, and Consumer Culture*. New York: Methuen, 1987.

———. "Whose Imaginary?" In *Female Spectators: Looking At Film and Television*, edited by Deirdre Pribram. New York: Routledge, 1988.

Katzman, Natan. "Television Soap Operas: What's Been Going on Anyway?" *Public Opinion Quarterly* 36 (1972): 200–212.

Kermode, Frank. *The Sense of an Ending: Studies in the Theory of Fiction*. New York: Oxford University Press, 1967.

Kitto, H.D.F. *The Greeks*. Edinburgh: Penguin Books, 1957.

Kristeva, Julia. "From One Identity to Another." In *Desire in Language: A Semiotic Approach to Literature and Art*. New York: Columbia University Press, 1980.

———. *Powers of Horror: An Essay on Abjection*. Translated by Leon S. Roudiez. New York: Columbia University Press, 1982.

———. "Women's Time." Translated by Alice Jardine and Harry Blake. *Signs: Journal of Women in Culture and Society* 7, no. 1 (1981): 113–17.

Kuhn, Annette. *Women's Pictures: Feminism and Cinema*. London: Routledge & Kegan Paul, 1982.

Lacan, Jacques. *Ecrits: A Selection*. Translated by Alan Sheridan. New York: Norton, 1977.

———. *The Four Fundamental Concepts of Psychoanalysis*. Edited by Jacques Alain Miller; translated by Alan Sheridan. New York: Norton, 1981.

LaGuardia, Robert. *Soap World*. N.p.: Priam Books, 1983.

Laplanche, J., and J.-B. Pontalis. *The Language of Psychoanalysis*. Translated by Donald Nicholson Smith. New York: Norton, 1973.

Lévi-Strauss, Claude. *The Raw and the Cooked*. Translated by Johan Weightman and Doreen Weightman. New York: Harper & Row, 1969.

———. *The Savage Mind*. Chicago: University of Chicago Press, 1966.

McClelland, David. *Power: The Inner Experience*. New York: Irvington, 1975.

Martin, Wallace. *Recent Theories of Narrative*. Ithaca: Cornell University Press, 1986.

Metz, Christian. *Film Language: A Semiotics of Cinema*. Translated by Michael Taylor. New York: Oxford University Press, 1974.

———. *The Imaginary Signifier: Psychoanalysis and the Cinema*. Translated by Celia Britton, Annwyl Williams, Ben Brewster, and Alfred Guzzetti. Bloomington: Indiana University Press, 1977.

Miller, D. A. *Narrative and Its Discontents: Problems of Closure in the Traditional Novel*. Princeton: Princeton University Press, 1981.

Miller, Jean Baker. *Toward a New Psychology of Women*. 2d ed. Boston: Beacon Press, 1986.

Miller, Nancy K. *The Heroine's Text*. New York: Columbia University Press, 1986.

Modleski, Tania. *Loving With a Vengeance: Mass Produced Fantasies for Women*. New York: Methuen, 1984.

———. "The Search For Tomorrow in Today's Soap Operas." *Film Quarterly* 33, no. 1 (1979): 12–21.

———. "Some Functions of Feminist Criticism; or, The Scandal of the Mute Body." In *Femininism Without Women*. New York: Routledge, 1991.

———. *The Women Who Knew Too Much: Hitchcock and Feminist Theory*. New York: Methuen, 1988.

Morford, Mark P. O., and Robert J. Lenardon. *Classical Mythology*. New York: Longman, 1971.

Muller, John P., and William J. Richardson. *Lacan and Language: A Reader's Guide to Ecrits*. New York: International Universities Press, 1982.

Mulvey, Laura. "Afterthoughts on 'Visual Pleasure and Narrative Cinema,' Inspired by *Duel in the Sun*." *Framework*, no. 10 (Spring 1979): 3–10.

———. "Visual Pleasure and Narrative Cinema." *Screen* 16, no. 3 (1975): 6–18.

New Larousse Encyclopedia of Mythology. With an introduction by Robert Graves. Hong Kong: Putnam, 1968.

Outhwaite, William. "Hans-Georg Gadamer." In *The Return of the Grand Theory in the Human Sciences*, edited by Quentin Skinner. New York: Cambridge University Press, 1985.

Paglia, Camille. *Sexual Personae: Art and Decadence from Nefertiti to Emily Dickinson*. New Haven: Yale University Press, 1990.

Philp, Mark. "Michel Foucault." In *The Return of the Grand Theory in the Human Sciences*, edited by Quentin Skinner. New York: Cambridge University Press, 1985.

Pribram, Deirdre, ed. *Female Spectators: Looking At Film and Television*. New York: Routledge, 1988.

Propp, V. *Morphology of the Folktale*. Translated by Laurence Scott. 2d ed. Austin: University of Texas Press, 1968.

Radway, Janice A. *Reading the Romance: Women, Patriarchy, and Popular Literature*. Chapel Hill: University of North Carolina Press, 1984.

Reik, Theodore. *Masochism and Modern Man*. Translated by Margaret H. Biegel and Gertrud M. Kurth. New York: Farrar, Straus, 1941.

Rosen, Philip, ed. *Narrative, Apparatus, Ideology: A Film Theory Reader*. New York: Columbia University Press, 1986.

Said, Edward. *Beginnings: Intention and Method*. New York: Basic Books, 1975.

Seiter, Ellen. "The Role of the Woman Reader: Eco's Narrative Theory and Soap Operas." *Tabloid* 6 (1981): 36–43.

Showalter, Elaine. "Feminist Criticism in the Wilderness." *Critical Inquiry* 8 (Winter 1981): 179–205.

Silverman, Kaja. *The Acoustic Mirror: The Female Voice in Psychoanalysis and Cinema*. Bloomington: Indiana University Press, 1988.

———. "Masochism and Subjectivity." *Framework*, no. 12 (1981): 2–9.

Smirnoff, Victor. "The Masochistic Contract." *International Journal of Psychoanalysis* 50 (1969): 666–71.

Spelman, Elizabeth. *Inessential Woman: Problems of Exclusion in Feminist Thought*. Boston: Beacon Press, 1988.

Stiver, Irene P. "Beyond the Oedipus Complex: Mothers and Daughters." In *Work in Progress* 26. Wellesley, Mass.: Stone Center of Developmental Services and Studies, Wellesley College, 1986.

Studlar, Gaylyn. "Masochism and the Perverse Pleasures of Cinema." In *Movies and Methods*, edited by Bill Nichols, vol. 2. Berkeley and Los Angeles: University of California Press, 1985.

Surrey, Janet. "Self-in-Relation: A Theory of Women's Development." In *Work in Progress* 13. Wellesley, Mass.: Stone Center for Developmental Services and Studies, Wellesley College, 1985.

Torgovnik, Marianna. *Closure in the Novel*. Princeton: Princeton University Press, 1981.

Turim, Maureen. *Flashbacks in Film*. New York: Routledge, 1989.

White, Hayden. "New Historicism: A Comment." In *The New Historicism*, edited by H. Abram Veeser. New York: Routledge, 1989.

Williams, Linda. "Feminist Film Theory: *Mildred Pierce* and the Second World War." In *Female Spectators: Looking At Film and Television*, edited by Deirdre Pribram. New York: Routledge, 1988.

———. "A Jury of Their Peers: Marlene Gorris's *A Question of Silence*." In

Postmodernism and Its Discontents: Theories, Practises, edited by E. Ann Kaplan. London: Verso, 1988.

———. "When the Woman Looks." In *Re-Vision: Essays in Feminist Film Criticism*, edited by Mary Ann Doane, Patricia Mellencamp, and Linda Williams. American Film Institute Monograph Series, vol. 3. Frederick, Md.: University Publications of America, 1984.

Index of Soap Opera Characters

229

Index

Compositor:	Keystone Typesetting, Inc.
Text:	10/13 Galliard
Display:	Galliard
Printer:	Haddon Craftsmen, Inc.
Binder:	Haddon Craftsmen, Inc.